THE POLITICAL ECONOMY OF MODERN SPAIN

Policy-Making in an Authoritarian System

THE POLITICAL ECONOMY OF MODERN SPAIN

Policy-Making in an Authoritarian System

CHARLES W. ANDERSON

◦⑤

THE UNIVERSITY OF WISCONSIN PRESS
MADISON, MILWAUKEE, AND LONDON
1970

Published by
The University of Wisconsin Press
Box 1379, Madison, Wisconsin 53701
The University of Wisconsin Press, Ltd.
27-29 Whitfield Street, London, W.1

ISBN 0–299–05611–2
LC 72–106036

for Jeanie

CONTENTS

TABLES AND FIGURES

Tables

Figures

PREFACE

THIS BOOK IS ABOUT SPAIN. It is also about the analysis of public policy, and it is a commentary on the role of experts in modern government. The reader is entitled to use it for any or all of these purposes.

The political system of Nationalist Spain is certainly entitled to detached analysis. Despite the research explosion in comparative politics during the last decade, this mutant case of Western political development has been almost entirely neglected. The few excellent studies, by Juan Linz and Amando de Miguel, Arthur Whitaker, Stanley Payne, and Benjamin Welles, stand out in a field that has been left largely to diatribe and polemic. It seemed to me worthwhile to try to capture something of how politics were done and policy was made in late Franco Spain, before this unusual political system passed from the scene or changed beyond recognition.

This study is not a comprehensive portrait of the structure and dynamics of Spanish politics. All I had the time or capacity to do was to look into a specific aspect of the nation's political eco-

nomic life. While I think what I have done provides some suggestions about how the system works as a whole, the larger job will
eventually have to be undertaken by someone more experienced
and skillful. My candidate for this task is Juan Linz, and I hope
he will accept the challenge one day.

However, my more immediate reason for going to Spain was to
examine an issue in contemporary political economics. In this era
of managed economies, do the institutions and processes of liberal
democratic politics make any great difference in economic policy
choice? The guidance of complex economics through the application of neo-Keynesian principles is still so new, and has been thus
far so successful in modern capitalist systems, that we have not
yet gained a perspective of the implications of this style of policy-
making for the political economic traditions of the West.

In conventional typologies of political systems, the authoritarian system of Nationalist Spain and the liberal democratic politics
of other Western nations appear as categorically different types.
The one is characterized by the concentration of power, the
presence of hierarchic forms of political organization, and the absence of institutionalized means of political competition. The
other is described as a system of the pluralistic dispersion of
power, of representative forms of political organization, and of
open competition for influence among many competing interests
and political formations. The presumed distinctiveness of the two
forms of political system suggests critical questions to the political economist. First, are these differences of political structure
and process apparent in the formulation and execution of macroeconomic policy? Second, does either of these political contexts
seem to have peculiar merits or liabilities in providing for economic development and the management of the affairs of a complex, industrialized society? Did the unique institutions and processes of Spanish authoritarianism make any difference in the capacity of leaders to make appropriate choices on public policy?

During the period from 1957 to 1967, which is the focus of this
study, Spain undertook a rather thoroughgoing transformation of

its political economic system. The Spanish state launched a massive retooling of its approach to economic affairs, along lines more compatible with the neo-Keynesian economic principles then coming into vogue throughout the Western world. This period was also one of rapid, though not untroubled, economic growth in Spain. The world economic community began to discuss the "Spanish economic miracle" and to compare it to the German *Wirtschaftwunder* of the 1950s. During the decade 1957–67, the Spanish economy grew at an annual average rate of 9 percent, one of the highest in the Western world.

My problem, then, is to assess the problem-solving and policy-making capabilities of the Spanish political system during this period. In comparison with the rest of the West, how well did the institutions and processes of Spanish authoritarianism serve her leaders? Did they provide an "environment of choice" in which critical problems for public action could be identified, alternative courses of action assessed, problems and consequences foreseen? Did the system provide policy-makers with the means of effective and appropriate decision and action, or was the success of Spanish economic development policy something of a triumph over the political context?

To get at this problem, I will consider two acts of choice that are central to the conduct of modern government. The first involves the selection of measures appropriate to the achievement of public purposes from among the capabilities of the state. We will examine the range of possibilities—the richness and flexibility —present in the Spanish political economy in comparison with that of other Western nations. Then we will see how the Spanish policy-makers contrived a selection from these possibilities for the achievement of the purposes they had in mind, again comparing their choices with those of their contemporaries elsewhere in the West. I describe this process as "policy instrumentation," and our analysis will follow rather closely the approach and comparative categories provided by the Dutch economists Jan Tinbergen and E. S. Kirschen and his associates.

However, there is a second act of governance that somewhat precedes the choice of policy instruments to be employed. This is the decision on how to decide, on what processes are to be gone through in evaluating alternative objectives of political economic action, searching for and assessing the plausibility and feasibility of different programs, coming to a conclusion on one preferred policy format, and then evaluating what has been done in the light of its consequences. This process, which I shall describe as "procedural instrumentation," will be handled in much the same way as the question of choice of policy measures. I will first appraise the range of decision-making procedures available in the "equipment" of Nationalist Spain and then examine the particular choices of policy-makers in contriving decision processes for specific situations. Their work will be compared with Western practice generally in the same period.

This framework provides an approach to policy analysis that is jointly political and economic in character. By extending and refining the analytic technique of Tinbergen and Kirschen, I hope to bring the interests and concerns of political scientists and economists in decision-making a little closer together, to bring them into focus on a common problem.

This study was also conceived of as something of an experiment in comparative policy analysis. There is a renewed enthusiasm today among political scientists for building greater powers of policy evaluation, analysis, and recommendation into their discipline. I intend this study to be a limited demonstration of my conviction that this interest should be pursued through comparative analysis, that policy analysis would profit greatly by examining the ways in which different political systems and cultures have tackled problems common to all societies. The procedures of choice followed in other cultures, the way problems are defined, the solutions attempted, and the comparative evaluation of outcomes are necessary parts of any sophisticated and sensible assessment of the issues of one's own time and place.

Some of the leading parts in our story will be played by the technocrats. To see the practitioners of the new economics at work in the Spanish context should suggest some interesting things about the role that this new cadre of experts is coming to play in other modern nations as well. To see their art practiced in the somewhat distinctive setting of Spain is instructive, I think, of the particular power and also the limitations of this approach to policy. At the same time, political science has not yet come to grips with the role of this new expertocracy in the conduct of modern government. We are not yet sure how this new political resource of skill in the management of the macroeconomy affects the operation of the larger political system. In this study, I shall try to point up both the political and the economic significance of the role the technocrats played in Spain.

The documentary sources used in this investigation are primarily matters of public record and may be found in the libraries and archives of relevant agencies in Spain. The primary repositories used were the archives and files of the Instituto de Estudios Políticos, the Hemeroteca Nacional, the Universidad de Madrid, the Comisaría del Plan, the Organización Sindical, the Banco de España, the Ministries of Hacienda, Comercio and Industria, and DATA, S.A., a Spanish social science research organization. Although documentary sources were supplemented with interviews with relevant public officials, I have tried to restrict the evidential base of the study as much as possible to matters of public record, because I believe that policy analysis must remain a contemporary and on-going practice, and one subject to immediate scholarly criticism. Hence the preferred approaches must be those which do not depend on extraordinarily costly, time-consuming, or difficult-to-replicate modes of inquiry. The translations from Spanish are mine.

Many other hands have contributed to the preparation of this book. I would first acknowledge my intellectual ancestors, whose writings guided me toward this approach. This list must include Albert Hirschman, Robert Dahl, Charles Lindblom, Jan Tinbergen, E. S. Kirschen, Harold Lasswell, and Theodore Lowi.

In Madrid, I was grateful for the cooperation of the officers of the Comisaría del Plan, the Ministerio de Hacienda, the Banco de España, the Organización Sindical, and the Instituto de Estudios Políticos. To single out names is somewhat unfair, for everywhere the process of assisting me seemed to be a team effort. However, the constant aid of María Delores Jiménez of the Instituto de Estudios Políticos requires special note. Amando de Miguel and Juan Linz were generous with support and friendship.

Financial support from the Ibero-American Area Studies Program of the University of Wisconsin, through a grant from the Ford Foundation, made it possible for me to travel to Spain for the research.

In this enterprise, I was blessed to an unusual degree with excellent criticism and advice. Those who helped me by reading earlier drafts of the manuscript include Philippe Schmitter, who saw more clearly than I what I was trying to do and provided a much sharper and clearer focus to the entire book. Juan Linz, from his expert knowledge, gave a much-needed, detailed critique. Kenneth Dolbeare raised essential questions from the point of view of a student of policy analysis. Terry McCoy and Richard Hartwig provided useful insights on the first chapter.

Mrs. Jeanene Alery typed the manuscript and did a particularly competent and craftsmanlike job with it.

Finally, to Jeanie, who loved the country as much as I did, this book is dedicated.

Charles W. Anderson

Madison, Wisconsin
May 1969

THE POLITICAL ECONOMY OF MODERN SPAIN

Policy-Making in an Authoritarian System

THE FOLLOWING LIST contains the abbreviations used for institutions and organizations that are mentioned frequently throughout the text:

ECM   European Common Market

IBRD   International Bank for Reconstruction and Development

IEME   *Instituto Española de Moneda Exterior*

IMF   International Monetary Fund

INI   *Instituto Nacional de Industria*

OCYPE   *Oficina de Coordinación y Programación Económica*

OECD   Organization for European Cooperation and Development

OEEC   Organization for European Economic Cooperation

RENFE   *Red Española Nacional de Ferrocarriles*

Chapter 1

AUTHORITARIANISM AND THE TOOLS OF STATECRAFT

THE CONVENTIONAL INTERPRETATIONS OF Spanish politics should be embarrassing to students of comparative politics. Most opinions on Nationalist Spain were fixed at the end of the Civil War, and as long as Franco remained in power, it seemed unnecessary to revise them. To a large extent, political analysts lost the thread of the story of Spanish politics sometime in the late 1930s. In the usual idiom, Nationalist Spain is frequently portrayed as the residual survivor of the Fascist and Nazi movements that, mercifully, are no longer at the center stage of world events. For a generation that thought in terms of two basic schemes of political organization, liberal democracy and communism, Spain under Franco seemed an archaic, contextless survival of a controversy that had passed.

Of course the issue of the significance of this regime is not so easily resolved. First, political authoritarianism, the class of governmental forms to which Nationalist Spain quite properly belongs, does not seem to be a waning political style. Authoritarianism characterizes many newly independent or less developed nations. It has reappeared with new vigor in recent years, even in

3

such larger more sophisticated nations as Argentina, Brazil, and Greece.

Second, to classify Spain with other forms of undemocratic politics leads to fundamental misunderstandings. One must at least establish the distinction between an authoritarian and totalitarian political system. Juan Linz defines the crucial difference as one of intentional mobilization and politicization of the population to the purposes of a totalitarian system, while on the other hand, "stabilized authoritarian regimes are characterized by lack of extensive and intensive political mobilization. . . . Membership participation is low in political and para-political organizations. . . . Rather than enthusiasm or support, the regime often expects . . . passive acceptance."[1]

The role of party and ideology was never as central in Spain as in Germany, Italy, or most communist countries. The structure of power has been considerably looser, based as much on a balanced coalition of forces that antedate the regime as on institutions created by it. There was much less inclination in Spain to sublimate social institutions to the state. Conversely, in totalitarian systems basic institutions of economy, society, religion, family, and so on, are to be transformed to fit the requirements of the political design.

The practice of Spanish authoritarianism is not inconsistent with its political theory. The heritage of Roman Catholic, corporate thought recognizes a functional differentiation of the various social institutions. Each has an appropriate role to play in the social order, and the state must ensure the proper relationship among these institutions. However, it must not subvert their appropriate autonomous role. In a sense, there are legitimate limitations on the power of the state recognized in Spanish authoritarianism, while totalitarianism connotes a state whose legitimate powers are theoretically unlimited.[2]

Finally, and perhaps most significantly, a lot has happened in Spain in the last thirty years. No political system is static. Though essential continuities of structure and process are readily identifiable, the dynamics of politics have changed in subtle but important ways. Furthermore, during this period the character of Spanish economy and society has been transformed to a striking extent. Spain is no longer the country it was in the 1930s, when it was at the dramatic center of world political events. And what Spain has become, and how it got there, raises important questions, I believe, not only about the recent history of Europe but, more importantly, about the present character of Western industrial civilization.

Within the last generation, Spain apparently has made good at that task which has singularly engaged the efforts of all Western nations in the postwar period, the generation of sustained economic growth and development. While it is probably premature to speak of the economic transformation of Spain, for the country is far from achieving European levels of living and welfare for its population, it is probably true that in the decade from 1957 to 1967 Spain passed through that invisible barrier which separates an underdeveloped nation from one capable of sustained economic growth. It was in this time that Spain's approach to the government's economic role was drastically restructured by adopting first, in 1959, a stabilization program linked to a strategy of economic liberalization, and then, in 1963, a design for growth based on national economic planning. During this period, per capita income grew at about 9 percent per year, one of the highest growth rates in the world. Industrial production and capital formation rates both exceeded 10 percent. Spain, virtually bankrupt and registering chronic balance of payments deficits at the beginning of the period, had achieved a strong currency backed by substantial reserves by the end of the decade. All of the symptoms of quickening social and economic change began to appear. An historically static rural population began to migrate toward the cities. The proportion of the work force engaged in agriculture declined from 49 percent in 1950 to about 30 percent in 1967. Spain acquired the distinctive stigmata of modern society—a new middle class demanding and receiving the amenities of mass consumption, chronic traffic congestion, air pollution, housing shortages, inflationary pressures, and weekends in the country.

This is the story of the process of rapid political economic development that took place in Spain during the decade 1957–67. Specifically, it is a study of the policy-making process in Spain and of how political leaders chose to deploy the powers of government to generate and direct the processes of economic growth. The central question of our analysis arises from the fact that the Spanish policy-makers attempted to apply the techniques that ostensibly had led to rapid economic progress elsewhere in Europe within the context of an authoritarian political system. As Spain sought to duplicate the extraordinary postwar economic progress made in the rest of Europe and in North America, was the distinctive political system a help or a hindrance? Did the context of political authoritarianism make any difference in the capacity of policy-makers to reach appropriate decisions concerning the direction and management of the national economy?

The management of complex economies has changed a great deal in the past thirty years. It may be that the critical problems of political economy are no longer political but technical. The great issues of wealth, its generation, organization, and distribution, have been central to Western politics since the industrial revolution. The characteristic institutions and processes of liberal democracy evolved, in some good measure, as responses to these problems. The typical party spectrum of most Western democracies was organized basically around distinctive approaches and ideologies concerning the political economy. The key interest groups emerged as spokesmen for the various factors of production in the economic process.

What seems to have happened with the emergence of what Andrew Shonfield calls "modern capitalism,"[3] called by others neo-Keynesianism, or in the United States, the "new economics," is that most of the objectives and programs that were historically issues of political contention have been affirmed as potential purposes of public policy.

The formulation of policy has become a matter of measuring the desirable realization of any one objective against its effect on all the other members of the set. Thus, redistribution of income, or the dedication of a higher proportion of national wealth to labor remuneration, will be pursued as long as it does not have detrimental consequences for economic growth, the balance of payments, or the cost-of-living index. Political economic questions become less either/or choices and more matters of extent. The panaceas and programs of earlier years, such as the nationalization of industry or comprehensive planning, are regarded less as ideological issues than as potential instruments of policy, whose applicability to any specific public problem is to be weighed in terms of the various objectives deemed to be at issue. The calculation of the potential impact of any single measure on all the factors in the equation requires specialized skill and familiarity with the special conceptual logic of modern economics. Neo-Keynesian economics is but one potential doctrine of policy, to be sure. However, the important point is that the "rules of the game" which it set for economic policy were largely accepted by the critical political contenders in the Western democracies during the last generation.

Thus, it may be that the paraphernalia of liberal democratic politics is not at the present time particularly pertinent to economic decision-making. Parliaments, in general, no longer have more than a residual role in economic choice. Partisan ideologies have largely been subordinated to a more general calculus of economic statesmanship. The center of gravity in the conduct of economic affairs has shifted from political authorities to central banks, planning agencies, and the economic ministries. Relations between interest groups and the state have been routinized.

It is such speculation that a study of economic policy-making in contemporary Spain is designed to test. Is the effect of the larger context of political system and process evident as Spanish policy-makers tried to recreate the successes achieved by modern economies elsewhere in the West? In what ways, if at all, did the "environment of choice" of an authoritarian system affect the capacity of policy-makers to identify problems, perceive relevant relationships among problems, formulate potential strategies, choose among alternatives, implement programs, and revise policies in the light of consequences?

This approach to public policy analysis is a bit unorthodox. It rests on a combination of modern political science, economics, and organization theory. In the remainder of this chapter, I will try to spell out the implications of this approach and the procedure I will follow in the examination of policy-making in Spain.

The Instrumentation of Public Policy

Let us look at the making of public policy as a matter of adapting the capabilities of the state to the achievement of public purposes. From this perspective, the institutions of government, the legal system of a country, and the state's capacity to tax and to spend become the equipment provided by a society to its leaders for the solution of public problems. They are tools of the trade of statecraft.

The skillful statesman is one who finds in the repertoire of powers and resources of his political system the means appropriate to the objectives he seeks. Furthermore, seen in this way, the capacities of leaders are conditioned by the richness of the equipment that the political system offers them.

Ideology, tradition, and constitutional convention of course delimit the range of possibilities open to the statesman. They also emphasize the propriety of specific policy options. In some societies, to spur production by the coercive mobilization of labor is simply beyond the range of legitimate programs open to the government. In other nations, the same objective may not be sought by encouraging the competition of private entrepreneurs. In some nations, the accepted way of making production decisions will be by transmitting authoritative commands through a bureaucratic hierarchy. In others, such techniques may be deplored and the manipulation of taxation and monetary systems deemed more satisfactory instruments of economic influence and control.

On the whole, public problem-solving is probably more an adaptive than an inventive art. As one surveys the way nations cope with problems, one is struck by how seldom a really original or revolutionary approach is to be found. Be the nation communist, socialist, or capitalist, in the end most problems are handled by prosaic means.

Perhaps this is the normal course of public decision-making. March and Simon suggest that in large organizations, decision usually can be characterized as a search through a long sequence of means and ends until a way of taking action is found in the existing repertoire of programs of the firm or government. "Metaphorically, we imagine a whole warehouse full of parts in various stages of prefabrication. The plan for the new structure must be carried to the point where it can be specified in terms of these stocked parts."[4] We will suppose that this is the way policy-making normally proceeds. And if this is so, it points up the importance of the heritage of means, available and legitimate, in any individual nation. Basically, this sets the bounds of possibility for the solution of a public problem.

There are, of course, ways in which the statesman may expand the equipment available to him, which is to say, his problem-solving capabilities.[5] First, he may borrow from the established equipment of other nations. The international diffusion of the basic techniques of monetary and fiscal management is a pertinent example. Second, ideology or social theory may suggest new sets of public equipment and technique. The impact of John Maynard Keynes on the policy-making machinery of the West is illustrative. Finally, pure political invention may occur. A totally new tool may be created for the solution of a public problem, such as the concept of the multipurpose river basin authority in the United States.

In examining the craft of economic policy-making as practiced in Spain, the focus will be on two fundamental acts of public choice. Policy instrumentation involves the selection of those means appropriate to the fulfillment of public purposes from among the legitimate resources and capabilities of the state. The adjustment of taxation rates to redistribute income or the creation of a new agency to stimulate or regulate a certain type of industry or commerce are pertinent examples. Procedural instrumentation concerns the structuring of a decision-making process, selecting techniques for the identification of public problems, searching for and assessing the plausibility of different public programs, choosing a specific course of action, and evaluating what has been done in the light of its consequences. Committees or commissions, surveys, referenda, hearings, and so on, may be used as procedural instruments. So may various types of statistical analysis, logical models of social trends, or public activities. The basic political structures and institutions, legislatures, elections, government agencies, may be regarded as procedural instruments when they are either implicitly or explicitly assigned a specific role in the formulation of a program of public action.*

Of course, there is no airtight distinction between policy and procedural instrumentation. One can easily imagine a policy instrument serving also as a procedural instrument. For example, this is precisely what happens when the state consciously relies on the market mechanism as a means of pricing the products of public enterprise. The market is the means of carrying out a public function, in this case the distribution of goods produced in

* The formal definitions of the key concepts in this analysis are as follows:

Equipment: the sum of state resources and capabilities, potential instruments, or sets of instruments.

Instrument: a specific capability or resource actually available to the government in power.

Policy instrument: the means available to a government to carry out a public purpose by affecting social or economic processes.

Procedural instrument: the means available to a government for arriving at a commitment on public purposes.

Public policy: a general strategy of action or decision, involving a set of policy instruments.

Public program: a delimited or focused range of public action, affecting a specific sector of society.

Decision system: a set of procedural instruments, organized so as to provide a decision-making process.

state-owned factories. On the other hand, it is also a decision-making instrument, since this mechanism will be used to guide choices on future production. Conversely, procedural instruments often have intended policy purposes in the mind of the decision-maker. If the question is one of drawing labor organizations closer to the regime, a wage policy adjustment, a more progressive taxation system, or enhanced labor participation in economic planning may be interchangeable or complementary ways of pursuing the objective.

One should not be too troubled by the fact that our classificatory scheme does not neatly divide two different types of political phenomena. Policy-making is an adaptive and, to some extent, an inventive art. Of course leaders are going to use the tools available to them for a variety of purposes and are not apt to be constrained by classificatory neatness in building policies and programs. The critical point, then, in establishing the kind of instrument we are dealing with, is the use or function of an instrument, seen in a specific policy-making context, from the vantage point of the decision-makers.

Policy Instrumentation

In comparison with the mixed economies of the West, how well equipped was Nationalist Spain for the practice of modern economics? Which of the policy instruments characteristic of modern capitalism were available to Spanish leaders, and which were not? What policy tools were added to the paraphernalia of the Spanish state, when, and under what conditions? It may be that there were rigidities in the authoritarian political style that denied to the Spanish public authorities certain policy potentials characteristic of more pluralist societies. On the other hand, the structure of the Spanish state may have made available policy instruments that were not characteristic elsewhere.

Despite the diversity of the postwar economic policy experience in Western Europe and North America, it is possible to establish a reasonably complete checklist of the policy tools available to Western policy-makers, in a sense to inventory March and Simon's "warehouse full of semi-fabricated parts." Following from the analytic work of Jan Tinbergen, a group headed by E. S. Kirschen has developed a useful taxonomy to catalogue the techniques of policy used in Western economies since World War II. The scheme is not intended to be universal or exhaustive. It is confined to those political economic systems that are identified with the neo-Keynesian approach to economic policy-making. It would of course be useful to have a scheme that could specify the types of instruments available to any government. However, although some general designs for classifying policy instruments are available, with varying claims to logical exhaustiveness and analytic utility,[6] the problem is really one of trying to devise a satisfactory taxonomy for a logically inexhaustible field, since the adaptation of public powers to public problems is essentially an innovative art, and sometimes an architectonic one.

The Kirschen scheme was developed by comparing the postwar economic policy experiences of nine nations—Belgium, France, Germany, Italy, Luxembourg, Netherlands, Norway, the United Kingdom, and the United States. In a sense, what I will do is add Spain to this comparative framework, though I will not cover systematically each of Kirschen's comparisons but choose those that are critical for the total analysis.

The Kirschen group poses the problem of postwar Western economic statecraft as a matter of the selection from and reconciliation of twelve basic policy objectives, to be implemented by choosing from among some sixty-three "available" instruments. The objectives[7] specified are as follows:

1. Full employment
2. Price stability
3. Improvement in the balance of payments
4. Expansion of production
5. Increase or promotion of
   a. Internal competition

    b. Coordination*
    c. Mobility of labor
    d. Mobility of capital
    e. International division of labor
  6. Satisfaction of collective needs†
  7. Improvement in the distribution of wealth and income
  8. Protection and priorities to regions or industries
  9. Improvements in the pattern of private consumption‡
10. Security of supply
11. Improvement in the size or structure of the population
12. Reduction in working hours

The inventory of the instruments available to policy-makers in achieving these objectives is arranged according to five families of instruments, subdivided into categories, and is shown in Table 1.

Within such a comparative context, the process of policy instrumentation in Nationalist Spain will be explored, and the substantive policy package fashioned by the policy-makers will be examined.

Procedural Instrumentation

A procedural instrument is a technique employed by a policy-maker to help make choices between alternative courses of action and to assist in judging the wisdom or prudence of a possible move. Just as one task of statecraft is selecting and blending public powers to respond to public problems, so another is fashioning the process by which decisions will be made. Here again,

---

* Defined as the reduction of the disorder and waste of resources which competition is alleged to create in certain circumstances, such as unlimited competition in public utilities, transport, etc.

† Defined as needs that the population cannot or prefers not to satisfy individually in the open market, such as education, health in some countries, etc.

‡ Defined as cases where "governments feel that they can judge consumers' needs better than the consumer himself"—prohibition of alcoholic beverages, etc.

TABLE 1. An Inventory of Instruments Available
in Western Economic Policy-Making

Families	Categories	Instruments
Public finance	Balances	1. Current 2. Overall
	Government expenditure	3. Public investment 4. Subsidies and capital transfers: enterprise 5. Transfers to households 6. Current purchases 7. Public stock changes 8. Wages and salaries 9. Transfers to the rest of the world
	Government revenue	10. Direct taxes on household and 11. Enterprise income 12. Indirect taxes on internal transactions 13. Customs duties 14. Property taxes 15. Transfers from the rest of the world 16. Social security 17. Succession duties
Money and credit	Borrowing and lending	1. Lending abroad 2. Borrowing abroad 3. Domestic lending 4. Domestic borrowing
	Operations in existing debt	5. Open market operations, short term securities 6. Other open market operations
	Interest rate	7. Bank rate 8. Legal maximum rate 9. Government loan guarantees
	Bank credit creation	10. Reserve ratios 11. Loan approval 12. Quantitative "stops" 13. Other directives, regulations, persuasion
	Other interventions in credit	14. Controls on local authority or nationalized enterprise borrowing 15. Control of private company borrowing by new issues

TABLE 1. (*Continued*)

Families	Categories	Instruments
	Other interventions in credit (*cont.*)	16. Control of installment purchase 17. Control of other financial institutions
Exchange rate		1. Devaluation 2. Revaluation
Direct control	Foreign trade, exchange and immigration	1. Private imports 2. Private exports 3. State imports 4. Exchange control 5. Immigration control
	Price control	6. Goods and services 7. Dividends 8. Rents 9. Wages
	Other internal controls	10. Investment 11. Operations 12. Natural resources exploitation 13. Quality controls and standards 14. Raw material allocations 15. Working conditions 16. Rationing
Changes in the institutional framework	Involving other instruments	Changes in the: 1. system of transfers to households 2. system of enterprise subsidy 3. credit system 4. tax system 5. direct controls
	Directly affecting conditions of production	6. Land reform 7. Changes in labor influence on management 8. Changes in competition 9. Changes in extent of public ownership of industry 10. Creation of national institutions 11. Creation in international institutions

Adapted from Kirschen et al., *Economic Policy in Our Time*, 1, Chapters 2–7. A useful "map" of the critical relationships between the objectives cited above and these instruments is presented in Table VII.1 at p. 148.

the society makes certain "equipment" available to policy-makers. There is the constitutional structure of due process of legislative enactment, the most general statement of how all classes of decisions committing the state will be taken. Generally, this constitutional level of decision equipment is designed more to constrain than to enable the leader. It is a set of procedures he is required to pass through in enacting public policy. However, these constitutional procedures will also provide the basic institutions that he will adapt to his purposes in making policy.

Constitutional procedures are normally quite general. Additional specifications may be made for particular kinds of decisions, such as consultation with economic advisers or central banking authorities for certain types of economic decisions. There may be certain conventions or customs relating to consultation between major groups in the society. All of these are part of the "procedural equipment" of a society. In addition there is a complex legacy of possible forms of consultation, investigation, study, and deliberation that may or may not be invoked, largely on the basis of the specific content of the decision at hand and the judgment of those involved as to what is appropriate under the circumstances.

The procedural equipment is to some extent malleable. Generally there is considerable latitude for specific processes to be devised and for the steps in the required process to be rearranged to fit the issue at hand. Just as the effective policy-maker selects from the capabilities of the state those appropriate for the resolution of a certain problem, so another skill of statecraft is the fashioning of procedural instruments into patterns for obtaining an adequate policy choice on a specific issue.

For example, let us examine the relationship between the policy initiator and the legislature. One policy initiator may feel that his task is done when he has prepared a technically competent proposal. It is then up to legislative leaders to generate political backing for the measure. In other words, the policy-maker would use the legislature to generate consent for his proposal. A second policy entrepreneur might see the role of the legislature a little differently. He may understand his job as that of presenting the legislature with a politically feasible proposal. For him, it would be perfectly appropriate to introduce an intermediary step into the policy process, creating, let us say, an ad hoc committee of the powerful to refine the "administration proposal" into legislatively acceptable form. From the point of view of this policy initiator, the only use planned for the legislature is that of formal ratification of the measure.

For our purposes, the significant characteristic of legislatures, economic councils, public hearings, interest groups, and the like, is their potential use by a policy initiator in perfecting his design for public action. Table 2 lists the potential uses of procedural instruments by the decision-maker. Some hypothetical characteristics are noted, including the probable structure, membership and participation, and powers of each type of political instrument.

Although Table 2 might seem to be a series of steps in the policy-making process, I do not intend to use it in this way. It is not a descriptive model. I am not saying that all of these processes can be identified in any public decision, and, particularly, I am not saying that there is some reason that they must occur in this order. It is true that this scheme is adapted from attempts to identify the stages in the policy-making process.[8] However, there is by now enough evidence that a policy-making model based on a specific sequence of stages creates more trouble than it is worth.[9] Therefore, this scheme merely indicates some of the purposes for which these tools might be used by policy initiators, and does not predicate expected behavior.

There is, of course, a potential difference between the intended function of an instrument and the role it actually plays in the decision process. In any collective body, one prime source of conflict is the role that the group is to play in the policy-making process. Thus the policy-maker, attempting to guide a proposal through a decision system, may feel that an informal meeting with legislative leaders is to serve merely an aggregative function, to reach an

TABLE 2. Some Potential Uses of Procedural Instruments

Function	Hypothetical composition	Hypothetical powers
Initiation and Problem Recognition (Provides a flow of suggestions for possible public actions. Ex.: parties, interest groups, advisory bodies, mass media)	Relatively fluid and flexible in structure and participation to provide open flow of information	Quite limited, if any powers to commit system
Formulation (Selects and develops one policy proposal. Ex.: planning agencies, technical teams, etc.)	Limited and specialized membership	Seldom can commit system as a whole, may have power to commit participants to "collective responsibility" to proposal
Consultation (Apprises of potential consequences were proposed action to be undertaken. Ex.: advisory committee, board of directors of agency representing diverse interests)	Fairly open membership, though relevant test may be critical "interest" in proposed policy	Low power to commit group or system since discord and criticism functional
Aggregation (Wins support of critical power holders for proposed activity. Ex.: ad hoc meeting of legislative leaders)	Limited to relevant elites	Characterized by potential veto power of participants
Collaboration and Coordination (Synchronizes action of private and public agencies whose action anticipated by proposal. Ex.: "indicative planning")	Limited to those performing relevant functions	Effort to commit group to future actions, for each participant can detrimentally affect program realization
Ratification (Ex.: legislature, monarch)	These are the instruments empowered to legitimate a public action. They sanction formal commitment of public resources and signal that the system is committed to a certain course of action.	
Feedback	Provides decision-maker with information on actual consequences and implications of policy. May perform any of first five functions.	

agreement on the substance of a proposal. However, the legislators may question the substance of the proposal (consultation), or perhaps they may attempt to initiate a brand new approach to the problem.

From the policy promoter's point of view, the problem in designing a procedural system is to reduce the possibility of the activation of politics. He wants decision instruments to serve the purpose of perfecting and enacting his design for action. He would use the participation of others as a means of simplifying his problem and of winning their support. He seeks to reduce dispute, conflict, skepticism, doubt. To introduce new elements into his program at the point of consultation is painful. It requires effort to create a consistent design for action in the face of disharmonious demands. It also delays the realization of the desired program.

Of course, it is the pluralist's belief that the policy-maker's drive to fashion a frictionless, efficient decision system should be resisted. In the democratic scheme of things, the purpose of a decision system is to simplify only eventually the problem of public action. The fundamental desire of the democrat is to resist the decision leader's tendency to simplify the problem of policy by requiring him to consider the fuller complexity of the heterogeneous demands and perspectives of various sectors of the society.

The tension between policy initiator and pluralistic interests is expressed in conflict within political instruments. Decision systems that work reflect a tentative reconciliation of these tendencies. The policy-maker bows to criticism and revises his plan to account for it. The interests accept compromise with the dominant design for action in order to achieve resolution of the issue and to share the fruits of collective action.[10]

Just as there is a repertoire of policy techniques that are more available (more acceptable, institutionalized, established) to statesmen in some systems than in others, so we should expect to find that some procedural instruments and some forms of decision system come more naturally in some polities than in others.

I shall expect that the same principles apply to a society's procedural equipment as apply to its policy resources. Thus there is probably more of a tendency in Latin Europe to repeat the use of the semi-corporate "council" of experts and organized interests than to experiment with such techniques as referenda among involved parties, the open public hearing, and the strong legislative role in substantive policy, all more characteristic of the American tradition of "grass roots" democracy. Nonetheless, I would also expect to find a normal process of diffusion of decision instruments from their area of origin into countries facing similar types of policy choice problems, but given the sanctity that attaches to public institutions, I would expect greater resistance to borrowing in this field than in that of policy instruments and would expect more diversity and contrast in comparing the problem-solving techniques of various political systems.

Again, the hypothesis can be tested in the Spanish case. Although the economic equipment of Spain might have been different from that of the rest of Western Europe in the postwar period, even more apparently distinctive was the Spanish political system. Hence, it could be initially expected that Spain's way of making policy choices might have differed from that prevalent in Western Europe, that the procedural instruments employed by Spanish statesmen might have been unlike those characteristic of the rest of the Western world.

One final type of procedural instrument must be considered. Every group of decision-makers must reach some agreement on the "context" within which the performance of economy, society, and polity is to be evaluated. A problem appears within a certain frame of reference—an image of what the social order looks like, what ought to be done about it, and by whom. Some would call this an ideology; others, given the type of policy we are dealing with, an economic theory or model. Yet ideology normally conveys too much, implying, as it does to so many, a systematic and total world view; and economic theory has the difficulty that some of the ideas to be discussed do not have an established place in the literature of the discipline of economics, and to use these terms would perplex the academic economist.

So I will use the term "problem context," at times interspersing "ideology," "model," "theory," or "strategy," as whim and specific need dictate, to describe the way in which groups identified critical political economic relationships and defined desirable or undesirable changes in these relationships.

A number of questions are in order concerning these problem contexts in the Spanish case. What alternative economic strategies or contexts were available in the political process? Which contexts normally available in the West (perhaps socialism, communism, or liberalism) were not available to Spanish policy-makers, and did this make a difference in the outcome of the decisions under consideration?

The Tests of Adequacy

This study is designed so that we may render a judgment of the problem-solving capabilities of the Spanish political economic system. The problem of evaluating the performance of a government is, of course, a knotty one. I shall not try to assess the wisdom of the policy choices taken by the Spanish policy-makers. To do so, a standard would have to be erected for the policies that a nation in development should pursue, and that process falls beyond the scope of this study. The problem of whether a certain course of action is or is not optimum to the public interest of a society is, of course, an old one in political analysis.[11]

Therefore, the "tests of adequacy" that will be applied pertain primarily to the policy-making process, rather than to the content of policy. To assess the difference, if there is a difference, between the policy-making process in Spain and in the constitutional democracies, three evaluative tests will be used.

The first test follows naturally from an assessment of the policy equipment available to the decision-maker. Was the Spanish political economy as rich in alternatives as other Western systems? Were some kinds of policy technique less available because of the character of the regime? Conversely, did the Spanish system provide additional possibilities for public decision or action not characteristic of other states?

Does an authoritarian regime have a greater capacity to react quickly and decisively to a public problem than a democratic one? This historic supposition is a second test of the adequacy of the Spanish decision-making process. I shall examine the time lags that occurred in moving through the various stages of the policy-making process, from the recognition of a problem to the execution of measures designed to cope with that problem. Observations of the time consumed in economic policy-making in Spain will be in a form directly comparable to the Kirschen study of time lags in eight Western democracies.[12]

The third test of adequacy concerns the fit between the intention and the outcome of public policy. We assume that no public policy is perfect, that every action will have unanticipated consequences,[13] and further, that better policy choices correctly anticipate and provide for more of the consequences of choice. Furthermore, we must assume that policy-making is an ongoing process, that one must consider a set of choices on the same subject made over a period of time.

Let us then examine two points in the decision process, time X and time Y. In an important sense, the consequences of the policy made at time X become the problem to be solved at time Y. If we are following the same subject of public concern, in our case national economic policy, we can say that the statement of the problem that appears at time Y represents the unfinished business, the unforeseen consequences, of the decision made at time X. Let us then examine the problem of why the problem posed at time Y was not solved with the decision made at time X. We may find that the situation has changed in ways that no policy-maker could reasonably have anticipated. But we may also find that part or all of the new problem represents a situation that was known or knowable at the time the first policy was adopted. If this is the case, there is a series of questions that can be put to evaluate the adequacy of the decision system in use at time X. Was information available at time X which, if properly accounted for, would have advised of the problematic outcome? What happened to this information? Did it ever come to the attention of decision-makers? If not, was the search process of decision wanting? How was the information processed if it was considered? Was the problem context employed such that these considerations were disregarded? Would an alternative policy package have had different consequences? Was such an alternative considered? Why was it not adopted?

Straightforward as this all seems, it can be a terribly misleading way of judging a policy-making process, if it is not used with great care and sophistication. Normally, indeed inevitably, public problems are not settled by one action at one time. Instead there is a chain of decisions, as a government revises its response to a certain type of problem in the light of experience. As Hirschman puts it, the implementation of a policy is in a very real sense a "voyage of discovery."[14] Lindblom's notion of "disjointed incrementalism" simply presumes that things work better if one does not try to solve a problem once and for all, but rather if various groups and interests confront bits and pieces of the overall matter when they appear problematic.[15] And the whole cybernetic metaphor developed by Karl Deutsch and David Easton implies that the political system is an apparatus that learns by the effects of its actions, which of course change the situation in previously unknowable ways.[16]

Because the policy process is ongoing, because each choice is a "leap in faith," because each decision creates something new, the most important effects of which are not precisely knowable in advance, it would be incredibly crude and inappropriate simply to evaluate the efficacy of a decision by looking at what happened that was not supposed to happen. Our judgment of the first decision must be conditioned by relating it to the adaptive capacity of the system as a whole, as reflected in the way the "corrective" decision is handled. Thus we do evaluate the decision made at time X in terms of the problem stated at time Y, but we do so by taking into account the way in which the decision-making process activated between times X and Y helps correct for the deficiencies in the first policy. The Spanish case includes two basic sequences of public problem-solving. The economic planning effort of the 1960s was in part designed to cope with some of the unfinished business of the stabilization program of 1959. Also, the stabilization program itself was part of an ongoing sequence of economic policy actions. Hence the "adequacy" of the stabilization decision may be examined by viewing the problem-solving process that culminated in the economic plan. But the adequacy of earlier decision systems can also be traced by examining the stabilization plan as a statement of a problem that had to be resolved. By this process, something can be learned about the evolution of the problem-solving capabilities of the Spanish state in the postwar period.

Chapter 2

THE POLICY EQUIPMENT
OF NATIONALIST
SPAIN

IN THE MID-1950s, economic conditions in Spain were changing rapidly. The Western boycott on trade with and assistance to Spain had ended with the United States military bases agreement of 1953. A certain amount of economic aid came with this pact, and this aid, together with the growth of the Spanish economy itself and the beginnings of the tourist traffic that was later to be the bonanza industry of Spain, brought the first hints of prosperity after years of hardship. The middle class, at least, was beginning to share the prosperity of postwar Europe. At the same time, Spain was introduced to the typical economic problems of other European nations: the cost of living rose markedly, and balance-of-payments deficits were registered more frequently as demand for industrial and consumer products outran domestic production.

Around Spain, the economic world was changing. European integration, begun under the Marshall plan, was showing its first fruits. In most of Europe there was a general shift in the context of public policy, a change from the economics of reconstruction to that of development, from a political economy of survival to one of growth. European policy-making was going in a new direction, and it was going without Spain, for Spain was not asked to join, nor did it choose to participate in the new trend of events elsewhere in Europe.

Today it is possible to define the principal factors involved in the economic change of that era with some assurance. However, my task is not to write an economic history but to analyze the problem-solving capacity of Spain at that time. Hence, instead of seeing this period through hindsight, it should be seen as it appeared to the policy-makers of that day, that is, from within the system in which they worked and which helped frame their understanding of what was going on and what their response to changing circumstances should be.

Let us begin by examining the tools which were most readily available to the Spanish policy-maker of the mid-1950s. These tools include the techniques of public economic management which were characteristic of Nationalist Spain, those which were legitimate within the system, whose utility had been established, and whose use represented the skill of the leaders of that period. The prevalent problem context or economic ideology that provided the main decision rules and framework for understanding the public role in economic management must also be examined. And we should examine the decision-making systems present and prevalent and the procedures through which problems requiring public attention were identified and processed and programs were enacted. All of this means that to examine the decisions of the mid-1950s, we should look first at the momentum and the legacy of political economy that had been building up since 1939.

The Problem Context: Economic Nationalism

The problem context of a period is part of the equipment of statecraft. It simplifies the number of variables that must be taken into account in making public policy. For the policy-maker, it helps to sort out the significant or relevant from the extraneous or incidental in his perception of heterodox reality. The problem context also provides decision rules for preferring some policy options to others, thus simplifying the choice among possible alternatives.

Most observers seem to agree that Francisco Franco was guided by no rigid economic orthodoxy and that his approach to economic problems was flexible, adaptive, and pragmatic. Nonetheless, there was a "statement of the economic problem" that characterized the first decade of the Franco regime. This orientation toward political economy outlined the tasks for Spanish policy-makers in the period after the Civil War and probably served also as the model of political economy initially used to deal with the changes that came in the 1950s.

Some observers have described this early economic policy as one of autarchy, and autarchy implies the attempt to achieve economic self-sufficiency and independence for purposes of national power. Although Spain cultivated economic self-sufficiency and emphasized armament production in this period, the official position is that these policies were a matter of economic necessity rather than ideological predilection.[1]

Spain emerged from the Civil War destitute. The timing of the conflict, in terms of the larger economic cycle, had been unfortunate. The nation had entered the war from a situation of prolonged depression. From 1936 to 1939, when other nations were beginning their recovery, Spain suffered complete disruption of production, destruction of transport and communications, and the depletion of gold and foreign exchange reserves.

The outbreak of World War II, only months after the Nationalists had consolidated their victory and restored order, precluded foreign trade and assistance as a basic strategy of reconstruction. Traditional trade relations were ruptured. European nations were devoting their full productive capacities to war and could no longer act as suppliers of capital goods and manufactured products, even if Spain could have paid for them. Agricultural recovery, for example, required equipment and fertilizer. Imports of natural phosphates declined from a base of 100 in 1933–35 to 43 in the 1941–45 period, and artificial nitrate imports, from 100 to 16.[2]

Spanish exports also were affected by the war. Traditional luxury agricultural products, such as wine and grapes, were no longer in demand, although such revenue losses were partially offset by increased exports of raw materials, particularly iron.

Spain's success in maintaining wartime neutrality prevented further deterioration of the economy. Indeed, this was a singularly significant act of statesmanship. However, to be effective the neutrality policy required a substantial investment in armaments. Such investment, coupled with the need for internal security, diverted productive capacity that might have been used for civilian recovery.

The end of hostilities in 1945 brought no change in the conditions that made a policy of economic nationalism necessary. Devastated Europe was in no position to resume trade with Spain. While the reconstruction of the rest of the continent was accomplished through massive infusions of American aid, the restoration of international trade, and the first steps toward a policy of economic integration, Spain, whose government was anathema to the victorious allies, was excluded from these efforts. An international boycott of the Franco regime ruled out any alternative to a policy of economic reconstruction through domestic effort alone. As Table 3 suggests, the boycott further postponed Spain's capacity to build economically through trade with the outside world.

The postwar ostracism of Spain is central to the official thesis that the policy of economic nationalism was a matter of necessity rather than intention. The argument deserves at least passing ex-

TABLE 3. THE EFFECT OF WARTIME AND POSTWAR BOYCOTT
ON SPANISH FOREIGN TRADE

Year	Index of export volume	Index of import volume
1935	100	100
1941	46	45
1945	68	47
1948	73	70
1950	98	64

Source: Antonio Robert, Perspectivas de la economía española, p. 106.

amination. If Spanish policy at that time is to be regarded as fully pragmatic, and if economic reconstruction is to be regarded as a preeminent objective, the argument could be made that the taking of credible initial steps toward political liberalization might well have been sufficient to bring Spain into full participation in the general postwar reconstruction effort. The target of the boycott was, after all, a regime deemed incompatible with the West, not Spain as a nation.

There were, then, ideological boundary conditions on the range of options open to Spanish policy-makers. Economic policy possibilities were not infinitely flexible and pragmatic; rather, the objective of establishing the corporate state set metes and bounds for the legitimate range of actions that might be pursued. If economic reconstruction is postulated as the central policy objective, and if reintegration into the world economic system is deemed a promising way of achieving that goal, then political liberalization can be regarded as a pertinent program for achieving that goal. The policy of economic nationalism is rational only if we postulate two coequal objectives—economic reconstruction and the consolidation and perpetuation of a nonliberal political system. These objectives must be reconciled in any political economic program. To the extent that the second objective limits the alternatives appropriate to achieving the first, then economic nationalism becomes a necessary policy.

As it worked out, the Spanish response to the postwar boycott was quite successful from the point of view of the reconciliation of these two objectives, and the allied effort was a failure. Instead of stimulating dissatisfaction with the regime, the boycott was successfully interpreted as an attack on Spain, rather than its government. As a result, the capacity of Spain to rebuild eventually on its own, in the face of concerted external opposition, became a source of considerable pride in achievement and probably contributed to building support for the regime.[3]

And as has so often happened, patience and intransigence eventually paid off for Francisco Franco. Eventually the boycott was lifted, and by 1953 the United States at least had opened the doors of international cooperation in Spanish development. Gradually the lines of normal intercourse with Europe and the world were reestablished, although Spain is not yet a full participant in such arrangements as the European common markets. The costs of the policy were largely lags in incorporating Spain into the postwar international economy, but from the point of view of the regime, these costs were, no doubt, more than offset by the fact that Spain was required to make no major structural changes in its political system. Finally, the very effort to achieve development through self-sufficiency, under the challenge of national crisis, probably helped to generate internal productivity and economic development that might not otherwise have been achieved (see Figures 1 and 2).

While it is true that Francisco Franco was not guided by a carefully developed economic theory, it should be noted that his program did draw from the basic interests and beliefs of those who supported the Nationalist cause. Franco's resolve to maintain a distinctive Spanish course of action in a hostile world meshed well with the antipathy of traditional and Falangist groups toward both liberalism and communism. The desire of most Nationalist elites—military, traditional, and Falangist—for a regime of unity and order was compatible with the program of extensive direct control applied to economic affairs in the reconstruction period.

Franco did accept the fundamental principle of economic organization of the *Falange*. Point nine of the twenty-seven point program of the *Falange española y de los JONS*, of October 1934, had called for the organization of labor and management along Italian Fascist, vertical syndicate lines:

We conceive the economic organization of Spain in terms of a gigantic union of producers. We shall organize Spanish society on a corporative basis by means of a system of vertical syndicates, arranged in accordance with the various branches of production in the service of the national economic integrity.[4]

The syndical idea became the primary instrument of labor and industrial coordination in the reconstruction period. Beyond this,

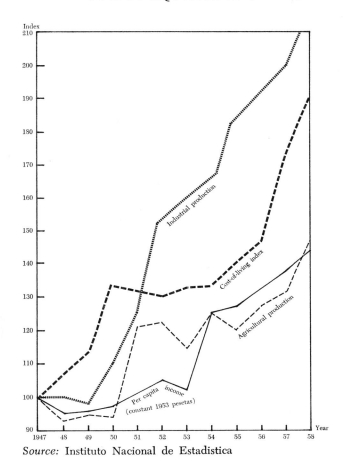

Source: Instituto Nacional de Estadistica

FIGURE 1. MAJOR ECONOMIC INDICATORS DURING POSTWAR PERIOD

Falangist economic thought was more a matter of passionate conviction than well-articulated economic theory and would have provided little clear guidance for economic decision in any event. Franco and the *Falange* parted company primarily on the latter's demand for certain radical reforms. Rather than pursue a populist program against monopoly in big business and big banking, which the *Falange* sought, Franco made these groups central forces in his program of recovery. Moreover, Franco did not ac-

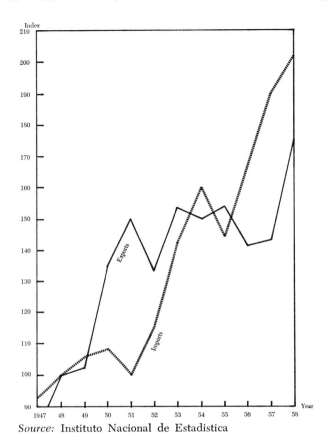

Source: Instituto Nacional de Estadistica

FIGURE 2. SPANISH FOREIGN TRADE DURING THE POSTWAR PERIOD

cept the *Falange* demand for a radical agrarian reform, although here the record is more ambiguous, for the views of José Antonio Primo de Rivera, founder of the *Falange,* on the agrarian question were really not that discordant with the eventual Nationalist program.[5]

Certainly there were ideological implications to the economic policy process in Spain between 1939 and 1955; it was not merely a question of practicality or expediency. Of course ideological commitments did not cover the full range of policy choices, and it is probably fair to state that the only decision that was compelling on ideological grounds alone was that autonomous labor and partisan organizations would not be permitted and that the forms of political economic association would be prescribed by the state in accord with the principles of corporate organization.* Beyond this, the main guidelines for policy-making would seem to be that reconstruction be accomplished by the generation of domestic productive potential (a counsel of necessity) and that economic policy be compatible with the pacification of the country and the consolidation of the regime. Within these confines, there was substantial flexibility to pursue the practical in economic policy.

These policy guidelines, this statement of the "problem context," was in no sense a departure from the main course of Spanish policy in the twentieth century. Under the circumstances, it was the least adventurous, the most prudent line that could have been taken. Protection, the stimulation of self-sufficiency, was the historic and characteristic Spanish response to economic crisis and a culturally preferred way of confronting economic problems.

Despite experiments with economic liberalism in the nineteenth century, the economy did not readapt from its colonial, mercantilist orientation. Spain had few potential export products. Geography and climate limited agricultural possibilities, and in any event the agricultural sector was hard pressed to supply the rapidly expanding home market. Minerals were not a great resource, and Spain, a late starter, did not become industrially competitive. Furthermore, Spanish businessmen were notably unventuresome about export trade. (One notes the predominance of foreign names in both mining and the export wine industry even today.)

The crisis of 1898 consolidated the more historic Spanish approach to public policy. Protectionist groups won over export-oriented businesses and the liberal intelligentsia and established an economic policy orientation that was to be pursued consistently

---

* In terms of the Kirschen scheme, we would describe this as the promotion of coordination through instruments affecting changes in the institutional framework.

throughout the first half of the twentieth century. Despite the political turmoil of the period and the acute ideological variations in the temper of governments, all endorsed a generally protectionist orientation.

Almost all the instruments of the Nationalist economic policy have precedents in this earlier period. The highly protective tariff of 1906, the 1907 policy which reserved public sector purchasing to Spanish industry, and the "Law of the Fleet" which promoted shipbuilding and naval construction were early elements of the policy. The protective tendency was reinforced during World War I. When Spain found herself shut off from outside suppliers, domestic production was encouraged and nationalization of foreign investment undertaken, particularly in transport.[6]

Precedent for much of the Nationalist economic policy can be found in the record of Primo de Rivera's dictatorship of the 1920s. This regime sought to promote national self-sufficiency, engaged in state industrial intervention and promotion, and tried to organize business and enterprise along corporate lines that were, in design if not in accomplishment, strikingly similar to those of the Nationalist period. Some of the most prominent "national interest industries" date from this period, as does the state petroleum monopoly. Efforts at agricultural price control and the regulation of basic commodity markets are strikingly similar to those of the later period, as was an agricultural policy centered on state investment in irrigation.[7]

Thus, Francisco Franco's strategy of reconstruction entailed no fundamental reorientation in economic policy, but was the most prosaic thing that could have been done under the circumstances. A better example of the point that public problem-solving is more apt to be adaptive than innovative could not be found. Necessity and ideology served to reinforce what was, in any event, the established Spanish way of doing things.

The Economic Instruments of Nationalism

Spain's post-Civil War economic policy was a response to an emergency situation. It was necessary to provide the requisites of life to a country ravaged by war, to repair and restore public services and the facilities of production and commerce. There was a desire to avoid inflation and to insure social tranquility through full employment and a fairly equitable distribution of consumer goods. These were the short-run objectives of policy. For the longer term, the policy was also designed to expand production in a poor (by European standards) nation and to improve Spain's historically difficult balance-of-payments position.* In pursuing these goals, Spanish policy-makers attempted to affect the economy at a number of points, using a variety of instruments.

THE CONTROL OF FOREIGN TRADE

Seeking relative self-sufficiency, Spain established a veritable arsenal of tools for controlling international transactions. Although Spain traditionally had been a high tariff nation, fiscal devices seemed an insufficient restraint in the 1940s. In this period of experimentation with direct controls and monetary techniques, the tariff was virtually forgotten. Hence, the tariff of 1922 remained in existence, hardly modified, until 1960.[8]

It is likely that the tariff was seen primarily as an instrument of revenue, not as a control of foreign trade. Spain, like most Latin nations, historically has relied on indirect taxation, finding direct taxes difficult to enact and enforce. In the mid-1950s, about 43 percent of revenues came from indirect taxes, 42 percent from direct taxes, and about 28 percent from tobacco, gasoline, lottery, and purchase taxes.[9] In fact, it may be that policy-makers were reluctant to weight the tariff with too heavy a burden of control, so as not to jeopardize the predictability of its revenue function. Of course, the tariff mechanism remained in the background and reinforced the effect of other techniques of control.

* In Kirschen's language we would describe this set of objectives as: improvement in the balance of payments, expansion of production, improvement in the pattern of private consumption, price stability, full employment, and the achievement of collective needs. We will assume that these were the more important objectives of Spanish policy-makers and that the other goals specified by Kirschen were secondary or derivative from the pursuit of these.

Direct controls were more critical in the strategy of foreign trade regulation. At first, the primary instrument was a system of individual licensing of all imports and exports and was linked to a network of bilateral trade agreements establishing quotas for trade with specific countries. These techniques were, of course, not unique to Spain. Initiated in Germany, they became characteristic of most Western nations in the period before a more coordinated system of international trade was established after World War II.

It would appear that the primary function of this device was to adjust trade to exchange availability. The problem was one of directing exports toward those nations that were capable of satisfying Spain's requirements for food, basic consumer products, and capital goods. Then the problem became one of controlling the flow of imports. It was necessary that they come from countries where Spain had sufficient foreign exchange earnings, and that priority be given to those goods essential to the reconstruction effort. Quotas were fixed both by country and product. Country quotas were the lever by which policy-makers could adjust foreign trade to exchange availability. There was also an element of bargaining in such relationships, as policy-makers attempted to gear trade relations to the most advantageous national deals they could construct. Quotas by product, then, became the instrument to affect the quality of trade. Quotas encouraged specific producers of export items, restricted imports to critical products, and, peripherally, provided an additional means of protection to domestic producers.[10]

Although this device of quotas might have been useful for the purposes of coordinating Spain's trade with the outside world and coping with a difficult crisis, the technique was not adequate in itself for a long-range program of self-sufficiency. Borrowing a policy instrument apparently invented in Latin America during the depression crisis of the 1930s,[11] late in 1948 Spain adopted a program of multiple exchange rates, ostensibly to provide incentives to selected exports and to provide a further means for limiting imports to critical items and encouraging domestic manufacture.[12]

The system provided for a scale of official export rates ranging from 10.95 to 21.90 pesetas to the dollar, and 11.22 to 27.38 for imports. At this time, all foreign exchange had to be traded through the *Instituto Española de Moneda Exterior*. This practice was modified with the establishment of a free market rate, alongside the official rate of exchange, primarily for tourist use. From 1951 to 1957, seven groups of exchange rates existed for imports and five groups for exports, varying according to the percentage of exchange the trader was permitted to sell in the free market and the percentage that had to pass through IEME at official rates.

In theory a multiple exchange rate could function as a refined and precise form of devaluation. The gross effect of devaluation in stimulating exports and discouraging imports would seem to be a rather blunt instrument to employ on the Spanish economy, which was geared historically to price inelastic export products and was critically in need of specific imports for reconstruction and sheer survival. The multiple exchange rate system should have provided the public authorities with a selective mechanism of devaluation or revaluation to be used to stimulate strategic exports and should have made the necessary imports readily available while discouraging superfluous ones.

Unfortunately, the Spanish system never worked this way, for eventually all official rates were set below the free market rate. Hence exports were still disadvantaged and imports subsidized relative to free market prices. It was usually more profitable to import than export. (A related short-run effect of the effort to diversify exports was that Spain's highest cost exports were subsidized while its lowest cost exports were taxed. Coupled with the bilateral trading system, which often worked to force Spanish businessmen to buy in the highest cost foreign market, the entire Spanish economy tended toward a higher cost structure than might otherwise have been the case.) Given the specific use of the multiple exchange rate instrument, one wonders whether the policy-makers' primary purpose might not really have been designed as an alternative to devaluation for a regime so cautious, so eager to appear solid, competent, and "in control." Both at home and abroad, any weakness in the currency would appear as a weakness in the regime as a whole.

And it should be noted that Spain was faced with unusual problems of monetary management in this period. The difficulties of reconciling the Republican and Nationalist currencies, and the related unfreezing of accounts after the Civil War, led to a sharp increase in the money supply. Public deficit financing for reconstruction, the freezing of Spanish assets abroad, the expansion of credit during World War II in anticipation of imports that never materialized, all contributed to the difficulties of maintaining monetary stability.[13]

INDUSTRIAL DEVELOPMENT

Industrial growth was central to the strategy of self-sufficiency. At issue was not only the reconstruction of plants destroyed in civil strife, but also the creation of domestic goods to substitute for imports in a period of foreign trade crisis and the generation of a higher level of employment and consumption for Spain as a whole.

The Nationalist emphasis on industrialization under state direction was the reassertion of a historic theme of economic policy that had been somewhat neglected during the Republic. Granted that the 1930s were hardly an auspicious time for the pursuit of a conscious program in this field, it does seem that the Republican governments, preoccupied with agrarian and educational reform and political questions, did not recognize industrialization as a privileged problem, nor is there evidence of bold ideological or policy statements in this policy area. The selection of industrial self-sufficiency as a critical policy objective is then apparently a marked shift in policy strategy developed by the Nationalist regime, and it would seem that "reasons of state" had much to do

with its specification as a priority problem. The difficulties of
achieving economic recovery while maintaining diplomatic neutrality were particularly acute for a nation that had close ties of
economic dependence with Europe in the stormy period preceding World War II. It is possible that the frustrations experienced
by Antonio Suanzes, later the head of the *Instituto Nacional de
Industria*, in negotiating on Spain's behalf with the German authorities, had much to do with the emphasis placed on industry in
the general autarchic program.

In pursuit of industrialization, Nationalist policy-makers fashioned a complex set of instruments, primarily involving direct
public investment, fiscal incentives, and direct controls, all sup-
plementing the basically protectionist design of foreign trade policy. The central tool was a public institute, or holding company,
the INI. Apparently borrowed directly from its Italian counterpart, the *Instituto per la Ricostruzione Industrial*, or IRI, the formal purposes with which INI was charged at its establishment in
1941 well reflect the overall policy strategy in vogue at that point.
The INI was to promote "economic autarchy" by establishing industry where private enterprise was incapable of acting, with
priority emphasis on import substitution and national defense industries. Some mention of creating public competition with private enterprise in monopoly circumstances was made, primarily
as a bow in the direction of the ideological principles of the *Falange*, with its populist antagonism toward Spanish capitalism.[14]

New industry was generated by the INI in a variety of ways.
Financed almost entirely, until 1957, by grants from the national
government (almost entirely based on government-created credits, with considerable short-run inflationary effect),[15] INI either
created firms outright or participated with private capital in the
new enterprise of the expansion of existing plants. At the end of
1954, INI owned 12 firms, held a controlling interest in 37, and a
minority interest in 12. To demonstrate the scale of these undertakings, it is important to note that 67 percent of INI capital was
invested in wholly owned enterprises, 31 percent in firms where

INI held a controlling interest, and minority participation accounted for only 2 percent of INI capital.[16]

INI's program does seem to have been geared strategically to autarchic principles and reconstruction. Primary investments were made in steel, hydroelectric power, shipbuilding, fertilizer production, the national airline, agricultural chemicals, autos, aluminum, and telephone and telegraph communications. In some fields INI can even be said to have fulfilled its mandate to provide competition for domestic monopolies, as in steel production, electric power, and in the development of artificial textiles to compete with a strong and traditional Spanish industrial sector.[17]

However, given the publicity, and to some extent the flamboyancy, that surrounded INI's operation, it is possible to lose perspective on its role in the total strategy of economic growth. In the first place, INI did not preempt much industrial terrain from the private sector. The primary investment areas were characteristic of public sector agencies in most of Latin Europe during the same period. Furthermore, the extent of INI's participation in total industrial investment was quite modest when compared to public industrial investment elsewhere in Europe. Between 1943 and 1960, INI investment represented an annual average of about 15 percent of total Spanish industrial investment. In contrast, public industrial investment accounted for 47 percent of total industrial investment in Austria, 45 percent in Turkey, 32 percent in the United Kingdom, 31 percent in France, 25 percent in Holland, and 20 percent in Belgium for approximately the same period.[18]

Thus, INI's role must be seen as only one component of a general strategy of industrial growth that relied heavily on the more conventional devices of incentive, direction, and control. Almost all the tools of conventional public policy were geared to the advantage of the domestic private industrial investor. Although Spanish industry traditionally had relied on high protective tariffs, the system of import licensing and currency controls virtually closed the country to competitive products. Strict direct controls on foreign investment effectively prevented competition from for-eign-based firms.

Labor costs were kept low by the denial of an autonomous labor organization and the right to strike. As we shall see, real wage rates, established by market demands for skilled workers, were often illegally rigged by employers to be far above officially established wage levels. Although Spain did provide a rather ex-tensive set of social welfare benefits to employees, the state ab-sorbed a higher proportion of the cost of these programs than was typical in the rest of Europe.

Price controls provided further incentives to industrial invest-ment. What seems to have happened was that a program origi-nally designed to protect the consumer in a period of scarcity be-came a policy that served to protect certain sectors of industry in a later period. Originally, price controls were set to assure the availability of critical products and to protect against inflation. However, it apparently became possible for organized sectors of industry to use official sanctions to underwrite price-fixing agree-ments within the sector. Of course, the corporate style of business organization, with its syndical organization of firms in common areas of production, in a sense legitimated what Americans would describe as "combinations in restraint of trade." Many indepen-dent sources suggest that few industrialists found price controls a constraint on profitability or expansion during the 1940s and 1950s.

For example, in the electric power field, it appears that the ini-tial rates set in 1953 were structured at the level of profitability of the more marginal firms. While this of course guaranteed the re-turns of the more efficient producers, later adjustments raised rates 25 to 30 percent in areas where there was public interest in increased electricity supply and established a general surcharge to cover the costs of investment in new facilities.[19]

At the same time, by permitting the Bank of Spain to exceed limits in credit creation, by supporting and stimulating the role of the private banking community in industrial credit, policy-makers sought to insure that entrepreneurs would not be hampered for want of money to invest.[20]

Finally, it should be noted that taxation on enterprises constituted a comparatively light burden during this period. In the pre-1957 era, taxation amounted to no more than 10 percent of national income,[21] and the high reliance on indirect taxation meant that the impact of taxation was less directed at corporate profits than would have been the case in most other Western nations.

Thus industrialists in critical sectors had available a remarkably congruent set of incentives and advantages as a consequence of the general structuring of conventional policy instruments. In some cases they were further advantaged by the Law of National Interest Industries which provided that firms deemed critical to the autarchy policy could have the advantage of forced expropriation,* tax reductions of up to 50 percent, a guaranteed yield of 4 percent on invested capital, and a reduction in tariffs for raw materials and equipment. The government obtained the right to intervene in management and to withdraw tax exemptions if earnings exceeded 7 percent.[22] However, it should be noted that this measure was primarily used to support INI financed firms. Up to 1959, only thirty industries had been approved for these privileges, of which twenty were owned wholly or in part by INI.[23] Finally, we should note a related law of 1945 which provided 50 percent tax reductions for enterprises in the fields of electric power and nitrogenous fertilizers.

Throughout, the policy-makers of this period tried to apply tight controls to the direction of industrial investment. As the distinguished Spanish economist Ramón Tamames suggests, what in effect happened was that private enterprise was regulated and controlled beyond liberal norms, and at the same time the private investor was provided with incentives and protection beyond liberal norms.[24]

---

* Government expropriation, at administratively determined prices, of properties selected by the firms for plant expansion or development.

Sometimes bureaucratic procedures could be incredibly frustrating. For example, no new industry could be established, expanded, or moved without the consent of the Ministry of Industry. However, for an industry dependent on foreign raw materials or equipment, authorization by this Ministry to establish a plant did not convey licenses for the requisite imports, which had to be applied for separately.[25]

AGRICULTURAL POLICY

For the first ten years of the Nationalist regime, agricultural policy was largely a desperate issue of recovery, a matter of using a small set of selected instruments to rebuild agricultural production and to feed the Spanish population on a very low level of production. By the end of the Civil War, Spanish agriculture was down to two-thirds of its prewar production level. Recovery was slow. Not until the early 1950s did production begin to return to the levels of the early 1930s.[26]

The critical public policy instruments in this first decade were state marketing institutions in basic commodities. Most important, and perhaps representative, was the program in wheat. Through the *Servicio Nacional de Trigo*, the government attempted to guarantee the supply of bread. Acreage requirements in wheat were imposed in relevant areas. The government trading enterprise purchased the entire crop at a guaranteed price, provided storage facilities to even out seasonal variations in supply, controlled prices to the consumer, and engaged in international trading to make up deficits in domestic production. The objectives to be reconciled in such a program involved protecting farm income, maintaining an adequate national supply, and keeping consumer prices low and stable.[27]

Initial steps in agricultural reconstruction included efforts to substitute domestic supplies of agricultural fertilizers and machinery for traditional imports that were cut off by wartime. The industrialization program of INI gave high priority to investments in these fields, and the start of domestic production in the late

1940s and early 1950s coincides with the beginnings of agricultural recovery in Spain. In addition, government stimulation, through shipbuilding, organization, and subsidy, advanced the fishing industry in this period to provide substitutes for protein foods not otherwise available. Beyond this, the Ministry of Agriculture maintained the policy format inherited from previous regimes, including sketchy programs in education, credit, extension, and research.

Only in the late 1940s did the Franco government undertake the set of massive irrigation works that was to be the distinctive feature of this era's agricultural policy. In such areas as Badajoz and Jaén, large-scale capital investment was combined with a program of directed colonization of small farmers on newly improved lands, the whole supported by a coordinated program of public organization, credit, and technical services. The objective was to create model agrarian projects and to raise the level of agrarian life in depressed regions, while increasing national agricultural output. That the projects were quite expensive in relation to productivity increases, and that the benefits of the public programs reached only a small proportion of the total population, would later become apparent.[28] At the time, however, they were dramatic and visible evidence of the government's progressive attitude toward agriculture.

The problem for agrarian policy-makers had both economic and political dimensions. While trying to increase production and control supplies and prices, the political effort at "pacification" required at least the image of attention to the demands that had generated radical politics in the Spanish countryside in the 1930s. The issue of agrarian reform had been central in the politics of the Republic and in the Civil War, and it was important to the ideology of the *Falange*. However, the issue was a knotty one, complicated by the diversity of agricultural conditions in Spain and the complexity of a vast number of different land tenure arrangements, while at the same time the problem of feeding the population was a day-to-day concern. In this perspective, the relationship of the Spanish landed class to the regime was at issue, but only part of the issue.

The policy response to agrarian reform was never one of tackling the problem head on, but rather of adopting a number of projects, none purely symbolic, to nibble at the more readily manageable parts of the problem. Irrigation schemes, providing for the resettlement of some of the more mobile and able farmers, was one component. Another provided for the consolidation of small holdings (*minifundia*). A quite ingenious project, it involved government assistance to any community seeking a more rational structure of land holdings, which in many parts of Spain had been broken into incredibly complex patterns of small parcels. One farmer might hold a set of completely discontinuous plots, the management of which would completely defy the use of machinery or other economically efficient techniques of cultivation. This consolidation program, instituted in December 1952, was extended to the entire nation in July 1955. Finally a law concerning "land capable of improvement" was passed in December 1953. Directed at the larger estates (*latifundia*) cultivated by traditional techniques, it provided for the expropriation of underutilized land unless the owners made recommended investments, for which they were provided subsidies. Though the law was applied gently and expropriation rarely if ever used, underutilization studies from 1954 to 1960 covered 216,000 hectares and resulted in the investment of PTS. 43 million.[29]

PUBLIC WORKS, TRANSPORT, AND HOUSING

Massive public works undertaken through direct public investment are often associated with the Nationalist regime. The regime made much of the highly visible, excellently engineered and constructed, high dams built for irrigation and hydroelectric purposes, of public housing, and of other facilities. Certainly there were real achievements in these areas. However, Spanish infrastructure investment policy through the 1950s was highly selective. Concentration on investment in intensive irrigation schemes was offset by a relative passivity in other areas, particularly highway construction.

Nationalist transport policy reflected the crisis of reconstruction, stressing maximum use of existing facilities rather than heavy investment in their improvement. Due to the destruction of vehicles in the Civil War, the problems of replacement of stock, and the difficulty of importing petroleum in wartime and after, railway transport was emphasized and road transport discouraged. This basic decision, quite consciously made and reinforced by investment emphasis, import policy, and rate regulation which definitely advantaged railroad over road carriers, was continued into the 1950s, long after the need for it had passed. With changing circumstances, Spain was left with a transport system quite unbalanced in comparison with the rest of Europe.[30]

The Franco government nationalized all broad-gauged railroads in 1941 and consolidated them into the single public system, the *Red Española Nacional de Ferrocarriles*. Railroad policy was to treat the system as a means to industrial development and not as an object of development itself. The program was one of maximum utilization of existing stock and facilities, with only such repair or improvement as was absolutely imperative. By the end of the 1950s, over 80 percent of the locomotives were still steam powered (in part reflecting the petroleum conservation measures), some over one hundred years old.

Highway construction was largely confined to minimal maintenance of the existing network, which was quite adequate in the 1930s. New construction did not reflect changes in automobile technology, and 1930 standards of width, engineering, and so on were generally applied.

Although housing was a high formal policy priority in Nationalist Spain, accomplishments until the mid-1950s were well below national needs and certainly below the comparative achievements of such nations as Britain and the Netherlands, though not so different from France and some other countries. The basic mechanism was public funding of rent-controlled housing, with priority given to construction by local governments and *sindicatos*. From the establishment in 1939 of the *Instituto Nacional de Vivienda* to 1954, an annual average of 16,000 units were constructed. Apparently this poor showing had more to do with materials bottlenecks than funding, for INI investments in cement and building materials helped to correct this situation. The First National Housing Plan of 1956–60 met 77 percent of its objective of 550,000 units, a quite impressive change in the pace of construction.[31]

Although the record was uneven and accomplishment varied from task to task, in general the public works sector was certainly one leading edge of Spanish economic reconstruction and development in the early Nationalist period. The intention to generate employment and general productivity through infrastructure development was realized. Production of electric power and construction activities expanded considerably faster than the economy as a whole to the mid-1950s, through a mix of policy instruments that included direct public investment closely linked to related INI industrial undertakings, a concentration of fiscal policy incentives in private activity in these areas, nationalization in transport, and regulatory measures that directed private activity toward public goals.

CONTROL OF THE ECONOMY

Price and wage controls were used extensively in the early Nationalist period to order and stabilize the economy. Again a certain perspective is necessary. The level of control was not totally pervasive and was not incomparable to those controls applied in most of Europe during the wartime and reconstruction period. Furthermore, the level of organization in Spain was such that enforcement was never thoroughgoing. Outright evasion, black marketeering, and informal, but accepted arrangements to thwart the intent of the controls were widely practiced.[32]

Direct price controls were confined to such basic essentials as coal, electricity, gas, minerals, metals, and building materials.

Other controls in industry were based largely on cost estimates by producers. The system of foodstuffs regulation has already been described. It covered primarily flour, bread, olive oil, and sugar. As Rogers states: "There [is] a wide field where authorities do not intervene. . . ."[33]

Despite these caveats, the use of direct controls in regulating productive activity, seen cumulatively, is impressive if not a little staggering. The Spanish producer, be he in industry, agriculture, or commerce, was subjected to authoritative regulation at almost every point in the productive process. In addition to price controls on some products, one must recall that many domestic supplies and most imported materials were subject to licensing and quotas. New enterprise or plant expansion required official permission. Relationships to other firms in the same sector were subject to syndical regulation which could affect, among other things, the share of the market, projected expansion or investment, and inter-sectoral transactions. Normal corporate and commercial organization and trade were covered by extensive regulation, in the civil law tradition. Fiscal policy provided other constraints and incentives. Finally, labor relations were closely directed and controlled by administrative regulations rather than by collective bargaining.

LABOR POLICY

Industrial relations in early Nationalist Spain involved an interesting interplay among ideological principle, the necessities of economic crisis, the objective of development with price stability, and the political goal of national pacification and social peace, which required the acceptance of the regime, if not enthusiasm for it, within the working class.

Since to the corporatist collective bargaining involved the "heresies" of class conflict and competition, and since a high degree of direct control was desired, until 1958 wages were set by official regulation, through negotiations that involved the Ministry of Labor and the syndical representatives of labor and management.

In general, Spanish policy may be described as a matter of rather rigidly restraining wage increases, at least until 1954, to preserve price stability. Offsetting this policy, extensive fringe benefits and protections were provided.

The general wage guideline seemed to consider 1936 the last normal year and set wages slightly ahead of 1936, but not by much. That such official wages were artificially low was evident throughout the Franco period. The market for labor was always ahead of public policy, and through overtime, bonuses, and various ruses, real wages quickly exceeded official ones. The Ministry of Labor would then periodically raise the legal salary levels to where they thought the real ones might be. Eventually, the legal rates came to be regarded as minimums.[34] Until about 1949, one notes a great number of regulations and changes in salary rates for specific jobs in specific industries. About 1950, the tenor of the policy changed. Across-the-board, cost-of-living increases became the dominant technique of wage policy, with only marginal adjustments in the interprofessional wage.[35]

To evaluate Spanish labor policy in any sensible way, we must consider benefits along with wages. In terms of protections against layoff and firing, holidays, and insurance and social benefits, the total package of welfare programs was comparable to most European practice. This is not surprising. The ideology of the Franco regime toward labor, as presented in the Charter of the Rights of Labor of 1938, reflected advanced European social thought the long way around, via German, Italian, and Austrian models. While the policy was of course illiberal and undemocratic—the right of strike and autonomous organization were forbidden—the agenda of public social action was similar to that of countries where socialist thought or social democratic thought had won policy victories. However, the proportion of the population excluded from such programs, primarily the agricultural sector, was probably greater than in other European countries.

What was the total effect in Spain of this labor policy in comparison with the rest of Europe? Unfortunately, it is virtually impossible to make comparisons for the early postwar period. The only studies that are helpful refer to the early 1960s and reflect accomplishments of the process we are about to analyze. Nonetheless, they do enable us to evaluate, in rough fashion, the general significance of the Spanish labor program.

If we look to the proportion of national income devoted to the remuneration of workers (Table 4), we find that Spanish policy led to a general distribution effect low for Europe, but not totally unrepresentative of this pattern.

TABLE 4. PERCENTAGE OF NATIONAL INCOME DEVOTED TO WAGES

Country	1958	1962
Austria	61	61
Belgium	57	58
Brazil	48	47
Denmark	59	—
France	59	61
Germany	61	64
Peru	38	37
Sweden	65	70
United Kingdom	73	75
United States	70	72
Spain	56	67.5

Source: H. París Eguilaz, Desarrollo económico Español: 1906–1964 (Madrid: J. Sanchez Ocaña y Cia., 1965). Though the source is friendly to the Nationalist regime, my own independent calculations using United Nations data indicate that it is essentially correct.

Perpina Rodríguez completed a more rigorous study of the same question, comparing Spanish and other European salaries in 1963. He found that nominal salaries in Germany and Belgium were about three times higher than in Spain, that French salaries were two and a half times higher, and Italian wages twice as high. However, taking into account relative purchasing power for prime necessities, primarily food, the difference of sheer wage rates is somewhat blunted (see Table 5).

Rodríguez goes on to note that Spanish labor practice includes payment of a full day's wage for Sunday, two additional monthly

TABLE 5. RELATIVE PURCHASING POWER OF AVERAGE
HOURLY INCOMES: EUROPE 1963
(Spain = 100)

Spain	100
Germany	206
Belgium	173
Netherlands	198
Italy	83

Source: Perpina Rodríguez, *Los salarios en la industria Española y en el
extranjero* (Madrid: J. Sanchez Ocaña y Cia., 1964), pp. 169, 178–79.

payments (July 18, to celebrate Franco's uprising of 1936, and
Christmas) instead of the single-month salary bonus conventional
in Europe, and that Spanish family benefits are generally higher
than in the rest of Europe.

Spain and Europe

Having set Spanish labor policy against the background of the
broader European experience, let us do the same for the economic policy equipment of Spain in general. The economic policy
experience of postwar Western Europe was, of course, quite diverse. It ranged from the vigorous neo-liberalism of West Germany to the maintenance and, some would argue, the extension
of the *dirigiste* tradition in France. Nonetheless, these distinctions
were largely matters of emphasis and style within a generally
common set of assumptions about the relations of state and economy. Although planning, public enterprise, market forces, fiscal
and monetary instruments, and controls were used differently in
the various nations, there was acceptance by all of a fundamen-
tally private economy, directed, shaped, and guided by a rather
common set of public policy instruments.[36]

Read against this background, the Nationalist regime did not
construct a totally distinctive political economic system. The set
of possibilities for public economic action was much like that of
Western Europe. The objectives that Spanish policy-makers pursued were compatible with their European counterparts. Spain

shared common policy approaches in the immediate postwar period with most of Europe. The imperatives of reconstruction, of generating productivity while maintaining relative price stability in a period of excess demand, of reconciling the historic demands of social reformers for social benefit while maintaining a basically capitalist framework were constraints and problems that affected Spanish policy-makers in much the same way as they did their European counterparts. Spain borrowed policy techniques from several European nations. Her approach to economic policy was a distinctive variant on European themes; nonetheless it was well within the range of possibilities of the common European experience.

Thus the elaborate system of foreign trade and exchange controls erected in Spain seems a unique program of autarchy only if we ignore the rest of the European experience and read the Spanish story in isolation. However, all the instruments of currency controls, import quotas, and bilateral trading agreements were commonplace in European policy from the late 1930s on. Originating in Germany, these instruments quickly spread to the rest of Europe before World War II. In the face of excess demand and dollar shortages, they were continued into the postwar period. The United Kingdom alone tried to establish convertibility shortly after the war, in 1947, and failed. Only in 1949 and 1950, under considerable pressure from the United States and with the beginnings of transnational economic policy experiments, in which Spain did not participate, did foreign trade liberalization become an important tendency in the rest of Europe.

Emphasis on public investment in industry was characteristic of some European nations in the immediate postwar period and not of others. The Spanish experience, of direct and mixed public capitalization through INI, has close parallels in France, Austria, and Italy. Nationalization under Labour in Britain and the modest Dutch efforts at public investment in steel belong to a similar category of events. The more rigorous reliance on private industrial activity in Germany, Belgium, and Scandinavia provides the other pole of the European experience. In general, the spirit and structure of public industrial activity in Spain is most similar to its Latin neighbors, France and Italy.

Direct price supports in agriculture were characteristic of all of Europe in the postwar period. Special regional programs of agricultural investment in Spain have close parallels in Italian experience. If anything, Spanish authorities were less active in support of agriculture than other European nations, where strong agricultural interest groups could require extensive public programs and advantages.

Extensive direct controls were a prime characteristic of Spanish economic policy, but they were important in the rest of Europe as well through the 1940s. Price controls and rationing practices instituted in wartime came to an end about 1949 or 1950 in most countries. Again, Spanish practice seems to have its closest parallels in France and Italy. Wage-control practice varied considerably in different European nations. Many countries rapidly decontrolled wages and relied on collective bargaining after the immediate wartime emergency had passed. On the other hand, the Netherlands used wage controls as a central instrument of economic planning into the 1960s. On the whole, Spain seems most closely to resemble France on this score for the immediate postwar period. Wage controls continued in France until February 1950. However, a freeze on wages was imposed shortly thereafter. By the mid-1950s, French wage policy was one of uniform interprofessional increases in wages and bonuses, much as in Spain.

In relation to direct controls, Spanish experience was distinctive in one respect. In most of Europe, controls were understood to be emergency measures, counsels of necessity, that should not be continued after the critical circumstances that led to their imposition had passed. In Spain circa 1950, on the other hand, one gets the impression that controls were conceived to be part of the systematic structure of the relation of state and economy, a normal and expected part of public regulation.

Evaluation of Policy Equipment

This, then, was the ongoing public economic activity, the established tried and tested body of techniques that Spanish policy-makers worked with. In the absence of active need to do otherwise, we would assume that these were the instruments to which Spanish policy-makers would have first recourse in solving the continuing problems of economic growth and stability. How rich, then, was the legacy of policy equipment that the first generation of Nationalist economic statesmen bequeathed to the second?

First, it should be noted that the boundaries of orthodoxy were not severe. Few possibilities were excluded in principle from the potential agenda of state activity. With the important exception of autonomous labor organization and collective bargaining, few techniques were excluded on the grounds of legitimacy alone. It was not so much a matter of pragmatism, but rather that the heterogeneity of the Nationalist movement and the political sense of its leader contributed to the basic flexibility of policy approach. The conservatism of the Movement made room for high capitalism, while the populism of the *Falange* required that some gestures toward social reform be made.

The composition of political support, historic circumstances, and doctrinal eclecticism made a mixed approach to the problem of government and economy not only appropriate but essential. There was no reason to attack established private enterprise or to pursue a program of nationalization. On the other hand, there was no reason to preclude massive public investment as a central part of a strategy of industrialization.

Certainly the regime had some ideological constraints. Nationalist Spain, one recalls, rejected the "excesses" of both "totalitarian communism" and "anarchic liberalism." Consequently, the devices and policies characteristic of both were excluded from the format of government, thereby eliminating on the one hand authoritative central planning or labor mobilization and on the other, extensive reliance on individual competition and market forces. But these taboos of the Civil War hardly interfered with the work of Spanish policy-makers. They merely helped, in their own exceedingly curious and roundabout way, to orient Spain in its own fashion to the "mixed economy" assumptions of postwar Western Europe.

The regime was basically unrevolutionary. It eliminated little and maintained much of the policy equipment of earlier periods. In such fields as irrigation, it emphasized historic commitments. It borrowed techniques of emergency and reconstruction economic policy from contemporary practice in other lands. It also adopted means of foreign trade control from its Latin American sister states and programs that were standard in the West. To this format it added innovations, mostly derived from corporatist ideology, such as the syndical technique of industrial organization. In most fields, a diversity of approach and a mixing of mechanism. Incentives and subsidies were often no more than the oblitical reasons. It may be that the spectrum of the appropriate in most policy fields was somewhat broader than it was in most communist and many liberal regimes of the same period.

However, despite this relative doctrinal openness, there was a strong tendency in practice to prefer instruments of direct control over more subtle devices of state regulation and direction. Ideology, the emergency conditions of reconstruction, and a *dirigiste* tradition that was more bureaucratic than military in its origins, all mutually reinforced a tendency in this direction. "Market forces" were a residual rather than an intentional policy mechanism. Incentives and subsidies were often no more than the obverse of programs of direct control, as in the case of pricing regulations that were designed to stimulate investment in electric power generation, or import and export licensing practices intended to give greater differential advantage to specific sectors or industries.

At issue here was the preference among instruments, rather than their sheer availability. Certainly Spain used monetary, fiscal, and credit policies to regulate the economy. However, Spain failed to borrow quickly the more effective techniques of monetary manipulation as they came into vogue in the rest of Europe and continued to emphasize direct controls while they were fading into the background of the policy mix elsewhere.

As we shall see, the interplay between the Spanish bureaucratic system and the syndical institutions more probably accounted for this preference for direct controls than did the emergency conditions of reconstruction, the military leadership of the regime, or Falangist ideology. The syndical structure presupposed negotiations and agreements among firms, rather than market competition, as a basic regulator of economic activity. However, it was not merely corporatistic decision-making but was such negotiation, superintended and reinforced by a bureaucratic establishment, that set the basic pattern of public action. The pattern was similar in the field of labor relations.

The bureaucratic, regulatory phenomenon was, of course, not simply a product of the Nationalist regime; it was a historic part of Spanish government. It had its roots in Hapsburg absolutism and was refined by the French tradition of a professional civil service in the Bourbon period and again during the nineteenth century when Spain began to develop a *grand corps* on the model of France. Spain shares facets of political culture with other Mediterranean lands. There is a bureaucratic ethos in such societies, in which the economic statesman feels vaguely uncomfortable with the fluidity of market forces and essentially autonomous and disjointed decision centers, and he is far more comfortable when things are clearly nailed down by a specific, written regulation.

Changing the format of Spanish economic policy in the 1950s was, then, not a matter of a radical restructuring of the agenda of state or of daring and creative innovation. The Spanish policymaker had available to him, in the established equipment of the state, most of the tools of modern economic policy. Some techniques were in need of repair and updating, to be sure; some were a bit rusty from disuse, particularly in the fields of fiscal and monetary policy. However, there were few taboos in system and few techniques were excluded on grounds of principle alone. In summary, the richness of the policy equipment of the Spanish state was not incomparable to that of the rest of the West. The "warehouse of semi-fabricated parts" was generally adequate to cope with the new issues that Spain was soon to face.

Chapter 3

THE PROCEDURAL EQUIPMENT
OF NATIONALIST
SPAIN

WHILE THE LEADERS OF Nationalist Spain were perhaps not particularly innovative in the economic realm, in politics they certainly tried to be different. The structure and logic of Spain's constitutional order were unlike anything that existed elsewhere in postwar Europe. Perón's Argentina was the only major contemporary parallel. In dealing with the governmental system of Nationalist Spain we are treating a distinctive case, not a variation on the way things were normally done in the West.

The structuring of the organic state was hardly an act of political originality. Those who developed the institutions of Nationalist Spain could find ample precedent both in the interwar experiments in Italy and Germany and in their own political heritage. The regime of General Primo de Rivera in the 1920s promoted, though only imperfectly implemented, a corporate scheme for political economic organization that strongly resembled the Nationalist undertakings in this field.[1] Falangist ideology concerning political structure probably owes as much to the institutional patterns propounded in this period of Spanish politics as it does to the inspiration of authoritarianism in other countries.

Furthermore, the ideological justification for the Nationalist political structures rested not on ideological creativity, but rather on the restoration of traditional usages. The corporate form of representation and the principles of authority and community that underlay the system were deemed to be the classic way of doing politics in Spain, temporarily perverted by inappropriate flirtations with foreign liberal models. The regime would eventually restore the monarchy, the traditional base of legitimacy and statehood. The prime decision bodies—the cabinet, council of state, council of the realm—were deemed continuations of the councils of the Crown during the fifteenth and sixteenth centuries. The legislative body would be called the *Cortés*, affirming an ancient and indigenous usage, not by the name and structure of an imported parliamentary model. The system of representation would resemble that of the medieval estates. From this point of view, it is liberalism and communism that are the contrived political experiments; resting not on centuries of usage but on "artificial and hypersymplified" theories of human motivation and social structure, liberalism and communism are the newcomers on the political scene. How much this credo of restoration of traditional political forms was actually conscious in the minds of the institution builders and guided their decision is, of course, conjectural. The important point is that the regime did not formally present its efforts as an act of political creativity. The new Spanish state was portrayed merely as an adaptation of perennial principles of government to contemporary conditions.

Of course, it would be hard to name a form of government for which relevant Spanish experience could not be cited. In the nineteenth and twentieth centuries, Spain had fluctuated between various forms of constitutional monarchy, republicanism, and military absolutism. Anarchism and communism, as well as socialism and other forms of both radical and conservative thought, had been strong domestic forces.

The Spanish political legacy was ambiguous concerning the nature of legitimate authority. Hence traditional monarchy, military rule, and liberal republican, as well as anarchist and Marxist, principles were all "available" bases of authority for the system. None really connoted an unprecedented step, yet none was the obvious, unquestioned pattern of political structure. Similarly, in labor organization, both syndical structure and autonomous, competitive labor organization had been present in the recent past. Neither was truly an innovation; neither was the accepted way of doing things. So broad and indeterminate had Spanish political experience become by this time that precedent could be cited for almost any institution or procedure.

In any event the Spanish policy-makers after 1939 had to undertake the construction of a new set of political institutions. Their task of devising policy-making procedures was not a case of normal politics. The accepted ways of formulating policy through republican process had been discredited. The critical associations that provided information and representation in decision making —the parties and labor organizations—belonged to the enemy. In devising decision systems, these policy-makers could not rely on an established reservoir of equipment, within a clear understanding of acceptable procedure. Particularly in the first years after the civil war, the dominant problem of procedural instrumentation was the construction rather than the use of political institutions.

In the following section we will look at the procedural equipment made available to Nationalist statesmen for the purpose of making decisions on economic affairs.

The Organic State and Basic Rules of Procedure

The idea of the organic state provided basic guidelines for fashioning all classes of procedural instruments. Stating its major principles should give us clues to the nature of procedure-making in Nationalist Spain, that is, to those processes deemed requisite in policy formulation and the limits of the appropriate in setting up systems of deliberation, consultation, and choice.

The concept of the organic state implies that the various sec-

tors or interests of society are not to be understood as autonomous, essentially apart from the state, though represented in the
process of government. Such a system is said to lead to the un-
predictability and disorder of liberalism. Rather, in the organic
state, the various sectors of society will be synchronized with,
meshed into, the state itself.

The principal objective of any structural arrangement would
seem to be the "harmonization of interests." Institutional engineering should lead to the blending of the basic interests of the
society into an organic whole. This blending must be intentionally created by interweaving the critical groups and "corporations"
into all forums of decision. The basic ingredients are the main
forms of representation in the system—family, local government,
and syndical—to which are added spokesmen for the prime institutions—the cabinet, the *Cortés,* the military, the Church, the
Movement. The prime structural technique is that of the interlocking directorate, with members of each major institution influential in the affairs of all others.

This, of course, is the inverse of American notions of political
pluralism and the separation of powers, in which the key concept
is to pit one center of power against another so as to prevent a
concentration of authority and control at any point in the system.
And as in the American case, where this constitutional principle
has been diffused throughout the society, and the establishment
of competing and plural centers of authority is deemed a basic
notion of organizational engineering, so in Nationalist Spain, the
idea of the harmonization of interests becomes a rather general
principle of organization for the society. (Hence, as we shall see,
the rather different Spanish perception of the significance of car-
telization in the economy.)

A second principle of procedural instrumentation in the organic state is that representation should be "authentic," that is, licensed. Only such groups as are legally recognized to speak for
their sectors can claim a role in the decision process. For each
aspect of life, there is to be a recognized institution of representa-

tion. Such groups as form autonomously or spontaneously in the community need not be heeded in official deliberations, unless political pragmatism counsels otherwise. Thus in economic affairs the only authentic vehicles of participation in the decision process are the syndicates and certain other recognized or tolerated forms of association.* Organizations that emerge outside of this structure are outlaws.

All of this, of course, is quite contrary to the liberal tradition regarding interest association. Leaving aside for the moment such technical matters as the registration of congressional lobbies in the United States, the presumption in liberal democracies is that autonomous and voluntary association is an expected and valued part of the system, and that such associations exercise the initiative of deciding to bring their demands and interests to policy-makers. Certainly the policy-maker in a liberal society has a broader latitude for bringing groups into the process of policy formulation, and the legal recognition of status is not a major criterion for assessing the propriety or utility of a group's participation.

A third principle of participation in the organic state is that representation is consultative and not controlling. Participation in policy-making throughout the system is mostly a question of advice and deliberation, and seldom the exercise of power. The principle that collective forums are advisory, and do not control executive figures, extends throughout the system. At the top level the cabinet serves at the pleasure of the Chief of State and is not responsible to a parliament. In various areas of policy-making, cabinet members may have advisory bodies, but they have no authoritative powers. In local government, the Spanish equivalents of city council (*ayuntamientos*) act primarily as consultants to local ex-

---

* A distinction should be made between formally authorized and tacitly permitted structures. Though the *Ley de Unidad Sindical* specified that all political economic representation should flow through the syndical bodies, this was not uniformly enforced. While the law was rigidly enforced toward labor, many forms of business, commercial, and associational organization were implicitly recognized as part of the representational structure.

ecutive authorities, although their approval is required for some types of decisions. In general, it would be most surprising to find any decision procedure in Spain in which a consultative body was created with power to enact and effect a specific course of action.*

In a more vague and indeterminate fashion, not only the associations that participate in decision-making but also the individuals who may do so are limited by public license. Formally, there is the expectation that the holders of all critical public posts, all those who stand for local government offices, or posts in the syndicates or *Cortés*, shall be members of the National Movement. While this requirement to some extent may condition the policy-maker's selection of participants in decision-making, this limitation on procedural instrumentation is much less compelling than the other three. Membership in the Movement became broad and relatively *pro forma* quite soon after the initial consolidation of power by the Nationalists.

While recognizing the obvious fact that existing liberal regimes do screen political actors for doctrinal conformity and that they do to some extent preselect the participants in the policy processes, let us simply summarize how the formal logic of liberal democracy differs from that of the organic state. Democratic liberalism sees procedure as a way of working out conflicts between diverse interests and points of view in the body politic. It presumes that the state should not identify the interests or their

* However, the new Spanish constitution, enacted by referendum in 1966, deviates from this principle. When this document becomes fully effective, the President of the Government (prime minister) may be responsible to some extent to a two-thirds vote of the Council of the Realm, a body composed of representatives of the Church, the military, the presidents of the Supreme Court and the Council of State, and various members elected by the *Cortés*. Similarly, under this new constitution, cabinet ministers will be responsible to the President of the Government and not to the Chief of State. However, none of these revised procedures went into effect during the period covered in this study. A thorough discussion of the new constitution is included in: Servicio Informativo Español, *Referendum 1966: Nueva constitución* (Madrid: Ministerio de Información y Turismo, 1966).

mode of impact on decisions, but that these should form auton-omously, act according to recognized and universalized proce-dural rules, and that they will be co-opted into the process by mutual accommodation with established groups. In the organic state, the basic interests in the community are defined in advance by political authority. Repression and exclusion, rather than co-operation and accommodation, is the formal norm governing re-sponse to interests that do not fit the predetermined structure of participation. This again is the formal logic of these systems. What happens in fact is often different.

Basic Constitutional Procedure

The constitutional order is the most general statement of how such guidelines will apply to the making of public policy. Therein are the requisite procedures that must be followed to give legiti-mate effect to a program of public action. Of course, the constitu-tional order provides only the bare bones of procedure, and it will be embellished and refined in each area of public concern.

The formal structure of the Spanish state in the Nationalist pe-riod can be stated quite simply. There is no written constitution; rather the regime is presumed to be based on a set of fundamen-tal laws.[2] The state is formally a monarchy, with the throne tem-porarily unoccupied. The purpose of the *Caudillo*, Francisco Franco, who occupies the position of Chief of State for life, is to restore this traditionally legitimate order. In addition to the office of the Chief of State, the critical institutions include the cabinet, normally of about eighteen members responsible to the Chief of State alone, and the *Cortés*.

Theoretically, all legislative powers are vested in the Chief of State. This would imply that all procedures of consultation are discretional for Francisco Franco. However, it is normally ap-propriate and customary for policy to be formulated in the cabi-net and submitted to the *Cortés* after approval by the Chief of State and the minister concerned.[3] Apparently only fiscal bills must be approved by the *Cortés*, in keeping with the *Fuero de los Españoles,* which includes the "no taxation without representation" principle. All other bills need not be approved by the *Cortés* to have the force of law. Formally, for a wide range of topics, debate, by the *Cortés* is at the discretion of the cabinet. The *Cortés* does have the right to initiate legislation, though only one such initiative was approved during the 1945–58 period. The law of the *Cortés* describes its role as one of "cooperation" in legislation. It has no definitive power. The *Cortés* symbolizes not the power of the people, but their participation in the affairs of government.

However, formal constitutional theory has never reflected the working relationship between Franco and the *Cortés.* Although the parliamentary body theoretically can be eliminated from "due process of law" (as can the cabinet for that matter), these are powers that are seldom used. The overwhelming body of legislation does pass through the *Cortés* and, particularly in recent years, government proposals are often substantially revised in the committees of the *Cortés.* While the Chief of State has the power to issue "decree laws" on his own initiative, this power is used mainly for certain types of fiscal, routine procedures. From 1943 to 1951, 1,423 laws (passed by the *Cortés*) and 223 decree laws were enacted. For the period 1952-1956, the figures are 616 laws and 133 decree laws. About two-thirds of the decree laws in the latter period dealt with *Hacienda* matters, mainly approval of public debt issues.[4]

Another procedure that the Chief of State can use at his discretion is the referendum. This public consultation on policy is designed to be used when the Chief of State believes it "opportune and desirable due to the exceptional importance of the laws of the uncertainty of public opinion." To date, the referendum procedure has been used only to give an extra seal of sanctity to fundamental or constitutional acts. Curiously, legislative process is required in the abrogation or revision of fundamental laws, such action requiring both a referendum and approval by the *Cortés.*[5]

However, the fundamental components of Nationalist Spain in the field of economic policy-making were the syndical institutions and the cabinet.

The Syndical Institutions

The syndicates are the key innovation in the Nationalist political economic system. Combining labor and management in a single organization, the syndicates were supposed to create a system of industrial relations based on negotiation and regulation rather than on "class conflict." Similarly, they were to eliminate "anarchic competition" by coordinating the relations of firms in a single industry or sector.

The syndicates were formally expected to be the link between the economy and the political system for virtually all purposes. In keeping with the philosophy of the organic state, they represent the "economic aspect of man's life" in all major institutions. From one-quarter to one-third of the members of the *Cortés* are selected by the syndical organizations. The syndicates are presumed to be a function of the National Movement, and the two organizations are closely interlocked at the topmost levels. During most of the period we are concerned with, José Solís Ruiz has been both National Delegate of the syndicates and Secretary General of the Movement, and he sits as a member of the cabinet in the latter capacity. Finally, it is normally expected that the syndicates will be consulted in the process of formulating administrative regulations, and this has often been at the heart of the process of economic policy.

With the exception of a few groups (government employees, the free professions, and domestic servants), membership in the syndical order is compulsory for both Spanish workers and employers. In 1964, about 9 million employees and 3.3 million employers belonged, about 92 percent of the labor force. Of the labor members, about one-third are in industry, two-thirds in agriculture, commerce, or self-employed.[6]

The national organization is divided into "economic" and "social" sections, the former for employers, the latter for labor. This national organization has branches in each province, and in some cities and rural areas. These local organizations also are divided into economic and social sections. Alongside this hierarchy are the twenty-six vertical syndicates for separate economic activities (textiles, banking, farming, etc.). Internally, the vertical syndicates repeat the division of economic and social sections, and most also have provincial and local organizations (see Table 6).

In addition to these representational structures, a section on syndical services (*obras sindicales*) engages in a wide range of activities. A large part of social assistance and welfare is adminis-

TABLE 6. STRUCTURE OF THE SPANISH SYNDICAL ORGANIZATION (1964)

Vertical or Industrial Syndicates	National Organization			Vertical or Industrial Syndicates
	Social Section	Economic Section		
	President (National Delegate)			
	Governing Board			
Central Social Section	Vicesecretary for Social Affairs	Vicesecretary for Syndical Services	Vicesecretary for Economic Affairs	Central Economic Section
	National Syndical Congress			
National Council of Workers	National Council on Cooperation		National Council of Businessmen	
	Provincial Organization			
Provincial Social Section	Provincial Vicesecretary for Social Affairs	Provincial Vicesecretary for Syndical Services	Provincial Vicesecretary for Economic Affairs	Provincial Economic Section
Local Section	Local Organizations			Local Section

Terminology and organization that used in 1964 reflecting minor changes from 1950s. Adapted from Carlos Iglesias Silgas, *Los sindicatos en España* (Madrid: Ediciones del Movimiento, 1966), p. 267.

tered through the syndical organization. They provide special recreational and vacation facilities, legal assistance, and placement services. The educational program is quite broad, including an apprenticeship system, five labor universities, and at least 120 craft schools. A network of clinics and sanitaria are operated, and the syndicates engage in public housing construction.

What did the syndicates reflect in the decision process, and how did they function in the process of policy choice in the mid-1950s? First, it is apparent that the syndicates did not provide an autonomous or decentralized mechanism for reconciling or aggregating the interest of labor and management at that time. Until 1958, with the creation of a limited collective bargaining capacity, the syndicates could not negotiate wages and working conditions policy. Rather these were prescribed in detail by the Ministry of Labor, sometimes regulated specifically for each factory, though more often set at either the provincial or national level for firms in common activities. In this process, the syndicates were expected to provide information and lobbying activity on behalf of their respective "economic" or "social" constituents.

In formulating bargaining positions for a specific industry in economic policy-making, the economic and social sections rarely if ever joined together to formulate policy. Questions of pricing, taxation, and industrial policy were handled by the economic sections of the vertical syndicates almost exclusively. Until 1961, no national congress of both economic and social sections had been organized to deliberate policy for the whole movement. In day-to-day operations, the critical locus of policy initiation and formulation was the economic or social section, at all levels.

On the labor side, there was ample room for skepticism about the syndicates' capacity to give an adequate picture of the demands, interests, and expectations of Spanish working groups. The syndicates had been organized largely by *Falange* militants, to substitute for the large anarchist, Catholic, and socialist labor federations of the Republican period. Most top level officials were appointed. The officers in the national body—about one hundred important leaders of the national syndicates and about two hundred syndical officials who headed the provincial syndical group-ings, including the fifty provincial chiefs—held their offices by ap-pointment. They were appointed either directly by Franco, or by appointees of Franco.[7] Holders of the middle-level posts were elected indirectly. Only the shop stewards (*enlaces*) were directly elected, and even here, until the 1960s, all candidates were scruti-nized for fidelity to the hierarchy, though the effectiveness and thoroughness of the screening has declined over the years.

Large questions then can be raised about the quality of repre-sentation in the syndicates. In 1956 the International Confedera-tion of Free Trade Unions condemned the undemocratic charac-ter of the Spanish syndicates before the International Labour Organization.[8] Deprived of the right to strike and other economic weapons, enrolled in a compulsory organization without legal al-ternatives, the important leaders appointed and the rest carefully screened, it does appear that the syndicates would be more effec-tive in interpreting the policy of the government and of their own hierarchy on labor policy than that of the working force.

And yet the conventional picture of unrepresentativeness and ineffectiveness can be greatly overdrawn. The government and the syndicates did not speak with one voice on public policy. The syndical leaders were expected by the system itself to play the role of militant spokesmen for labor. In 1954 and 1956 they won substantial, and perhaps seriously inflationary, wage increases over the strenuous objections of other members of the regime co-alition. By 1962 some syndical leaders were arguing vigorously for radical reform, including full-fledged internal democratization of the organization. In their language and style of militancy many of the syndical leaders were not unlike their counterparts in other Western nations. They were brokers, and they bargained for their clients, though in the last analysis they accepted the judgment of the constituted authorities. It was their task, then, to rally their followers to the official policy formula.

Some degree of militancy in the leadership of labor was pre-requisite to the operation of the system. If there was no pluralis-tic competition, nonetheless there were loyalties to prior organizations and a skepticism about the Nationalist order to be overcome. The leaders were expected to guide labor so as to create acquiescence in, if not enthusiasm for, the syndical experiment. This required some responsiveness, some payoffs from the system.

Futhermore, a description of labor organization in Spain cannot deal exclusively with the syndicates, since there was a free labor movement throughout the period. Though illegal and suppressed, this movement had an impact on public policy. In a sense, the free labor movement provided a pluralistic competitor in the system. Officialdom measured the level of labor dissidence and thus evaluated the performance of the syndicates. Spanish labor could compare the relative militancy and effectiveness of the underground labor movement and the syndicates. It is hard to estimate how widespread this unofficial activity was, but strikes, though illegal, were a constant phenomenon in the 1950s. The growth of the *comisiones obreros* in the 1960s was remarkable, particularly in the larger factories in the key industrial centers.

Unfortunately we have no hard information on the attitudes of Spanish workers toward the syndicates. However, we are in a somewhat better position to judge the quality of representation in the economic or management side of the organization, because of an outstanding study by Juan Linz and Amando de Miguel.[9] Although this study of the attitudes of businessmen toward the syndicates was made in 1960, and hence reflects the reform atmosphere of the period, it probably reflects feelings in the 1950s as well. Linz and de Miguel surveyed both the character of participation and the perceived quality of representation, not only in the economic sections of the syndicates but also in the other forms of legal business organization in Spain.*

* This included, in addition to the syndicates and their "subgroups" (provincial or local units, or branches of vertical syndicates) the Chambers of Commerce, Industry, and Navigation; the "consortiums" (some with international character, such as the International Cotton Foundation); the "leagues" of industrialists, primarily in the Basque region; and various "societies," corporations, or professional groups, such as the Catholic Association of Managers.

They found, in terms of participation, considerable apathy and lack of opinion and concern about these organizations. Although most of their sample of 460 entrepreneurs belonged to one or more such organizations (and of course membership in the syndicates is compulsory, and in others highly desirable), few took an active part in their affairs (see Table 7).

TABLE 7. PERCENTAGE OF PARTICIPATION IN SYNDICAL AND BUSINESS ORGANIZATIONS BY SPANISH BUSINESSMEN

	Syndicate	Syndicate sub-group	Chamber	Consortium	League	Society
Belong	79	23	71	36	21	21
Consider most related to interests	26	7	17	18	7	5
Of those *belonging* to each group						
Take active part	10	12	5	18	10	13
Hold or have held office	22	24	11	23	10	26

Adapted from: Juan Linz and Amando de Miguel, *Los empresarios ante el poder público,* p. 32.

Nonetheless, Linz and de Miguel looked for, but did not find, a small elite dominating the affairs of these organizations. Rather, participation of the businessmen studied, both in interest organizations and in public office, was relatively open. Of the sample, some 29 percent held or had held office in corporate bodies, 20 percent had held public posts (such as mayor, city councilman, *procurador* in the *Cortés,* etc.), but only 7 percent had held both public and associational positions. And there was little difference between moderate sized and large firms in this regard. Only about 44 percent of these entrepreneurs denied having some measure of formal or informal power in the system. On the basis of such considerations, Linz and de Miguel reject the idea of a power elite in the business community, a small set of leading, large entrepreneurs controlling interest groups and representative bodies, their power intertwining with that of public authority.[10]

About half of the businessmen studied had used the interest group to represent them before government, and over half of this group reported good results from this contact. Those who did not use the services of the interest group generally preferred to deal with government directly. Large firms were more apt to use their own representatives, and average sized enterprises to rely more on interest group representatives.

To some extent, the larger firms found the interest groups more effective, and particularly those in highly monopolistic sectors, such as electricity, paper, steel, or heavy machinery. Here we are dealing with those developmental industries where public-private contact was close, and incentives to the private sector extensive, in the postwar period.

It is also interesting that businessmen in industrial Spain (the North, Catalonia, and Madrid predominantly) found these groups more effective, but entrepreneurs in the less industrialized areas were most satisfied with the performance of the syndical organizations. The highly articulated industrial and commercial complexes of the former regions, of course, had forms of organization better suited to these sophisticated industries, but in the rest of Spain, the syndicates proved a more critical link to policy influence.[11]

What we have, then, is a picture of an associational system on the business side of the syndicates, not totally in the hands of a small elite of bureaucratic corps, but with considerable breadth if not depth of participation. The system is fairly responsive to the needs of its members and effective in meeting them. However, as Linz and de Miguel point out, "their defensive action against a drastic revision of the status quo probably . . . can be effective, but their power is not that of the creative formulation of general initiatives."[12] In other words, the syndicates were better at direct lobbying, but did not play a particularly useful role in aggregating a unified policy position for their clientele, or participating in the design of measures or objectives for the economy as a whole.

Looking at the syndicates as a tool of decision-making in the 1950s, the Spanish policy-maker might well have concluded that they were useful as a form of representation at the local level, but at the macroeconomic level, they probably reflected bureaucratic and partisan interests that could be heard equally well elsewhere in the system.

The Preeminence of the Cabinet

The second imperative component of decision-making procedures in Spain in the 1950s was the cabinet, the crucial policy-making forum in the Nationalist system. The cabinet served as the principal mechanism of innovation, since it contained the most active forces of the regime and since most policy emanated from the bureaucracy in any event. It was the focus of coalitional politics, the place where the disparate forces supporting the regime came together to seek common ground before the *Caudillo*. It was the key forum of policy consultation in the system, the critical place for analyzing proposals against a broad, national spectrum of interests and concerns. It was the only basic tool of administrative coordination and the one place where an effort could be made to overcome the historic, monolithic self-sufficiency of the Spanish ministries. In short, the cabinet was the focus of most of the critical functions of policy procedure.

Franco appointed all ministers, and they were responsible to him alone. In practice, he constituted a new government every five or six years by the appointment of new sets of ministers. Certain conventions have attached to the appointment of specific cabinet posts. The three military seats (army, navy, and air) were held by active officers, providing the armed forces with considerable weight in overall policy-making. One minister represented both the Movement and the syndicates through the office of the National Secretary of the Movement, though there was a tendency to allot the ministries of agriculture and labor, as well as housing, to individuals identified with the "populistic" side of the *Falange*. The economic ministries, *Hacienda*, Commerce, and Industry, which are our principal concern, have often been given to civilians associated with the business community, although they have been held by military figures and bureaucrats. Normally, these ministries, together with foreign affairs, have been the leading edge of liberalism in the cabinet.

We know little enough about procedure in the cabinet. Its deliberations of course are not public and have never been subjected to analysis. Yet conflicts within the cabinet often become public, and we can get some feel for the major cleavages that have arisen on critical issues. In general, Benjamin Welles's description is a good summary of how this body seems to have operated after 1958.

Cabinet meetings are held twice monthly on alternate Fridays. On the intervening Fridays, Franco presides over the cabinet's economic subcommittee. Cabinet meetings start at 9:00 A.M. and almost always continue through the night until dawn Saturday. . . .

Each minister reports in order of seniority. According to those present, no limit is set on the time consumed by any minister or on the topics he may discuss. The cabinet not only weighs such transcendental issues as renewal of the American bases agreements or Communist subversion, but even the size of a pension for a rear admiral's widow, or a medal for a deserving railway guard.

Hour after hour, the sessions roll on, and while some ministers occasionally step outside to stretch their legs, Franco himself has never been known to quit a cabinet session. This is how he rules Spain. From start to dawn, he remains imperturbably in his place, attentive, seldom interrupting, unruffled even when his ministers break into angry quarrels.[13]

As an instrument of economic policy-making the cabinet was far from perfect. The key problems seemed to involve, first, the difficulties of formulating policy in the cabinet itself, where so many political or irrelevant considerations muddied technical matters, and, second, the problems of coordination among the economic ministers themselves.

The latter question seemed almost unsolvable during the first two decades of Nationalist rule. One problem was simply that of bringing together the line ministries so that fiscal policy would bear some relation to industrial incentives policy, so that controls on foreign trade, prices, wages, and so on, would not all be working at cross purposes. This was difficult enough, given the jealous propensity of ministries to act as ultimate arbiters in their own fields, but it was only part of the problem. Much of the economic activity of the Spanish state was carried out by autonomous agencies, with budget and sphere of operation pretty much outside cabinet control.[14]

The Cortés

I have already commented on the peripheral role of the *Cortés*. It played a ratifying and legitimating role and, at best, was hardly an arena of aggregation or consultation. It did play one peripheral policy-making role, that of providing legal criticism on drafts submitted by the cabinet. My own examination of the effect of committee deliberation on a number of bills, though hardly systematic, suggests that the *Cortés* concentrated on perfecting and analyzing the legal implications of bills, refining language and criticizing minor points, and anticipating consequences on the body of Spanish law and in the courts.

This service was a useful one but hardly a critical legislative one. But the *Cortés* was not a legislature. About half of the *Cortés* was directly appointed by the Chief of State, the rest selected by an extremely indirect process of election, with most candidates eventually owing their position to some directly appointed official. As of the reform of 1957, the composition of the body was as follows:

7 officers (president, 2 vice-presidents, 4 secretaries), directly appointed;

18 cabinet ministers, directly appointed;

160 Councilors of the National Movement, directly appointed;

5 from the Council of State, Civil, and Military Tribunals, directly appointed;

178 syndical organizations, perhaps 120 directly appointed;

152 from local governments (1 from each provincial capital, 1 from all other cities in a province, 1 from the provincial council), indirect election;

553 total membership.[15]

Optional Components for Decision Systems

The syndicates and the cabinet were specified participants in economic policy-making in Nationalist Spain. Normally, the *Cortés* played a formal, sanctioning role. What else then, did Spanish policy initiators have to work with in formulating policies circa 1955, apart from the structurally requisite institutions?

In the field of economic policy one clear-cut candidate for participation was the great private banking system. Historically, the governing boards of these institutions had made critical decisions concerning the pace and direction of the private economy. As we have noted, Franco, upon taking power, was quite content to let them have a strong role in overseeing the reconstruction and development of the private sector. That these institutions had come to the financial support of the Nationalist cause in the most troubled hour of the civil war did not reduce his confidence in their capacity to play a strong role in economic affairs.

The position of these banks was really quite exceptional. In a country with a poorly developed stock exchange, these banks supplied over half of the capital needed by private enterprise. In 1956 five of these banks, the Hispaño Americano, Banco Español de Crédito, Banco Vizcaya, Banco de Bilbao, and Banco Central, controlled 51 percent of the capital in the country. These five, plus the Banco de Santander and the Banco Urquijo, made up the seven great banks whose enterprise groups included almost six hundred of the major firms in Spain. Overlapping directorates linked the major banks with the enterprises in their group.[16] Tamames estimated that in 1965 the seven great banks supplied 6 of 48 members of the boards of directors of major sugar companies, 27 of 77 directors of petroleum firms, 43 of 156 in electric power,

25 of 211 in fertilizer, 38 of 279 in cement, and 37 of 152 in steel.[17]

Linz and de Miguel's study seems to add evidence that the private sector was significantly guided by the banks in investment decisions. Of the 460 Spanish enterprises studied, 52 percent of the firms with over 500 employees and 18 percent of those with less than 500 workers had a member of the board of directors in common with some bank. Linz and de Miguel report that larger entrepreneurs saw the banks as important components of their own decision processes.[18]

What we have then is an associational network involving a good share of Spanish industrial capital. Through the common forums of interlocking directorates and the procedures of capital supply from the banks, a relatively high degree of communication and interaction, if not control, among the participants in this community could be expected, with a greater aggregational capacity in this group than in the syndical organizations. We would expect that the banks and the important firms in their groups normally would have sufficient access to relevant public officials simply to bypass the official syndical interest organization. The biography of Juan de la Cierva, a distinguished member of the Spanish high financial community, gives an account of the close relationships between bankers and government.[19]

Related to the banking community, but not exclusively so, is another group that is critical in the economic decisions of this period. This groups includes the "keepers of the macroeconomy," the technicians and experts, for the most part young, who had assimilated the perspective, language, and techniques of modern economic analysis. The movement started in the banks, particularly the Banco Urquijo, in the early 1950s. Frustrated by the failures and eccentricities of government statistical work and economic projections either nonexistent or very bad, a few banks began to produce basic analyses of foreign trade and economic trends, with a good deal of emphasis on events elsewhere in Europe. The growing influence, self-consciousness, and sense of *esprit de corps* in this group of technicians can be traced during the

1950s. They were soon to be found in special research sections, not only of the private banks but also in the Bank of Spain, private firms, in the major government ministries, and in the syndical organization.[20]

A word should be said here about the resources for expertocracy available in Spain in this period. Among the components of a decision process, most lacking was basic statistical information on the operation of the economy. Basic indexes were simply not available to decision-makers. National income calculations, through 1956, were based on indirect techniques, since Spanish statistics were not adequate for direct computations. No industrial census existed.[21] In 1961 the *Revista sindical de estadística* suggested that gross domestic product estimates of the National Economic Council could be off as much as 10 percent and that figures on active population, distribution of investment, and other basic indexes could be much worse.[22] (Perhaps the charges should be taken with a grain of salt, for there was strong rivalry between the organizations.) The first official estimate of income distribution was not made until 1962 when the research section of the Ministry of Commerce produced a rather rough analysis of income levels.[23]

Other problems were caused by the contradictions in figures and estimates used by different agencies. Estimates of the central government's income for 1959, made by the Bank of Spain and the Ministry of *Hacienda*, differed by about 20 percent.[24] Such problems could have policy consequences. For example, the National Economic Council in 1960 estimated industrial production as having risen 5.6 percent, and attributed a slight decline in gross national product to lagging agricultural production. However, the Ministry of Industry claimed a 2.2 percent decline in production for the year.[25] And one Spanish Minister of Commerce lamented:

> The most complex problem of all was that of potatoes. It has been very difficult to know the national production of tubers, since the

figures submitted by various public organizations differed. In some reports it was argued that there was practically no need to import and in
others that we would have to bring in hundreds of thousands of tons.[26]

Reliable indexes of economic activity are an essential input in any
policy-making system. And this type of instrument was simply not
available to Spanish policy makers.

Some Peripheral Components Briefly Considered

Let us touch on some other groups that might be considered
potential participants in an economic policy-making procedure
and note their significance. It could be expected that the Movement, as Spain's closest approximation to a partisan organization,
would have some role in such policy-making. Yet its influence and
activities were apt to be peripheral at best. By the mid-1950s, as a
partisan force, it had been shorn of most of its power and influence.[27] To some extent it was expected to promote corporate principles and the ideology of the state. And we have noted its function
in recruitment, as something of a screening device for candidates
for public office.

Generally, the Movement as an institution was more concerned
with political than economic questions, which were left to the
syndicates in the formal division of labor. In 1960, for example, a
critical year in Spanish economic decision-making, when economic issues overshadowed political ones in most publications,
the Movement newspaper *Arriba* devoted far more space to the
anniversary of twenty-five years of peace under Franco, questions
of syndical representation, Masonic conspiracies, the history of
the Movement, and Spanish foreign policy than it did to the issue
of the stabilization program of 1959.

However, the Movement, through its newspaper and other
publications facilities, did sponsor and promote the work of a
group of young reform-minded economists, who argued critically
against the established policy pattern and for sweeping reforms
along populistic lines. Somewhat later, the Movement press did

propagandize economic decisions taken by the government, in some cases through sophisticated and highly competent analyses by the technocrats. The Movement's most identifiable role was that of supporting popular reforms. Though this was, no doubt, of marginal utility in balancing the ideological mix of politics, most of the time the Movement was a rather ineffective proponent, particularly as the "new style" of Spanish political economics developed. Its rhetoric, leaden with bombast, offered little in the way of systematic analysis and persuaded few but the already commited.

Throughout the Nationalist period, the Spanish armed forces have played a steadily diminishing role in economic affairs. During World War II, and for some time after, high military officers had played key roles in economic strategy, and their impact was apparent in the initial emphasis on defense industries during the early period of autarchy. Through Suanzes, INI was closely associated with the military. However, by the middle to the late 1950s, the military as an institution had a much smaller role to play. By that time, the primary encounter of the military with economic questions came at the cabinet level, where its stance was usually conservative, though with important exceptions. Unlike some other countries, military officers played no role in official economic leadership, nor did the army have any prominent developmental, industrial, or civic action activities, though many individual officers had important interests in private economic activities.[28]

The role of Catholic organizations is a bit more complex. Perhaps one of the larger ironies of Francisco Franco's regime was that he anchored his system in the eternal verities of the Spanish tradition, the most stable of which was the Catholic Church, just before the church itself began to change. In any event, since Pope John XXIII, Catholic organizations have been among the more radical and effective forces for change in Spanish political and economic affairs.

Increasingly toward the late 1950s, various agencies of the

church became spokesmen for reform, and even the upper hierarchy has become increasingly pointed in its demands for more socially oriented public programs. More critical for economic policy was the lay organization *Acción Católica*, which, under the terms of the Concordat, must be free from political interference in the conduct of its "apostolate." Leaders of Catholic Action were influential in economic affairs at policy-making levels even before 1945. In addition, the organization is influential in journalism and other fields. However, its most critical and controversial activity has been the formation of labor organizations rival to the syndical groups, the *Hermandades Obreros Acción Católica*. Often led by militant, reform-minded priests or laymen, these workers' groups have been recurrently harassed and disrupted by the authorities. However, their association with legitimate church activities makes their suppression a most delicate issue. In any event, this activity really belongs to the period of the early 1960s, and was little more than possibility in the period under consideration. The more significant role of *Opus Dei* in economic policy will be explored in the next chapter.

Finally, institutions of local government were potential participants that should be considered. The possibilities of developing a more decentralized decision procedure were always open to the Spanish policy leaders. The issue here is not one of democratization. All provincial governors and local executive officers were appointed through the Ministry of Government, representing a good number of early party militants, some military men, though predominantly career bureaucrats by the 1950s. Weak advisory councils existed, the *ayuntamientos* at the municipal and the *diputaciones* at the provincial level. Despite the hierarchical character of the system, local government did add another perspective to Spanish policy. Local governments were often active in lobbying for their particular interests, and the syndicates at one point emphasized provincial interests in policy formulation. There is, however, a strong historic centripetal tendency in Spanish policy-making, particularly in economic matters. Public choice is seldom decentralized, and is rather jealously guarded by the authorities in Madrid. As we shall see, the potential political instrument of local government was never exploited by Spanish economic decision-makers, and when the time came to decentralize, new institutions were created instead of adapting existing ones.[29]

The Limits of the Appropriate

Let us now assess the procedural equipment of Spain, around 1955 to 1958, by setting it in the perspective of the more general Western experience. Of course, a clear evaluation of the total system will have to wait until we have had a chance to move beyond the static comparisons of structures and can see the relationships of these components in actual problem-solving situations. Nonetheless, it is possible to make a few preliminary observations.

For example, it will not do simply to contrast the powerless *Cortés* with the elected, sovereign parliamentary bodies of Europe. Especially in the field of economic policy, the European parliaments were becoming less active as forums of policy deliberation throughout the postwar period. We must distinguish two parliamentary roles here. In economic policy-making, the critical capacity of European parliaments in economic affairs occurs at the beginning of the policy-making process, not at the end. It is the capacity of partisan majorities to form governments, and in this way to elect from among alternative economic policy formats, that marks the real impact of parliament on policy and distinguishes the other European cases from Spain. However, the role of a parliament at the end of the policy-making process, as legitimators and ratifiers of programs worked out by the government, primarily in the forum of the cabinet, was not totally incomparable to the Spanish pattern. Only in the United States, of the Western nations we are considering, does the legislature really maintain a vital role in economic policy formulation, apart from the question of selection of the government.

Similarly, it is not the predetermined nature of interest group representation that distinguishes Spain. Throughout Europe and the West, contacts between governments and interest groups were increasingly institutionalized in the postwar period. Implicitly, at least, certain associations were authoritatively chosen as competent to speak for specific sectors of the population. Deviant groups were ignored in the policy process, though the process of outright suppression of the "unchosen" was nowhere as prevalent as in Spain.[30] Thus, in most of the West, a group outside the establishment could mobilize political resources and seek entry into the circle of institutionalized policy consultants. However, even this process was not totally absent in Spain. In the 1962 Asturian strikes, for example, the government finally bypassed the syndical leaders to deal directly with the leaders of the miners.

A clear contrast between Spain and other Western nations is the degree of decision-making autonomy left in the hands of private associations. Only in the Netherlands is the wage structure subjected to central control in a way that invites comparison with Spain. However, we must note also the degree of autonomy given the private banking community in matters of private-sector investment in Spain, where it is certainly higher than the European norm, although parallels are certainly possible both in Germany and Sweden.

The hierarchical internal structures of interest groups do not, of course, set Spain totally apart from the European norm. Real choice between alternative leaderships in interest group organizations was the exception rather than the rule in the West. Spanish interest groups are distinctive because they are usually both compulsory and noncompetitive. However, we have noted also that Spanish labor leaders were constantly competing in a very real sense with prior loyalties and with the possibility of underground movements. Although in the last resort the regime permitted itself the luxury of extensive coercion for noncompliance, the syndical leaders seemed to be working for worker support against what were, for them at least, very real alternative possibilities.

Competitive parties, offering alternative public choices of general economic policy formats which could be enforced by control of government and parliament, were of course the critical missing link in Spanish practice. However, in economic policy particularly, the "end of ideology" politics of the West often did not offer really vivid differential choices for public decision. In addition, there was a remarkable stability of basic coalitions in some Western nations, particularly in Germany, Norway, and Britain after 1951, where one party remained in power during the entire period we are considering. Austrian politics were based on an interparty compact. Even in systems more apparently open to alternative designs for policy, as in Fourth Republic France and in Italy, the participants in the political coalitions were drawn from a relatively stable pool of contenders. The actual changes induced by shifting coalitions in these nations did perhaps have a greater impact on economic policy design than the comparable changes occasioned by cabinet shifts in Spain, but it is an incremental rather than an absolute distinction.

I do not raise these considerations to minimize the real difference between Spain and other Western systems. However, it is clear that the sharp edges of formal difference are blurred a bit by an appreciation of the concrete operation of the system, and particularly so in the realm of economic affairs.

Viewed in this perspective, the decision equipment of the Spanish policy-maker was certainly in the same universe as that of his European counterpart, particularly when the contrast is made to Eastern European, Soviet, or Asian systems of the same period. Throughout Europe, and in Spain, there were structured expectations of what interests would be consulted in policy-making. Economic policy-making was becoming increasingly systematic and routinized in all nations in this period. Certainly there was more richness and diversity and hence, we would expect, a higher probability of introducing a broader range of policy initiatives and perspectives in countries where there were plural and competitive parties, interest groups, and the like. Yet, as we shall see, even this consideration does not clearly distinguish the Spanish case.

It is in the arena of public debate, open-ended and unspecified by institution, that we find the sharpest contrast between Spain and the rest of the West. Just as authoritarian Spain through the mid-1950's was reticent about the unstructured, undirected use of the market mechanism in economic policy, so it was uneasy about the open, unstructured public process of debate on policy. Thus we find that, to most observers, the control and censorship of the press and other media of communications, the rigid restriction of the right of assembly, and the limitations put on intellectual activity most clearly distinguish Spain from any other Western nation. The open, churning, pondering argument that serves as a prime vehicle of policy initiation, criticism, and formulation was clearly constricted in Spain. The average Western policy-maker gets many of his good ideas, or finds arguments that urge caution, simply by reading the daily newspaper and considering the opinions of journalists or others who, of their own volition, without any particular institutional or representational license, express another possibility, an opinion, or concern. The Spanish policy-maker, particularly in the 1950s, had to work with only a minimum of information of that kind.

And yet the real limitations on public debate in Spain had many curious characteristics. What was in fact excluded from the public forum and what was not? The greatest heresy was ideological argument, which was deemed a challenge to the regime itself. Yet dispute and criticism were considered appropriate, particularly when they took place inside corporate institutions. And curiously, one could argue almost any case as long as it was not identified with the taboo ideological formations. Early in the 1950s, one could state the case for the most radical of reforms, including the nationalization of industry, as long as this was presented as a Falangist, not a socialist or Marxist, inspiration. Furthermore, technical as distinct from political debate was appropriate and included most areas of economics. This particular distinction, we shall see, had far-reaching implications for Spanish politics.

In comparison with his Western counterparts, the Spanish policy-maker lacked the unroutinized, unsystematic aspects of an otherwise not entirely dissimilar set of decision implements. The spontaneity, freshness, and occasional novelty of suggestion that could come from a relatively free press and an open, undefined public forum of ideas, the different departures that occur when men set about to solve problems for their own communities or interests, not thinking of the larger public interest at all, these components of disjointed incrementalism were simply not as vital in Spain as in any other Western nation.

Chapter 4

THE FORMULATION
OF CHANGE

THE SPANISH POLICY REVOLUTION is usually dated from 1959 and the stabilization program of that year. A regime dedicated to autarchy turns outward; a system based on bureaucratic regulation is liberalized. Spain appears to make a complete about-face in economic policy; yet the change is in many ways more apparent than real. Deep continuities with earlier policies are evident. To understand the significance of what happened, one must look at the interwoven pattern of political and economic events of the 1950s. Here, and in the following chapter, I will trace the process of making the stabilization policy and the development of policy and procedural instruments in that process.

The Process of Problem Recognition

Surveying the Spanish economic scene in the early 1950s, one could conceive a wide range of possibilities for future policy concern. First of all, there was the unfinished business of the Nationalist policy. Spain's standard of living was still one of the lowest in Europe, and industrialization had neither filled domestic demand nor enhanced exports. Much remained to be done on infrastructure reconstruction and development. Almost half the labor force was still in farming, and the agricultural sector was marked by low productivity and investment. The transport and commercial systems of the country were antiquated. There had been no real change in the composition of Spanish exports since the late 1920s. The peseta continued to deteriorate, price rises were becoming significant, and the public sector ran large, though disguised, deficits. Spain's financial structure was not appropriate for modern needs, and the level of red tape, administrative drag, and cynical evasion of regulations was high. There were also the unfulfilled social promises of the *Falange*—full-scale agrarian reform, control of monopolies, and other populistic measures. Certainly, the high level of savings of the country was not related efficiently to investment, nor were taxation policies very progressive. On the other hand, one could bemoan, as some churchmen had begun to do, the breakdown of the fiber of Spanish culture as urbanism, industrialism, and "Americanization" changed old patterns of life. The nature of the political system was not a totally closed question for a great many.

In every country, at every time, there is a virtually inexhaustible list of things that could be done, or undone, to improve the lot of the people and the civilization of the land. The initial problem of public policy-making is to choose some issues to work on, to identify some facets of the nation's life as problems and to define the rest of the field as "the way things are." This is the process of problem recognition. One is interested in learning which groups or agencies identify an aspect of the nation's political economic life as imperfect and problematic, and envision public action as an appropriate remedy. Of all these initiatives in the system, which logically range, I suppose, from two neighbors grousing that "there ought to be a law" to a central bank advisory to the cabinet, which reach competent public authorities and which are selected by them for action?

It is important to recognize that the process of Spanish policy-making had never been static. Although the context of decision had remained relatively constant since 1939, there was a continual reassessment of programs, objectives, and instruments in every period. New problems became the focus of attention; older issues faded into the background. In the 1951–56 period notable new departures in policy had begun. The bases agreement with the United States in 1953, and attendant economic assistance, and the massive across-the-board wage increases of 1954 and 1956 are particularly prominent. In addition, in this period rationing came to an end, reforms in foreign commerce controls were carried out, an effective import program maintained stable food prices, and, of course, there was a marked acceleration of investment in public works and industry.[1]

One should recognize this ongoingness of the policy process, for case studies so often give the impression of an abrupt beginning and end. In fact, there were many incremental shifts in policy, working in the same direction as the one strand of the process we isolate here.

There is, however, a logical point of departure for an analysis of the policy process that culminated in the cabinet changeover of 1957 and the stabilization plan of 1959. Examination of the record of economic discussion, as revealed in public pronouncements of leaders, newspaper commentary, and specialized business, interest group, and scholarly publications, clearly discloses a pause in the process of problem recognition covering approximately the period from 1953 to late 1955. Economic commentary conveys the urgency of reconstruction and development, and the achievement of self-sufficiency, along the lines of the Nationalist policy format. Afterwards, we shall be subjected to a virtual bombardment of problem recognition—critical, analytic, admonitory —from all sides. But for a period of some three years, the atmosphere is one of economic euphoria and satisfaction in the overall policy format. The dominant tone of communication to policymakers about the state of the economy as a whole is that things are going rather well.

One index of this pause in problem recognition is found in the Spanish economic press.[2] In all such sources there is a general

satisfaction with the Spanish economic situation. Criticism, lobbying, or policy suggestion is most infrequent. When mention is
made of incipient inflationary problems or agricultural difficulties,
the assumption is normally made that the authorities are competent to meet the problem.[3] Only *España económica's* early cham-
pioning of a return to liberal economic principles stands out, but
even it argues that Spain's entry into the growing European trend
toward modern capitalism must be moderate, judicious, and
timely.[4]

It might be argued that any publication would have been hesitant to criticize in this period of Spain's political evolution. At the
time, the bland, unprovocative tone of these economic journals
was echoed in everything that was published in Spain. It may be
that the absence of initiatives in the economic policy process was
due to censorship, and that things were not quite so quiet as they
seemed. However, the economic press seldom dealt with taboo
political themes; it could remain on the permissible technical
level. And, as we shall see, within a few years, with no change in
the political system or in censorship, these journals would become
deeply immersed in policy criticism and controversy. Censorship
and authoritarianism may have dampened criticism in the mid-
1950s, but the economic euphoria was also very real.

The publications of the syndical organizations reflect the same
tone and communicate satisfaction with existing policies rather
than criticisms or suggestions for new departures. Representative
is Antonio Robert's analysis of Spanish economic policy circa
1954. A distinguished economist associated with the Movement
and the syndicates, he puts extreme emphasis on industrialization
as the key to development and urges mechanization and scientific
practice in agriculture. Beyond this, and urging more flexible
credit policies, he presents no new policy initiatives. He foresees
none of the problems that are to dominate economic discussion
later in the 1950s.[5]

The commentary and analyses of the great private banks reflect
this same temper of the times. I have already noted the

prominent and powerful role of these institutions, and I have indicated that, to a large extent, they took over the field of economic analysis in the absence of competent governmental sources of information. The year-end reports of the banks and their special studies have been viewed by the Spanish economic community as the single most important source of information on economic trends. Their annual appearance is eagerly anticipated, and their presentations are closely scrutinized.

Again, the reports for 1953 and 1954 reveal a serene contentment with trends and a satisfaction with public policy. Economic growth has been good, and has been accomplished with relative price stability. Spain, with the United States bases agreements and the expansion of exports, is back in the world economy.[6] There were exceptions. Pablo Garnica of the Banco Español de Crédito stressed the precariousness and deceptiveness of the balance of the budget and suggested that public deficits might threaten industrial recovery.[7] But this was a mild qualification in a generally enthusiastic report. Similarly, one detects a growing concern for Spain's place in world trade, her balance of payments, and the relationship of her economy to the new capitalism of Europe. Andrés Moreno, member of the board of the Hispano Americano, underlines the need for foreign investment to supplement the nation's scarce capital resources.[8]

In the background, questions were being asked about the overall tendency of Spanish development. The bankers had formed a corporation to prepare a comprehensive study of Spain's relationship to European integration,[9] and a group of younger economists had begun to publish critical analyses of the going economic concern in the Movement newspaper Arriba.[10] Furthermore, the United States after 1953 had been urging a liberalization of economic policy in Spain. The economic section of the Pact of Madrid committed Spain to stabilize its currency, balance its budget, remove excessive regulation, discourage monopoly, and encourage competition.[11] Ambassadors of the United States urged such programs and encouraged Spain to lift prohibitions on foreign investment. Such representations were fairly constant, and they increased in intensity and publicity after 1955.[12]

All in all, these were limited exceptions to the dominant tone of the period. For most of this time, if a Spanish official had been diligently searching for new ideas to feed into the policy-making mill, he would have come up with little from the basic idea and criticism-generating instruments of the system.

Signaling New Problems and Possibilities

If one follows the indicators of economic opinion closely, the point at which the dominant mood changes from satisfaction to concern is quite clear. If we use *España económica* as a bellwether of the economic press, the first decisive expression of urgent policy anxiety appears in October 1956. The subject is rising prices and inflation.[13]

However, the critical turning point in the discussion of Spanish economic policy probably is marked by the Banco Urquijo's comprehensive research project on the state of the nation's economy, *La Economía Española: 1954–1955,* published in Madrid in early 1956. The report is suggestive in a number of respects. First, it shows the new role of the economic experts. Second, it illustrates the comparative style that was to be characteristic of much of Spanish policy analysis in this period.

A word should be said about this comparative style. Spanish publications of all types devoted more effort to examining and analyzing political economic phenomena elsewhere in the West than in Spain itself. Both in the daily press and in specialized political and economic materials, the American studying Spain was struck by the comprehensiveness of reportage and the depth of analysis of events in other nations, and by the paucity of information on Spanish affairs. There are a number of reasons for this contrast. First, social analysts are simply more interested in events in neighboring nations in Europe and in the United States. Second, the Spanish, and particularly Spanish intellectuals and liberal statesmen, have been prone historically to consult European experience rather than indigenous tradition in political and economic matters.

However, I believe there is a third reason for this pronounced use of comparison in policy analysis. In a regime of censorship, where high standards of adherence to the system were expected, particularly of the intelligentsia, one was on safer and freer grounds commenting on foreign affairs than domestic issues. Furthermore, one's interpretations of foreign affairs could be developed by contrast and comparison into a commentary on what was happening in Spain. The pattern is so consistent that I really believe it was practiced intentionally. As late as 1967, part of the press-run of *ABC* was confiscated after it published an analysis of liberal constitutional monarchies throughout Europe. Spain, to my recollection, was never mentioned. Yet the point, in the midst of discussion of the succession problem, by the leading liberal monarchist newspaper, was unmistakable.

To see this practice in economic affairs, we have only to examine the Banco Urquijo study of 1956. The study begins with a commentary on the changing temper of public policy in the rest of Europe, stressing the "recovery of economic liberty," the renewed use of monetary and fiscal instruments rather than direct controls.

Of England, the report says:

Not a few observers were sure that the English process of socialization was irreversible, that it was in the mainstream of the spirit of the times, and that a non-Labourite government could brake it but not reverse it. The truth is that five years of Conservative government have been able to raise the prosperity of the English people without needing to deny, much less destroy, the authentically fecund social advances, but suppressing the more troublesome and misspent interventions. . . .[14]

Similarly, Germany is the "most eloquent example" of "how the socializing and nationalizing criteria, so much in vogue for so many years, have been overcome through an intelligent return to free economic activity."

All of this is contrasted, not to the state of affairs in Spain, but in Argentina, out of context in this review of great power economics, but a close ideological ally of the Spanish regime.

Successive nationalizations and public controls characterized the economic and financial policy of the technical team that advised General Perón. In 1954, the failure was visible from any angle. In 1955, the surgery of correction was felt with anguish. That administration, provoked by events, found no occasion to change its methods. Its successors are declared partisans of economic liberty.[15]

Need the point be put any more clearly? Yet so far we are merely dealing with the state of the world economy. Spain has not yet been mentioned. The report goes on to discuss the inflationary problems of all Western nations and shows how monetary and fiscal instruments have been used with great success in meeting this problem.

Turning to the Spanish economy, satisfaction is expressed with the growth achieved during the biennium, growth which is attributed to abundant rainfall, monetary expansion, the maturation of important investments made in previous years, and United States aid. Then the report turns directly to the problem of the Spanish economy, raising the issue that despite the development recently achieved in Spain, her standard of living is still far behind the European norm and her rate of growth less impressive than the freer economies of Western Europe.

What can be done about it? This problem of the estimation, increase and redistribution of national income is surely the most complex and intricate of those facing Spain. On this subject, the President of the Banco Urquijo said to the General Meeting of Shareholders at the end of the last period: "We believe it urgent to pursue a responsible, orderly, serious study of this economic problem. Its complexity requires subtle and exceptionally sensitive techniques served by teams of specialists. For the moment, we will not add a single word."[16]

Or, the "new economics" of those who have the tools to provide it is the key to economic reform and improved growth.

Let us examine these first signals of policy reconsideration, which entered the process in late 1955 and early 1956, for the themes and the agents of policy initiation will remain durable in the process to come. Recalling that Braybrooke and Lindblom hypothesize that the policy process begins with recognition of a new problem, means, or objective, we note that all of these were present in these early initiatives. Recognition of inflation as a problem had been a constant concern of many business groups and policy-makers throughout the Nationalist period. The concern was renewed, and it became widespread by late 1955, but particularly after the across-the-board wage increases of October 1956. To this looser problem recognition was now added a new statement of means, of possible instruments, potentially to be borrowed from the recent and successful experience of Western Europe. And especially for the larger Spanish enterprises, this suggested a new desired objective, the liberalization of the economy, though they would always argue that liberalization was the means to accelerated growth with stability rather than the end itself.

Also incipient in the policy initiatives of 1955–56 was a shift in the initiative-generating structures of the system. The influential style of policy analysis was about to move from economic microanalysis to macroanalysis, and with it there would be a change in the forms of expertise relevant to moving a problem into the realm of policy consideration. Gradually, the lobbyists of the syndicates would be phased out as the prime suppliers of policy initiatives, to be replaced by the experts and technocrats working in the banks and the government bureaucracies.

From 1945 to 1955, with increasing reliability in the latter half of the period, the initiative-generating system of Spain worked pretty much as it was supposed to. The syndicates provided initiatives and feedback for the adjustment of ongoing policy. They were capable of transmitting information on the wishes, plans, and criticisms of various industries to policy-makers. The Minister of Commerce during this period, Manuel Arbúrua de la Miyar, often cited the advantages of direct grass roots representation.[17] Linz and de Miguel observe that such direct representation was often satisfactory to businessmen. Tamames provides information on the utility of the syndicates in coordinating public and private economic efforts.[18]

However, the syndicates were competent to speak only to problems of implementation of established policy. They were not designed to criticize the overall tendencies of national policy or urge new departures.

It was this terrain that the economic experts occupied. They introduced a new level, a new type of initiative into the policy-making process. The measure of this shift is found in the changes that take place in the vocabulary and perspective of Spanish policy-making. The relevant indexes of Spanish economic activity change from statistics measuring growth in various industrial sectors and reflecting the syndical system's interests to a preoccupation with gross national product, the balance of payments, price structures, and monetary system, the macroindicators of national economic activity.[19] There is an increasing tendency to see Spain in comparative perspective and to measure Spanish achievements against those of Europe, rather than against the background of reconstruction and the changes accomplished by the Nationalist regime.

The syndical leaders saw or sensed the political implications of what was happening. As early as the spring of 1956, the national leadership began to organize a national meeting of the organization's economic sector to debate overall policy questions.[20] However, such meetings take time to prepare, and the congress did not meet in full session until December 1957, by which time it could do little more than add its voice to problems and projects that had already been well defined by other parties. It was also in this 1953–57 period that the syndical organization began to recruit and organize its own corps of economic experts, skilled in the new economics that was being practiced elsewhere in the system.[21]

Between 1955 and 1957, the newly activated agents of policy initiation refined and extended their analyses. Now a steady flow of problem statements and policy recommendations entered the public forum. The temper of economic commentary had changed radically from the quiescence of 1953–55. Early raw messages of concern about inflation were being rounded into full analyses of related problems and potential solutions.

In fact, the Spanish system of signaling economic problems was quite efficient in the short run, although, as in most modern nations, it was incapable of seeing incipient problems very far ahead. The tranquility of 1953–55 was not misplaced. Spain was achieving a constant, stable annual growth rate of about 5 percent.[22] In fact, it was the achievements of that period that led to the problems of a later period. During these years, an economy of hardship had begun to move toward prosperity. As the middle class in particular began to achieve a European standard of living, pressures on imports began and were compounded by the demands of the new industries for raw materials and machinery. The pressure on food imports arose because of a steadily rising level of nutrition in all levels of society. In the total program, concentration on domestic needs, rather than on exports, further compounded the imbalance in foreign trade. Release from austerity and the demand for a higher level of living, now within reach, put pressures on prices.

This inflationary pressure was accentuated by the expansionist credit policies and by the magnitude of direct public deficit investment, much of it in public works and other large-scale projects which would only be amortized and become productive over the long run. Coupled with this was the political requirement that the labor force share in the new prosperity through higher wages.[23] The Spanish reluctance to pay taxes or to undertake fiscal reform that could have brought public budgets closer to balance added further to the potential for inflation.[24]

Price instability was a product of the cumulative impact of the Nationalist reconstruction and development policies. While it is true that few cautionary signals were raised, except by foreigners, about the built-in excesses of the program, when the critical indicator of prices changed, criticism was not long in emerging. Although the exact point at which price increases became significant is a bit uncertain, the most identifiable beginning of the inflationary trend probably came in the last quarter of 1955. First signals of this problem were seen in the first months of 1956, with the publication of the bank reports, and the more general demand for action from the private sector occurred about six months later. While this is not a particularly rapid response to change in the economic environment, it is comparable to the speed of problem recognition in most of the rest of Europe at the same time.[25]

The Selection of Priority Problems

In any political system, the decision-maker is subjected to a heterodox barrage of demands. The raw field of possibilities for public action is diffuse and contradictory. The sum of initiatives offered in the political process provides no compelling focus for the policy-maker.

Because a new set of policy initiatives introduced between 1955 and 1957 has been the area of concentration, the clarity of these demands has been overstated. From the point of view of the policy-maker, the movement recorded here probably appeared to be a series of disjointed episodes in a system generating many rival messages concerning potential policy action. Perennial problems of growth in specific sectors, of public investment programs, and so on, continued to preoccupy most economic actors.

The process of generating initiatives does not solve the problem of public action. The policy-maker requires some basis for selecting and ranking possibilities and problems. He needs a framework, a context, for finding pattern and relationship in what is otherwise a random field of unordered possibilities and problems. He must simplify and economize, thereby reducing the number of variables he must hold in mind.

I have already noted problem contexts (or ideologies, or economic theories) among the instruments of decision, the procedural equipment of the state. I have suggested that one measure of the richness of a system's decision equipment is the number of problem contexts that are available to decision-makers. Therefore, in dealing with a system of less than total doctrinal rigidity, the decision to select one problem context rather than another becomes a central act of policy choice. It becomes a critical act of procedural instrumentation, for it will set the rules for future choices of which problems to consider and which alternatives to prefer. This becomes clear if we consider the problem contexts available to Spanish policy-makers in 1956–57.

Three Available Problem Contexts

Basically, there were three "grand options" open and legitimate in Spain at this point, three hypothetical ways of defining the political economic situation of the nation as a whole.

ESTABLISHMENT FALANGISM

Of course, the most natural and incremental action would be to maintain the decision rules and policy format of economic nationalism. In Chapter 2 I detailed the rationale and approach that dominated Spanish economic policy-making from the end of the Civil War until the late 1950s. Now in 1956–57 some of the critical assumptions of this economic strategy were called into question. The response was a renewed elaboration and articulation of the premises of that policy, an intellectualization of a policy approach that had not been assisted previously by much in the way of formal theory.

The term *establishment falangism* is my own contrivance, and to my knowledge no Spaniard has ever used this expression. The most articulate spokesman for this point of view was no doubt Higenio París Eguilaz, chairman of the National Economic Council and the National Council on Income until 1957. In less systematic form, similar themes occur in the writings of Antonio Robert and other economists of the syndical movement, some university economists, and in the statements of economic ministers in the 1951–57 period.

Establishment falangism rests on the proposition that Spain is to be regarded as an economically underdeveloped country. Its standard of living and production is significantly below that of Western Europe and North America.[26] Furthermore, in relation to world trade, it stands as a nation of the "periphery" as described by Raul Prebisch. As an exporter of primary products and an importer of manufactured goods, it is condemned to a chronic imbalance in its terms of trade. The value of its agricultural products and raw materials and the possibilities of market expansion for its classic exports are distinctly limited, compared to the open-ended possibilities of innovation, diversification, and reinvestment available to the countries of the "center," or the industrialized world. Spain then, like any underdeveloped nation, must fall further behind the ever rapidly accelerating productive potential of the industrial world unless it creates basis structural changes in its economic system. The well-known remedies are import substitution and export diversification. Spain must build industries and expand agriculture so that it produces more of the products for which it has relied on foreign suppliers. Spain must conserve its foreign exchange, concentrating imports in those fields where it is absolutely disadvantageous to produce domestically. Furthermore, Spain must develop new exports as a further rectification of its systematic disadvantage in trade.[27]

This, of course, is what the Nationalist policy was all about. The Nationalists stressed import-substituting manufactures, buttressed by an arsenal of policies of protection, exchange manipulation, and the like, which constituted an orthodoxy in economic development theory through the 1950s. The role of the state in stimulating basic industry, and its tolerance of the moderately inflationary consequences of this program, could be justified, explained, and made congruent and coherent by reference to current doctrine on economic development technique.

From this point of view, to emulate the liberalization, currency convertibility, and integration appearing in industrial Europe would be folly. Citing Gunnar Myrdal, París argues that "the nations that propose that all countries suspend their regulations on foreign commerce are really seeking the paralysis of the economic development of the backward nations."[28]

Like París, Antonio Robert sees a need for foreign investment to provide sufficient capital for further development. He too feels that liberalization or integration with Europe can only be considered after Spain reaches a European level of development.[29] To open Spain economically, without condition, would permit more competitive European industries to destroy the weaker Spanish producers. Industrial Europe would become richer from the exploitation of Spanish markets, and Spain would continue to be a dependent, agricultural region.

Furthermore, liberalization would endanger Spain's distinctive system. Though this point would not have been made by either París or Robert, many partisan Falangists would see in Europeanization a threat of contamination of Spain's unique political and social structure. It was sometimes suggested that Spain's natural trading partners were in Latin America, not Europe, where Spain would find natural marketing advantages due to shared language and cultural sympathies.

THE STRUCTURALISTS

During the 1950s, a fairly self-conscious school of younger Spanish economists began to develop. Nearly all had received their professional training at the Faculty of Political Science and Economics of the University of Madrid. They identified with the structuralist persuasion in economic analysis. For the most part, they allied themselves closely with the Movement, and particularly the national revolutionary or reform wing of the *Falange*. Their stance was one of criticism of the prevailing policy orientation in Spain in the 1950s. Among the more prominent members of this group were Enrique Fuentes Quintana, José Luis Sampedro, Juan Velarde Fuertes, and Ángel Rojo Duque. Ramón Tamames must also be counted as a member of this school, though he was not so intimately associated with the rest during the formative years.[30]

The approach they offered for the analysis of Spanish economic policy has much in common with the "structuralist" critique of "monetarist" development policy that was coming into vogue, particularly in Latin America, at about this same time.[31] They shared with the establishment Falangists a reluctance to pursue economic integration with Europe through rapid liberalization, and doubts about the adequacy of monetary and fiscal tools in generating economic growth and stability. They too felt that Spain would be seriously disadvantaged in open competition with industrial Europe. However, unlike the establishment Falangists, they did not believe that the existing policy format of economic nationalism was an adequate guide to continued development.

For them, major and radical changes in the structure of the economy and society were a precondition to full and meaningful development. The concentration of economic wealth and economic power in Spain was a critical bottleneck to further modernization. The great banks and their privileged groups of industries used their economic power to maintain their own advantage, not to advance development. The structuralists early favored the nationalization of banking. Monopolistic conditions in industry, backed by public policy, further concentrated economic power and encouraged inefficient production. The structuralists advocated policies to restore competition, including public enterprise, though they accused INI of being insufficiently aggressive in this field.

This concentration of economic power prevented needed reforms that would both vitalize development and diffuse the returns from growth to a wider spectrum of the Spanish population. Fundamental agrarian reform was essential to break the grip of the rural oligarchy, which was unconcerned with the productive potential of their lands and satisfied with the minimal results of traditional techniques of organization on the great estates. Furthermore, agrarian reform was needed to bring the rural population into the modern life of Spain.

Progressive taxation, educational reforms, and constructive social policies also were part of the agenda of the structuralists. The inequities of the Spanish socioeconomic system, the concentration of wealth in a few people in a few regions of Spain, also were central points in their critique.

It is interesting to contemplate the basis of legitimacy of this political economic position. The structuralists were vehement and radical in their attack on established economic elites. What they urged would elsewhere be described as a revolutionary program. Their style and approach was often obviously influenced by Marxist analytic techniques and their remedies paralleled those offered by socialists in other nations. They were open and unabashed in their attack on the "power structure," and they cited C. Wright Mills approvingly and drew the necessary parallels.

And yet the structuralists were successful in not having their program identified with the taboo ideologies of socialism and Marxism. They linked their criticism to the reformist principles of the *Falange* and to structuralist economic development theory. Never did they suggest that their reforms would imply political democratization. Many who said the same things under a different ideological aegis were dealt with harshly by the Nationalist regime. However, the leaders of the structuralists achieved positions of respect and influence in the universities and as economic advisers to the state.

This alternative conception of Spanish development remained available and vital throughout the entire period we are considering. Just as the establishment Falangists intellectualized the program of economic nationalism and elaborated it into a more or less respectable theory of development, so the structuralists claimed merely to be working out the implications of the ideals of José Antonio in terms of modern economic analysis.

NEO-LIBERALISM

From the banks, from the managers of some larger industries, from some academic economists, and from the important order of Catholic laymen *Opus Dei* came the third problem context for understanding Spanish economic problems in the late 1950s. The advocates of this approach to further development had one prime characteristic in common. They were interested in, or connected with, economic leaders and authorities in Europe and North America. The members of this movement identified as much or more with the international economic community of central banking, modern enterprise, and technical economics as they did with events and institutions in Spain itself. The bankers had close and necessary connections with colleagues in Geneva, London, Paris, and New York. Spanish entrepreneurs often associated with industrial managers in France and Germany and saw the contrast between the modern capitalism thriving in these lands and the situation of Spain. A new troop of economists was developing competence in the techniques of European "economic doctors" whose impact and apparent success were becoming a central theme of postwar economic management.

In adopting the term *neo-liberalism* to identify this group, I do not imply any similarity to the small and abortive neo-liberal movements which began to appear in Northern Europe during the 1960s. These latter groups sought a return to classical, liberal orthodoxy in economic matters. Rather, I choose the term *neo-liberalism* to denote the affinity of this group of Spaniards to the modern capitalist, Keynesian position then dominant in economic policy-making in most of Europe.

The critical premise of neo-liberalism is that Spain must join in the new processes of growth in Western Europe, or be left behind in an increasingly integrated, prosperous, international industrial economy. The new economics had found the way to sustained growth with relative price stability and without excessive government intervention. Currency convertibility and the removal of restraints on trade had led to larger markets and greater economies of scale, perhaps as a first step to true economic integration. New technologies were changing the patterns of production so that industrial processes only a few years old might be hopelessly obsolete.

Spain was beginning to pay an exceedingly high price for its reconstruction policies. However well advised these policies might have been in 1940, they were no longer suitable to a radically changed environment, domestic and foreign. High levels of protection encouraged the continuation of inefficient technique. Government interventions had distorted the overall pattern of growth, so that Spain's industrial structure favored certain high-cost industries deemed critical for public policy, while industries that produced at a comparative cost advantage were often hampered.

Spain was not a wealthy nation, and it could not afford the luxury of misdirected development. The country might prove its capacity for self-sufficient development, but at what cost? Was it necessary to deprive the Spanish people of the best standard of living and the optimum rate of growth so that Spain could demonstrate its capacity to stand in isolation from the rest of the world? The consequences of uneconomic development programs and persistent public deficits were now visible in inflationary pressures and trade deficits. Only by subjecting both public and private activity to the disciplines of economic rationality could Spain achieve further growth. This meant that the peseta would have to reach its real value in the world monetary market. It meant undoing the labyrinth of controls, subsidies, and regulations; it meant opening the Spanish economy to foreign competition.

These were a few of the imperatives of neo-liberalism. The key was a return to the price mechanism as a basic instrument of economic guidance and organization, cushioned and directed by public policy as necessary to smooth the process of growth.

One should reflect for a moment on the significance of this spectrum of problem contexts available in Spain about 1957. This was, after all, the country that had "outlawed" the major economic ideologies of the Western experience—communism, socialism, and liberalism. A naive model of the Spanish political economy might have hypothesized that this would be a critical bottleneck, that Spain, unlike parliamentary democracies, could not draw on the alternative interpretations of public economic action that had developed out of the partisan conflicts of Western industrial society. One would propose that the procedural equipment of Spain would be less abundant in this respect than that of more open systems.

And yet, the spectrum of general models for economic change was not much different from that effectively available to other Western nations in the same period. Nowhere in Western Europe was a Marxist option really viable after 1948, if at all, in the postwar period. The effective choice was between democratic socialism and various neo-liberal options, represented by Christian Democratic, Liberal, or Conservative parties, depending on the country. When examined carefully, there is little difference between the model offered by the structuralists and the democratic socialists elsewhere in Europe. (Although it was always a bit sub rosa, many of the leaders of the structuralist movement had fairly close contact with socialist parties, particularly in Italy and France.) And the neo-liberal option in Spain was based on direct imitation of European practice.

To legitimate their approaches, the advocates of these positions simply translated ideological argument into the language of economic theory. The former was forbidden in Spain, but "technical" economic disputation was an appropriate concern and activity. And all, of course, were supported and sponsored by groups that held real power in the coalitional politics of the regime.

Of course, this is not to argue that there was no meaningful difference between the procedural equipment of Spain and the rest of the West in this respect. Obviously, the choice among the available policy models would be related to popular election in every other Western nation. In Spain the choice would ultimately be made by the *Caudillo*, based in part on his reading of what was acceptable to the prominent members of the regime coalition. However, the point is simply that the "boundaries of the appropriate" established by the Nationalist regime did not critically circumscribe the range of problem contexts available in this system in comparison with other Western nations.

The Choice of a Problem Context

In February 1957, about one year after the first signals of economic distress appeared in Spain, Francisco Franco announced a major change in the composition of his cabinet. Each of the major economic ministries passed into new hands. Alberto Ullastres, a Catalan economics professor earlier associated with the *Instituto de Economía Política* group, became Minister of Commerce. Mariano Navarro Rubio, a director of the Banco Popular, one of the lesser of the major banks (though its size and importance grew enormously during Navarro's tenure) became Minister of Hacienda (Treasury). Laureano López Ródo, a professor of public administration, became Technical Secretary General of the Presidency. There were related appointments. Three months earlier, Franco had replaced París Eguilaz with Pedro Gual Villalbí as head of the National Economic Council and Minister for Economic Coordination. However, attention focused on the first three figures.

They had interesting similarities. None had previously been prominent in Spanish public life. All were in their late thirties or early forties. All were identified as technical rather than political appointments. The house organ of the College of Economists suggested that "now Spain will use economists to solve economic problems."[32] Ideologically, all were European oriented and neoliberal in inclination. Personally, they were austere, hard-working, businesslike in demeanor. Paul Hoffman of the *New York Times* described them as "managerial types who look rather out of place in Madrid's majestic and somnolent citadels of bureaucracy."[33] The image of efficient, disinterested public service which they conveyed contrasted sharply with the public impression of their predecessors, and particularly the Minister of Commerce, Arbúrua, who was felt to be corrupt, inefficient, and compromised. To what extent the technocratic team lived up to its image of austerity is a topic of wholesome conjecture among Spaniards. Certainly, some of the businesses with which they were associated prospered during their tenure in office, but whether the opportunism was theirs or was that of their clients and potential clients is totally a matter of conjecture.

However, the most distinctive feature of the new economic team was that all were identified with the Catholic organization *Opus Dei,* a lay order whose members, though they may take religious vows, remain in secular vocations. The organization came into existence in the 1920s, some suggest as a Catholic counterpoise to the Communist parties of the West, organized around a small, dedicated elite, operating in secret and interested in exercising influence over the decision centers of the society. The group became significant in Spain in the late 1940s and 1950s. It sought to recruit the "up and coming," the potential leaders of the society, and soon individuals associated with *Opus Dei* were becoming prominent in university and cultural affairs, business and journalism, and in economic management.

Since the order had something to do with initiating economic policy and recruiting economic policy-makers in the 1950s, the organization should be considered as something of a procedural instrument, or at least as a form of interest group. The operations of the order are quite secret. No membership figures are revealed—most *Opus* members claim that none are kept—and members are often reticent about identifying themselves. Judgments on its role in policy-making vary widely. At the minimum, it is described as little more than a discussion group, whose members seek ways of bringing religious imperatives to bear in their professional lives. At the maximum, it is seen as a conspiracy to control the seats of power and effect a premeditated plan of social reorganization.

Most *Opus* spokesmen claim that the group has no political significance, that its members make no corporate decisions on political questions. However, the solidarity of the group, its strong capacity to win influential positions, and its pattern of recruitment from among the potentially prominent argues for some political motive. Although spokesmen insist that there are great differences of opinion within the group on socioeconomic questions, such disputes appear to be within a rather limited range of opinion. The arguments to which I have been referred seem to concern the incremental mix of economic and social concerns within neo-liberal orthodoxy. But whether or not there is agreement on policy, there is homogeneity of recruitment from men with similar upper-middle class backgrounds and "modernizing" aspirations. There is a corporate sense of identity which leads *Opus* leaders in one area to reinforce and advance the position of those in another.

Although to most Spaniards *Opus Dei* appeared as something of a monolithic force during the period of its rise to national influence, it is becoming apparent that there are strong factions with different orientations within it. One suspects that the more doctrinaire, rigid, and potentially undemocratic branches of the organization, with which its public image is often associated, are particularly important in cultural and intellectual affairs. It is possible that the groups in *Opus* associated with economic matters are more cosmopolitan. It may be, in fact, that Franco selected *Opus*-associated economics ministers as an alternative to giving them a more politically volatile ministry, such as information or education. In any event, we know that Francisco Franco selected men identified with *Opus Dei* to lead the Spanish economy in 1957.

Franco now becomes our policy initiator, and the new economic team a procedural instrument. What was his purpose in undertaking the cabinet change of 1957? Was he consciously choosing the new political economic model of neo-liberalism in this way? There is no direct answer to our question, since Franco never explained or justified his cabinet choices. His decisions usually came as a complete surprise, even to the principals involved. New appointees, and discharged ministers, have occasionally learned of their fate from the newspapers. Whom Franco consults in such matters is not made public, nor is it even a subject for informed speculation in the political gossip of Madrid.

Hence, we work from inference in constructing the most plausible explanation of this reworking of the context of decision in Spain. First, certain factors not directly related to economic policy must be considered in explaining the decision to change the cabinet in February 1957. Student political unrest was becoming apparent toward the end of 1955. It became a considerable political issue in 1956, and on one occasion even threatened a confrontation between the army and the Falangist militants. Confrontations between dissident students and Falangist militants did occur in the Faculty of Law of the University of Madrid after the official slate of candidates for the student syndicate election was defeated. A survey indicated that 70 percent of students entertained at least reservations about the Franco regime.

The events in the university were perhaps symptomatic of increasing political tensions throughout the system. A state of political unrest continued in Madrid, and activists of the Movement felt challenged by the increasing boldness of liberal and monarchist commentary and activity. It may be that the restructuring of the cabinet indicated an attempt to restore the balance of forces within the governing coalition. Thus, before the major cabinet transformation, General José Luis de Arrese had replaced Fernández Cuesta as Minister Secretary General of the Movement, with the explicit charge of revising the Fundamental Laws to establish the place of the Movement in the system. In the cabinet change of 1957, in addition to the overhaul of the economic ministries, important adjustments were made in other portfolios to the apparent end of establishing a new equilibrium between the contending forces.[34]

However, beyond the political explanation, what reasons might have been in Franco's mind as he selected an entirely new set of economic leaders for the nation? From this point of view, we must consider the cabinet as a procedural instrument in Franco's scheme of decision, and ask what purpose this change in personnel was designed to achieve.

Of the various functions that procedural instruments may perform for the decision-maker,* we can reject the hypotheses that the cabinet change was designed to enhance problem recognition (initiation) or for feedback. The neo-liberals had quite adequate access to decision centers. Franco hardly needed this change to avail himself of their counsel.

More attractive is the possibility that the purpose was political and aggregative. Franco's style was accommodative and pragmatic. It is possible that he felt that the dissent on economic policy of the 1955–57 period required that leaders identified with the key policy critics come into the cabinet to restore the harmony of the regime coalition. However, had this been his primary objective, he could certainly have found more prominent or symbolic figures. On the other hand, the common identification with *Opus Dei* meant that the new ministers were not merely liberals, but also that their orthodox economics were rooted in Catholic thought, an important factor for legitimizing their participation to the defenders of the "traditional order."

More impressive is the hypothesis that Franco sought to improve the procedural equipment for the formulation, coordination, and implementation of economic policy in general terms, without having the approach of neo-liberalism specifically in mind. The economic problems then manifest surely suggested the need to tighten and invigorate an obviously loose-jointed, flabby, unresponsive, occasionally corrupt system of policy formulation. One could interpret the replacement of París Eguilaz, an eloquent defender of establishment Falangism, by Gual Villalbí, a professional economist of internationalist and liberal bent, as a trial balloon in the direction of neo-liberalism in December 1956, prior to the more massive cabinet readjustment, though this also may have been a gesture to satisfy Catalan discontent. However, the move was generally seen as a way of revitalizing the National Economic Council, of using incremental means to bring about greater coordination in economic policy.[35]

* Initiation, formulation, consultation, aggregation, coordination, implementation, and feedback. See Chapter 1.

It is also worth noting that López Ródo is said to have come to Franco's attention through his treatises on administrative reform, which are mainly arguments for organizational reform along classic public administration lines. In fact, López Ródo plays an especially significant role in the emergence of the *Opus* group as a whole. He entered the government first in December 1956, as technical secretary general to Admiral Carrero Blanco in the Ministry of the Presidency. It seems not unlikely that Carrero Blanco, one of the more persistently liberal members of the cabinet and sometimes regarded as the *eminence gris* behind Franco in this period, was in some measure responsible for promoting the fortunes of the *Opus* group within the inner circle of Spanish policy-making.

Finally, one notes that the first action of the new cadre of ministers, made by February 25, 1957, was the creation of a new structure to promote coordination of economic policy-making at the cabinet level. A system of delegate committees (*comisiones delgadas*) was fashioned, one for economic affairs, which included the ministers of Hacienda, Agriculture, Industry, and Commerce, and others in transport and communications. An Office of Economic Coordination and Programming was created under the Secretary of the Presidency. A committee of technical secretaries of the presidency and the economic ministries was established to begin economic planning.

It may be that Franco intended to create a policy revolution and used the cabinet change of 1957 as a way of adopting neoliberalism as the model for future economic policy-making, but it is difficult to reject alternative explanations for his action. Such a definitive choice would have been somewhat out of character in view of Franco's characteristic deliberateness of political style and the level of sophistication in economic matters generally attributed to him, which was not very high. Hence, it seems inappropriate to view this cabinet change as a choice of policy model, and a better explanation of Franco's action was a desire to strengthen the capacity of the system to make policy, with the particular type of policy less clearly in view. Certainly Franco knew the ideological inclinations of his ministers in general terms. However, it seems more satisfactory to regard the adoption of the neo-liberal approach as a "second level effect," in the economist's language, and to realize that the extent of the commitment to neo-liberalism probably was largely unanticipated by Franco himself. In the course of subsequent events, Franco's apparent hesitation at critical points to move as radically as his ministers wished, until persuaded that no alternative course was open, tends to add credence to this explanation.

It may be that those who urged the appointments on the *Caudillo* knew perfectly well what they were doing. It may be that they presented these men as serious, competent, technically qualified, knowing full well that they would bring with them ideas that would lead to a general overhaul of economic policy. Such an explanation would not be incompatible with the notion that *Opus Dei* and the "economic modernizers" accomplished a "revolution by stealth"* in reorienting Spain's economic policy format. But this much is totally in the sphere of conjecture.

The Formulation of a New Policy

From this point on, our analytic focus is on the *Opus Dei* group of economic ministers. They become the policy-makers or policy initiators, the central actors, seizing the initiative for the design of measures. We will analyze the process by which they developed their first landmark policy, the stabilization plan of 1959.

We know that the first actions of the new ministers were procedural rather than substantive. The organization of the cabinet committee on economic affairs was to bring coordination to policy-making, for ministers had often in the past worked at cross purposes. Below this level, the *Oficina de Coordinación y*

---

* The phrase is from Albert Hirschman's *Journeys Toward Progress.* If my assumptions about this case are correct, I find it an unusually appealing illustration of his point.

Programación Económica (OCYPE) and the committee of technical secretaries started to design measures to bring some planning and discipline to public investment and expenditure (see Table 8).

TABLE 8. A Chronology of Major Events
of the Stabilization Period

Date	Event
February 1957	New cabinet, including *Opus Dei* "technocrats"
April 1957	Simplification of exchange rate system
July 1957	Basic monetary measures: rediscount, etc.
December 1957	"Global" taxation system
January 1958	Spain associates with OEEC
July 1958	Spain joins IMF and IBRD
January 1959	Questionnaire of private economic community
December 1958	Credit regulations
February 1959	Visits by IMF team and Jacques Rueff
July 1959	Stabilization program
November 1959	Unemployment insurance enacted
Early 1960	Some increase in public investment to offset dampening effects of stabilization
Autumn 1960	Further measures to stimulate economy: increase of bank credit, abolition of global credit ceiling
March-June 1961	Visit of IBRD study mission
February 1962	Opening of negotiations with Common Market
February 1962	Appointment of Planning Commissioner
April 1962	Banking reform law enacted, Bank of Spain nationalized
September 1962	Publication of IBRD report
April 1963	Foreign investment liberalization
December 1963	Enactment of development plan
July 1964	General taxation reform

Appointment of the new ministers implied the recognition and selection of new, privileged problems, the control of inflation over expansion, liberalization, and the alignment of Spanish policy with the West over self-sufficiency. The period from 1957 to early 1959 was one of tentative and cautious exploration of these problems through the modification and adjustment of established instruments. As early as April 1957, the multiple exchange rates which had been in effect since 1951 were eliminated, though they were replaced by subsidies and deposit techniques to protect Spanish export industries from the impact of inflation. New budgetary procedures were established in an effort to make it possible to account for the full extent of public investment and, hence, of the true extent of the public deficit. Previously, the budget had normally been in formal balance, but it had not included the expenditures of many of the autonomous agencies which accounted for the lion's share of investment. A freeze on public sector salaries went into effect. By July, the policy-makers began to concentrate on credit mechanisms as the most immediately manipulable tool for controlling inflation. The rediscount rate was raised from 4.5 to 5 percent, and measures were taken to cut speculative credit. These were all short-run measures requiring little in the way of advance programming or design.[36]

At the end of the year, the first complex, new policy instrument was put into effect, a new plan for collecting corporate taxes, one which was ingenuity itself in adapting existing institutions to new purposes. It had always been difficult to collect taxes in Spain.[37] Businessmen often kept multiple sets of books, and the machinery of fiscal inspection was not adequate to enforce the laws. Now, instead of assessing direct business taxes on individual firms, taxes would be assessed "globally" on an entire sector of industry (corresponding, in most cases, to the syndical groupings). Discussions between the government and a committee of leaders would set the quota for each sector. It would then be up to the sector to allocate the burden among its members, and the sector as a whole would be responsible for payment in full. This clever policy invention of course corresponded to the corporate theory of sectoral solidarity, made use of established institutions in a new way, and made the older forms of tax evasion more embarrassing, if not more difficult. It was easier for the authorities to challenge the data provided by a sector than that of an individual firm.[38]

A leading economic journal summarized the first year of the new economic team as follows:

Little by little, the dispositions are coming forth pointing out the direction which from the beginning we felt the new government was going to give the nation. One has to note, however, that except for the new budgetary and taxation procedures, all the rest do not represent undertakings of importance or general repercussion. The tone is one of caution and carefulness, giving the impression that they want to proceed safely, and not fall into failures or things that need to be redone.[39]

Moreover, there were signs that these minor measures were helping to cool off the economy. The wholesale price index was 521 in 1956 but fell to 361 at the end of 1957. The cost-of-living index rose to 608 in 1956 but was 400 in 1957. The free-market value of the peseta leveled off at 59.40 at the end of 1957 after soaring from 51 to 60 between January and the end of November. The rate of increase of Bank of Spain bills in circulation was slowing.[40]

The rate of innovation of policy measures slowed in 1958, but programs whose design had begun earlier came to fruition. A commission including both public and private banking authorities was established to control the allocation of medium and long-term credit. A rudimentary plan for national investments was drafted and published in March 1959. However, the more significant event of 1958 was probably the entry of Spain into basic international institutions. On January 10, Spain became a member of the Organization for European Economic Cooperation (OEEC, soon thereafter to become the Organization for Economic Cooperation and Development, or OECD). On July 4, Spain joined the International Monetary Fund (IMF) and the World Bank (IBRD).[41]

It seems clear that the new economic ministers had no overall blueprint for immediate policy change. They took the more obvious and less provocative steps to check inflation and move Spain toward engagement with the world economy. Perhaps the pattern would have remained one of adaptive, incremental adjustments in established policy equipment had it not been for certain critical shifts in the environment, particularly beyond Spain's borders.

The first of these was the quickened pace of European economic integration. The Treaty of Rome, establishing the European Economic Community, was signed in March 1957, its institutions created in January 1958, and the first 10 percent reduction in tariffs among the six members was effected in January 1959. These events, accompanied by substantial international interest and publicity, were only the culmination of a long series of steps aimed at liberalizing trade among the nations of Europe, beginning with the relaxation of import controls and the creation of the European Customs Union in 1950, proceeding through the creation of the Coal and Steel community, OEEC, and other institutions. From all of these Spain had been excluded or had excluded herself. Particularly for the neo-liberals, with their European orientation, the Treaty of Rome was the symbolic act. It now seemed that Spain was to be omitted from the critical adventure in changing the economic structure of Europe.

The second significant event in the outside world was the French stabilization program of December 1958. Following a severe recession and stagnation, the French Finance Minister Antoine Pinay had entrusted a council of experts, led by Jacques Rueff, with the task of drawing up an overall report on the entire national problem. The result was a program that included tax increases, a 15 percent devaluation and the establishment of external convertibility of the franc, suppression of restrictions and controls on 90 percent of France's trade with OECD countries, the reduction of some subsidies and "social charges" in an attempt to balance the public budget, and other measures.

Depending on one's point of view, these events constituted either problems or possibilities for Spanish policy-makers. Either they were factors to be coped with or policy innovations occurring elsewhere which could be added to the arsenal of equipment of Spain. For the neo-liberals, with their European orientation and their envy of more sophisticated economic technology, these events appeared as innovations which critically changed the field of available policy instruments. The stabilization plan in particular opened a new possibility for policy instrumentation.

Events in Spain heightened the desire for new policy departures. While the internal economy was stabilizing and inflationary pressures diminishing, the reports published at the beginning of 1959 revealed that the external situation had become more perilous during the preceding year. Imports were rising despite the quota system and a 25 percent tax. Exports were falling rapidly, at the rate of 10 percent a year. Exchange reserves had reached rock bottom. At the end of 1958, Spain had only $10 million in reserves, and a $60 million net deficit, counting current obligations.[42]

It was in this environment that Spanish policy-making would take place in late 1958 and early 1959. Prior events had guaranteed that inflation and balance-of-payments issues, as well as internal decontrol and liberalization, would be privileged problems on the agenda of state. The scope of potential policy equipment had been expanded by the new policy initiators' attentiveness to recent innovations in Western policy equipment.

The Procedural System of Stabilization

The first instruments of consultation used by the policy-makers were international agencies. In December 1958, an OEEC team visited Spain. A delegation from the IMF arrived in February, and in the same month Jacques Rueff, father of the French stabilization, conferred with the policy-makers and made public statements. The involvement of these groups was designed to serve a number of purposes. Primarily, there was a need for genuine consultation, for technical information, advice, and ideas on how to adapt the tools of the new economic statecraft to Spanish conditions. As we shall see, this advice was remarkably effective. Though there was close accord between the Spanish policy-makers and their advisers in any event, the way in which Spain followed this international advice in detail is striking.

However, such consultations no doubt also had aggregative and coordinative purposes. Receptiveness to foreign participation in policy-making no doubt was designed as a signal to Europe that Spain had indeed turned over a new economic leaf and was now fit company in the new economic arrangements of Europe. And the rallying of prestigious overseas influence might also serve as a source of power in anticipated internal conflicts over the new policy directions. (Of course, this could backfire, and the opponents of the reforms did indeed concentrate some fire on "foreign influences.") It is probable that the policy-makers also anticipated potential IMF financial assistance for a program of currency devaluation and perhaps World Bank support for general development policies.

It could hardly be said that the agencies from which advice was sought were impartial as to the outcome of the Spanish policy deliberations. The OEEC was established at the time of the Marshall Plan to bring greater coordination in European internal and international economic policies. With the end of the Marshall Plan, it turned its attention to matters of European trade and payments. The organization was committed to a greater integration of European economic life, on the basis of neo-liberal principles. Hence it urged Spain to remove constraints on foreign trade and on currency convertibility and to bring its domestic policy format into line with that of the other member nations.[43]

The IMF, for its part, had been the leading advocate of trade liberalization and financial orthodoxy in the postwar period. Article VIII of IMF's charter had charged the organization to work toward the elimination of discriminatory currency practices or restrictions on convertibility. Members were to work toward convertibility and were required to report transitional restrictions to the organization. The IMF was interested also in sound monetary management and had made its support of governments passing through fiscal crises contingent upon the adoption of stabilization programs, usually involving both public austerity measures and decontrol. The "money doctors" had participated in such programs in Chile (April 1956), Bolivia (December 1956), Paraguay (August 1957), and Argentina (December 1958) prior to their consultations in France and Spain.[44]

While these international consultations were in progress, the process of policy deliberation was also going on within Spain. Prior to the formulation of stabilization, the new economic team had hardly been associated with the basic forums of participation in policy-making. In fact, most of their procedural actions had tended to restrict critical deliberations to the economic specialists, as in the case of the cabinet committee on economic affairs, which was intended to isolate economic policy formulation from full cabinet debate. Until 1959 there was little or no structured consultation on major policy departures. Both the tax reforms and Spanish membership in international organizations were received as announcements of policy. One infers from published reactions and preceding silence that key economic groups played no role in deliberating these decisions, and they evinced a bit of surprise when each occurred.

However, in January 1959, in relation to the stabilization program, an unprecedented instrument of decision procedure was unveiled by the Spanish policy-makers. A questionnaire was directed by the cabinet to the "most characteristically representative" institutions of the various economic sectors, soliciting their opinion on the probable consequences of liberalization and European economic integration for Spain, and their specific economic interest. The questionnaire went to the Syndical Organization, the Superior Council of Chambers of Commerce, the Bank of Spain, Spanish Confederation of Savings and Loan Associations, Superior Banking Council, Institute of Agricultural-Social Studies, INI, the Institute of Political Studies, the faculty of Economics of the University of Madrid, and the National Economic Council.[45]

The responses to this inquiry were so remarkable that we should dwell on them for a moment. There was unanimous and enthusiastic assent to Spain's pursuing a policy of liberalization and European integration. Spain's failure to join with Europe would mean isolation, long-run trade reduction, and that Spain would be out of step with modern economic dynamics. Although the uncompetitive character of Spain's economy was noted, there was generally an attitude of confidence that Spain could eventually compete on European terms. There was very little attention to measures to cushion the impact of integration, save for short-run transitional measures, but more on ways of making Spanish industry, agriculture, and commerce capable of competing successfully. The alternative model of establishment Falangism appears in two responses, but only as a straw man to be torn down.

What had happened? There had hardly been this degree of consensus on neo-liberal principles in preceding years, nor would there be again. One remarkable characteristic of the replies is their similarity in style. All are exercises in macroeconomic analysis, as though the terminology and concepts of modern economics were habitual in Spanish public discourse. What is also intriguing is that despite the open invitation to express the direct self-interest of the organization concerned, almost all neglected this and dealt with the problem in global, national terms. The syndicates gave absolutely no evidence of concern for the effects of stabilization on income or employment. (Actually, the syndical response to the questionnaire was based only on the attitudes of the economic sector which, as we shall see, had just prepared a major study on the state of the economy. There was absolutely no consultation with the labor sectors on stabilization, a point noted by Commerce Minister Ullastres who in 1960 said that "perhaps some day it would be convenient . . . to meet with the *social* directors of syndicalism" concerning the ramifications of stabilization.[46]) Other institutions were cautious about arguing the case of their specific sector. Perhaps the most striking was the report of INI, which in addition to being quite cautious on Europeanization, chose to act as spokesman for all Spanish industry and produced a ringing critique of current industrial policy. "For a great part of Spanish manufactures, one must go into a virtual labyrinth of assignments, quotas, etc., having many times to buy in the black market, where one gets low quality products, without guarantee, at fantastic prices."[47]

What kind of participation in decision-making did the policy leaders receive from this exercise? The structure of the question-naire suggests to me that they actually did seek consultation (advice on potential consequences of actions to interests) rather than the aggregative effect they achieved. Probably the product of this procedure can best be described as "positive feedback," a repetition and endorsement of the arguments the neo-liberals had been making over the past two years.

Probably the effect reflects an adjustment by those consulted to the unanticipated style of participation, and the fact that none was internally organized to represent its members at this level. Only the chambers of commerce and the syndicates reveal any sense of contact with their members in preparing replies. Several groups noted that the limited time provided for reply prevented extensive internal consultation on the matter. We may also be witnessing the mutual reinforcement of the economic technicians, for it seems that in many cases these replies were drafted by the staff economists of the organizations concerned. In any event, the policy-makers received from this procedure a largely uncautious, uncritical, overwhelmingly enthusiastic endorsement of the course they intended to follow.

How well did this representative procedure reflect real attitudes in the Spanish business community? One study of Spanish entrepreneurs made at about this time found generally liberal attitudes prevailing toward both foreign investment and European integration. For all sizes and types of firms, 40 percent of the entrepreneurs favored foreign investment without limitations and another 37 percent approved of such investment in a minority role. European integration was favored by 60 percent of the entrepreneurs. However, there were significant differences among firms. The most liberal on foreign investment were the service, mining, and metallurgy sectors, while chemicals, paper, construction, and construction materials industries were more conservative. Firms located in Asturias, Vizcaya, and Madrid were considerably more liberal than those in Catalonia. And the younger, more aggressive and innovative, elite firms, more closely connected with public affairs, were more liberal than the more traditional firms. One would expect that especially these last were somewhat overrepresented by the representative procedure.[48]

A second, and related, vehicle of consultation emerged independently of the initiatives of the policy-makers. The syndicates began organizing a conference on national economic policy as early as 1956. The political implications of this effort are clear. The concern of José Solís, national leader of the syndicates, about the potential preemption of the syndicates' dominant role in policy-making by the new economists is apparent. In his address to the Syndical Economic Council on December 14, 1957, and on many other occasions, he constantly repeated the theme of the syndical desire for more active participation in economic policy-making.[49]

The desire by the syndical directors to reassert their leadership in economic policy-making led to the convening of the ninth plenum of the National Syndical Economic Council in late 1957. This was the first true entry of the syndicates into the field of macroeconomic policy. Until 1952 this group met annually, always devoting its deliberations to specific sectors: coal and iron in 1948, cement, fertilizer, and seeds in 1950, gas and textiles in 1951, and foreign commerce in 1952. After 1952 its activity lapsed.[50] The reactivation of this instrument to debate global policy questions showed a vivid political awareness to the implications of economic policy debate in Spain in 1957.

The meeting took over a year to prepare. It was preceded by prodigious inquiries into the developmental needs of the various provinces of Spain and studies of specific sectors. A vast number of syndical leaders and members at all levels were involved in these studies, many of them showing considerable sophistication, all of them revealing attentiveness to local interests. As a source of intelligence on the attitudes and desires of a wide and deep spectrum of commercial and industrial opinion, this was an impressive work.

The overall conclusions of the meeting were quite compatible with the neo-liberal enthusiasm felt elsewhere. A primary objective of policy is that Spain enter the European and world economies. To this end, economic development is essential, involving a target growth rate of 5 percent. The modernization of structures and policies in many fields is required to meet this goal. Investment must be favored over consumption in the short run, for at least 24 percent of national product must go into current investment for development objectives to be achieved. Preferential treatment must be given to the more underdeveloped regions of Spain. Public austerity, balanced budgets, and a new fiscal system based on direct, personal taxation were called for, and a very strong statement advocating Spanish entry into the common market was included.[51]

Despite this prodigious effort, there is no evidence that the reports of the Syndical Economic Council played a role in the design of measures during 1958, and despite the political reasons for doing so, they are seldom mentioned in the statements of the economic leaders explaining and urging the program through 1959. Ullastres, at one point, admitted that he was not too aware of the proceedings in the Syndical Economic Council and had not kept in close touch with the deliberations.[52]

Hence, one must conclude that this activity was little more than positive feedback for policy-making. (However, we shall see that some of the studies executed at this time had long-range policy-making utility.) But the instruments of participation independently activated by the syndicates no doubt did help in rallying broad support for the liberalization program and in educating rather large constituencies in the rudiments of the new economic logic. The VI National Assembly of Brotherhoods (*Hermandades*) in the agricultural sector, meeting in 1957, also made a strong statement urging Spanish common market entry.[53]

There was some evidence of disquiet when the program was presented to the full cabinet. There was little love lost between some of the military and old Falangists and the new economic leaders. However, the cabinet made no significant changes in the program. The policy leaders had sought to displace the cabinet as a prime forum of economic policy-making and to reinstrument procedure so that it played essentially a formalizing role. They succeeded in so restricting the policy activity of the cabinet in this instance. There was no challenge to the role defined for them by the economic ministers, by the full cabinet.

By the end of June, the Spanish government submitted a statement to the IMF and OEEC of the measures it was prepared to take. The report reflected in detail the advice of these agencies, yet noted several items (such as retaining the special government marketing program in wheat) that were the initiative of the Spaniards.[54]

At the end of July, the various programs were enacted by decree law, thus eliminating the *Cortés* from the decision process. It would seem that this had more to do with questions of urgency than concern about the impact of *Cortés* deliberation on the decision. The ministers did explain their action to this body. Navarro Rubio emphasized the consultations of the questionnaire and, in a forum dominated by leaders of the Movement, showed its compatibility with the principles of the organic state:

> The entire nation, through its most representative and responsible institutions . . . freely expressed its viewpoint on the future orientation of our economy, arriving unanimously at the conclusion that [we must] align our economy with the other nations of Europe to do which it was necessary to achieve stabilization simultaneously . . . in this way the decision of the government becomes an authentic national agreement, in a political act of special and singular importance, because it shows the virtue and efficacy of the principles, at once organic and democratic, which inspire the doctrine of the Movement and on which are established the institutional equipment of the State.[55]

The Process in Perspective

The process of formulating the stabilization program of 1959 reveals some of the strengths and weaknesses of the decision systems devised by Spanish policy-makers when compared to Western counterparts. We have already noted that the regime's commitment to its prior policy format was not one of ideological rigidity, hence other perspectives on policy were available, and criticism of the going concern was possible without severe tension in the system. Certainly the debate among establishment Falangists, structuralists, and neo-liberals was fragmentary, sporadic, and unstructured, hardly a full and public exploration of the rival merits of the alternative policies as it might have been had these been partisan programs vying for power in a system of open communications.

Curiously, the neo-liberals, the "loyal opposition" under the circumstances, had the best of such public debate as there was. Their arguments and publications were dominant. The "government of the day" really made only a desultory defense of its program, and the structuralists were no more than an incipient factor at that point. The selection of this "opposition" group to become the government within two years of its emergence is a bit remarkable, but this is a commentary on the leadership style of the Chief of State and not on the structure of the system. In Spain, the principle of "one man, one vote" applied to only one man.

The syndical response to this competitive force did assure a rather full consideration of long-range global policy. The conclusions of the national syndical meetings indicate that the leadership of this group was not closely wedded to entrenched interests. Rather, the position taken by the syndicates indicates a great eagerness to "get on the bandwagon" of liberalization and Europeanization. Certainly one would not claim that the internal structure of these deliberations was democratic, yet examination of the provincial and sectoral reports reveals a wide scope of considerations and participation, many far from neatly tied to the package perhaps sought by national leaders. Whether these procedures, plus the supplementary vehicle of the questionnaire which extended the process to important economic groups not adequately covered by the syndical system, can be considered the functional counterpart of the national economic and social councils in such nations as Belgium, France, Italy, and the Netherlands, I will leave as a matter of conjecture. My own impression is that, in the quality and extent of considerations and representation provided to policy-makers, the several institutions are comparable. However, it is significant and noteworthy that there was no direct labor participation in these proceedings in Spain, and participation by this group was characteristic in most other Western nations.

Finally it must be noted that the absence of parliamentary participation is distinctive, though the parliamentary role was most rudimentary in the parallel stabilization program in Gaullist France. And in comparison to the active role of Congress in economic policy-making in the United States, we are dealing with a distinction not of degree, but of the nature of the decision-making system itself.

Certainly the procedure was adequate to assure the policy-makers of positive support from critical economic interests for the program they were about to undertake. Nonetheless, it is also true that they moved to decision in absolute ignorance of the potential reaction of labor or of the more generic attitudes that party organization might have provided. However, in a system as controlled as Spain, this was a less important consideration, at the margin, than it would have been in a more open society. Only an incredibly prudent policy-maker would have wanted to assure himself that a wave of strikes would not undermine the economic policy package, given the coercive machinery available to the Spanish state and the willingness of the regime to use it.

In terms of sheer efficiency, the procedural system was quite sufficient. Relevant expertise, domestic and foreign, was both timely and adequate. The time cost of decision was well within the bounds of European experience. It took about five months to effect credit and monetary controls in 1957, and the time for this process ranged up to eight months in other Western nations in the postwar period. It took only a few months to devise a totally new budget procedure. A plan for investment took about eighteen months, and even normal programming of government expenditures takes up to a year elsewhere. The new taxation plan was devised in no more than ten months, and Western experience in this field ranges from four to thirteen, on an average. The stabilization plan took essentially seven months to prepare, about twice as long as the parallel French program.[56]

Chapter 5

THE STABILIZATION
PROGRAM

THE STABILIZATION PROGRAM IS CONTAINED in a series of decree laws and administrative actions of July and early August of 1959. To attack domestic inflation, a regime of public sector austerity was declared. In the field of public finance, both current spending and deficit financing were to be cut. Total public expenditures would be limited to PTS 80,000 million for the following year. At that time another limit was set on the amount of public financing to be made available through the banking system. Previously a great part of the resources of general government, but more critically those of autonomous institutions such as INI and RENFE, had come from the private banks and the Bank of Spain. By curbing institutions at the source of their investment capital, the policy-makers were using the only instrument that seemed available for controlling these public sector agencies. A separate measure released the Bank of Spain from its prior obligation to guarantee automatically all emissions of public debt. Funding through the banking system was reduced from PTS 11,100 million in 1958 to 3,400 million in 1959. The wheat marketing service was exempted from these restrictions.

The total budget for the public sector was to be balanced by an increase in certain easily manageable taxes, specifically on tobacco and petroleum, which were government monopolies, and through tariff increases of up to 50 percent. These measures, along with United States aid and short-term credits, would create formal budgetary equilibrium.

Monetary management instruments were introduced to reduce the flow of credit from the banking system. A ceiling was set on the total amount of credit that the banks could make available to the private sector. The Bank of Spain was provided with somewhat greater flexibility on types of discount and interest. Together with an increase in the rediscount rate, these measures led to a quick increase in interest charges throughout the system.

To cope with the balance-of-payments crisis, a single, unified exchange rate of 60 pesetas to the dollar was established, in effect constituting a devaluation of the currency. Some of the diverse subsidies, special operations, and so on which had implied de facto multiple exchange rates, even after the end of formal differential rates, were eliminated.

In addition to these stabilization measures, a program of foreign trade liberalization was undertaken. Apparently the OEEC, backed up by the IMF and World Bank, was most influential in specifying a package of measures which would bring Spanish trade policy into conformity with other member nations. Quotas and other restrictions were to be eliminated from about 50 percent of Spanish imports from OEEC countries. Quotas, where they continued to exist, would be "globalized"; that is, limits would be specified for all imports of a certain product rather than by both product and country, as had been the practice in the days of bilateral trading. Membership in the European Payments Union implied currency convertibility with member nations, an end to bilateral payments agreements, and a consolidation of the Spanish exchange rate.

International liberalization would bring with it some reduction in state economic activity. Many public trading corporations, dealing in a wide variety of imported raw materials, were eliminated, nineteen in all by the end of 1959. An unemployment insurance program was created as a step toward loosening the rigid antidismissal procedures in effect, but its coverage and effectiveness were quite limited. And, of course, the elimination of some import, export, and exchange restrictions would cut down the red tape required in international transactions.

Other measures implied or specified in the program included an overhaul of the obsolete tariff law, general taxation reform, an antimonopoly law, greater incentives and guarantees to foreign investment, and an effort at long-range economic development planning.

Foreign support for the program included $75 million in IMF drawing rights, $100 million in OEEC credits, and $70 million in commercial credits, from the Chase Manhattan and First National City banks. The United States Import-Export Bank provided $30 million. Other OEEC members were willing to fund Spain's exchange indebtedness in the amount of $45 million. Ongoing United States aid programs amounted to $100 million, making a grand total of $420 million.[1]

Stabilization and Public Problem Solving

To specify the details of the program reveals little of its political and economic character. It was not self-evident to all economists, and it was certainly not self-evident to all interested parties in Spain, that liberalization was the only indicated remedy for inflation and exchange disaster. In fact, such a program ran counter to most of the conventional wisdom about Spanish economics accumulated domestically over the twenty years of the Nationalist regime. Moreover, the reasons for the political acceptability of this formula in Franco Spain are not at all obvious.

Therefore, we must analyze the logic on which these objectives, problems, and instruments were based. To many a stabilization plan may seem no more than a task of technical economics, but in fact it is also a rather intricate political act. The only political resource available to the economic expert in normal circumstances is his skill to demonstrate the urgency and utility of his proposals to the politically powerful (apart from his ability to cast a veil of "scientific" mystique over his product). It is the linkages to critical interests that enable the expert to form a coalition in support of his program. Examined from this point of view, the advice of experts appears as an intricate proposed solution to a problem that is jointly political and economic.

Consider the stabilization program as an interdependent set of objectives, problems, and remedies. The saliency and propriety of each component are enhanced by relations drawn to show that each one is critical for the achievement of any other. Because the set is stated as a closed system, it becomes a statement of privileged objectives, problems, and instruments. The pursuit of any other goals would be uneconomic to the optimum achievement of the elements in the set. The advocate of any "unprivileged" objective, problem, or remedy must demonstrate a logically compelling linkage to all the components of the initially specified set to make an argument as equally powerful as the "overlapping utility" of the measures initially proposed.

Let us start from the premise that inflation and the balance-of-payments crisis were the two most broadly recognized problems in 1958–59. However, for the policy-makers and their immediate allies, large industry and the banking community, internal liberalization and "Europeanization" were also critical problems, although this opinion was by no means widely shared by all other vital political forces. One problem to be solved, then, was the demonstration that the indicated solution to the privileged problems was domestic and foreign liberalization. This would have to be effected in a system where the historic, the adaptive response to inflation and foreign trade problems was an extension of public controls to regulate prices and wages and to control imports and exports toward increased self-sufficiency.

For the policy-makers, the five objectives specified were: internal equilibrium and sustained growth, balance-of-payments equilibrium, international liberalization, domestic liberalization, and the coordination and control of the public sector. The problem then was to solve all five objectives simultaneously. This is done by demonstrating that the remaining four objectives can be stated as problems inhibiting the realization of an objective, or as means to the achievement of a specified objective:

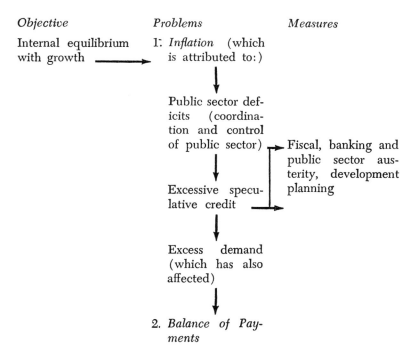

Objective	*Problems*	*Measures*
Internal equilibrium with growth ⟶	1. *Inflation* (which is attributed to:) ↓ Public sector deficits (coordination and control of public sector) ↓ Excessive speculative credit ↓ Excess demand (which has also affected) ↓ 2. *Balance of Payments*	Fiscal, banking and public sector austerity, development planning

Thus far, the indicated remedies to the problems of inflation involve "austerity" (making investment correspond to real savings). However, the problem of excess demand is linked to the deterioration of the equilibrium in foreign trade. The proposed solutions for this problem are either an expansion of exports or domestic substitution for imported products. (Since the first objective specifies economic growth, we cannot simply tighten our belts and do without.) Now our austerity program, to which we are committed as the indicated response to the first problem, constrains us from following historic policy. If investment must correspond to real savings, massive public investment or public subsidy cannot be an appropriate remedy. We must look elsewhere for measures to rectify the balance-of-payments situation.

Given austerity, our problem becomes that of lack of investment resources to reach the dual objective of growth and balance of payment equilibrium, since we can no longer use "potential savings" instruments. Foreign investment is one straightforward remedy, and it will require measures of internal liberalization, as well as relevant steps to build confidence and acceptance of Spain as an attractive locale for such investment.

However, solution of the balance-of-payments dilemma also requires the expansion of exports. The Nationalist economic policy, relying heavily on import substitution, squeezed the Spanish economy in two ways. First, by producing goods domestically, under protection and at prices higher than imports, the potential level of living and saving in Spain fell below that which would have been possible under free trade. Second, the higher prices and lower quality of Spanish products meant that they had to be subsidized to sell in the world market. Furthermore, many of Spain's traditional exports were in primary products, and there is a well-known argument that nations producing agricultural and raw materials are systematically disadvantaged relative to industrial producers in world trade. Finally, for Spanish industry to compete effectively abroad, it must be able to import advanced machinery and equipment easily.

The only available resolution of the problem, then, is to expose the Spanish economy to the world market, so that Spanish exports become competitive with foreign products and so that Spain may have the advantage of lower priced imports. And this in turn implies that internal policy will have to be less restrictive, so that Spanish producers are not hampered in their attempt to compete with foreigners. (Hence a new unemployment insurance scheme will be required, to substitute for classic restrictions on employee dismissal. However socially reputable, under the new order of things, Spanish producers will not be able to afford to absorb the costs of supporting redundant or inefficient labor.) Our statement of the problem now becomes:

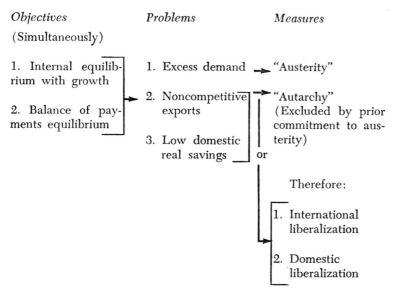

Objectives	*Problems*	*Measures*
(Simultaneously)		
1. Internal equilibrium with growth	1. Excess demand →	"Austerity"
2. Balance of payments equilibrium	2. Noncompetitive exports	"Autarchy" (Excluded by prior commitment to austerity)
	3. Low domestic real savings	or
		Therefore:
		1. International liberalization
		2. Domestic liberalization

One can also read the equation the other way around. If the postulated objective is international liberalization, or Europeanization, to bring Spain into the increasingly vital life of the rest of the Continent, then stabilization must be a requisite measure, for otherwise there would be a devastating run on imports if these were opened up under conditions of excess demands. All other objectives in the set appear as remedies:

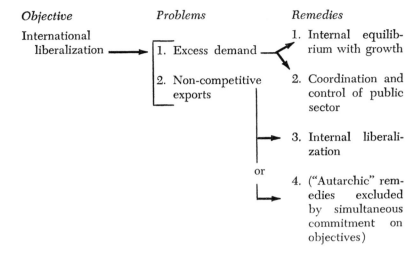

This logic, never as schematized as I have presented it here, was implicit in the statements of the Spanish policy-makers and their foreign advisers as they justified the stabilization program to their several publics in 1959. This extrapolation of the model of neo-liberalism appears persuasive and compelling, and, as we shall see, this had much to do with its political acceptability. However, the logic of the argument is not totally self-contained. There is a single major assumption underlying it, which is that Spanish producers were capable of responding to competitive forces to such a degree that balance-of-payments equilibriums could be restored. If this condition is not fulfilled, the entire formula becomes a counsel of economic ruination, for if Spanish producers do not, on the whole, outcompete foreign enterprise (which has a distinct advantage in the first period), all objectives in the set are jeopardized. Increasingly available imports, if more attractive, further disrupt the balance of payments and growth deteriorates, setting in motion pressures for controls over domestic and foreign trade and for public deficit financing of indigenous producers, with attendant inflationary pressures.

The Political Acceptance of Stabilization

What is most remarkable about the stabilization program is the degree of support it received from critical political forces. Certainly there was opposition and some bitterness in the cabinet, particularly from some military and Falangist ministers. Herbert Matthews reported at the time that "there is an influential group of businessmen and economic advisers close to General Franco who do not like the plan and are trying to sabotage it."[2] However, in most political arenas, assent and enthusiasm were evident.

I have already described the unanimous support reported in the questionnaire circulated by the economic ministers in early 1959. But there were even more significant affirmations of enthusiasm. The syndicates saw their role in policy-making preempted by the new technocrats, and we have already recorded their discontent at this turn of events. The Falangist social activists could only see the program as a strengthening of their classic antagonists, high capitalism and big business. And the dour, passionless new economic leaders were simply personally uncongenial to the "politicos" of the Movement and Syndicates.

Nonetheless, all sectors of the Movement and Syndical organization rallied to the program through 1959. Solís, head of the Syndicates and the Movement, adopted the tone that Spanish labor and industry must gird themselves for new challenges, to "fight for Spain." He seemed to be whipping up enthusiasm for something of a crusade for economic integration with Europe.[3] The economists of the Syndicates, in their journal *De Economía,* underscored the urgency of this response of European integration. Antonio Robert, once hesitant about Europeanization, now suggested that the Nationalist policy, while essential to infrastructure development and creation of consumers goods industries, left the export sector behind, and that this should be a critical priority in the coming period.[4]

José Antonio Suanzes, head of INI and in good measure the architect of the nationalist economic program, appeared as a prime critic of the going concern and an advocate of stabilization.[5] The young radical economists of the structural reform school pointed out the advantages of the market mechanism in creating competition and stimulating development.[6]

The generality of support for the program requires explanation. The political restraints of the system or the political culture of acceptance of hierarchically determined authority are tempting explanations, but they will not do, for within a year we shall see a massive and critical debate generated on economic issues.

Most commentators have attributed this overwhelming endorsement of the stabilization program to the critical nature of the economic situation. Whitaker writes, "Spain was now virtually bankrupt. . . . This situation probably contributed more than anything else to Franco's decision to submit his regime to the surgery of the stabilization plan."[7] Benjamin Welles, a bit more dramatically, puts it this way:

By June 1959, Spain's foreign reserves were gone, prices were climbing, and vital imports grinding to a halt. Disaster loomed and Franco finally capitulated. Ironically, it was the hated foreigners who saved him. Wall Street, Paris, London and the OEEC bailed him out. But on strict conditions. . . . This meant drastic reforms which, in turn, meant violent criticism and perhaps even agitation among the masses, for it was the low-paid masses who would bear the brunt. But there was no alternative. Time was running out. It was a grim, ugly moment. Franco turned wearily, angrily to the *Opus Dei* ministers, waiting for his decision: reform—or drift. "*Hagan lo que les da la gana*" he snapped. "Do as you want." He had crossed his Rubicon.[8]

Despite the appeal of urgency, there are other reasons for the program's acceptability to a wide variety of interests. Certainly for many interests, large, more efficient firms for example, liberalization was a breath of fresh air and a promise of reform. The young and reform minded, who might have had some reservations about the economic orthodoxy of the program, for the moment held their tongues, on the chance that this represented the first chink in the regime's armor, the first promise of changes to come. The greatest difficulty might be to explain why Franco, as well as the interests most closely identified with the Nationalist regime and policy style, accepted the program.

A Revolution Not as Great as It Seemed

And yet, viewed from a certain perspective, there is no reason that Franco or his closest allies should have seen stabilization as a reversal of their policies. While many observers chose to interpret stabilization and liberalization as a major change, virtually a policy revolution, the magnitude of the difference stabilization made can be easily exaggerated. There is really substantial continuity and compatibility with the major trends of policy under the Nationalist regime.

The system of rigorous economic control was never a matter of orthodoxy, either to Franco or to top economic leaders. Always it was presumed to be a pragmatic response to an emergency situation. There are persistent indications of interest in restoring "normal" economic programs. In July 1956, before the appointment of the new economic team, the Chief of State said, "We will try forcefully, in the least time possible, to reach a situation in our economy that permits us commercial liberty and in which we can return to the tariff as the automatic regulator of our commerce."[9]

Similarly, isolation had never been Franco's foreign policy objective. On the contrary, he persistently sought to restore Spain to her place as a European power. The rapprochement with the United States was considered one of Franco's major achievements. There is no reason to believe that he would have had serious reservations about liberalization, when it carried with it the real possibility that Spain would once again be accepted as a partner by Europe and the world economic community, even though he may have been unhappy about the extent of the control that the IMF and OEEC chose to retain over Spanish policy as a condition of their support.

There is another foreign policy dimension to the acceptability of stabilization by Franco and other conservative forces. The program was borrowed directly from de Gaulle's France, which Franco had come to see as a regime quite compatible with his own. During the period when de Gaulle had first come to power, there was a sense among some of the Nationalist elite that the world was at last catching up with the Spanish system.[10]

However, the most significant point concerns the meaning of liberalization in the Spanish context. Many foreign observers saw this as a renunciation of centralized economic control, perhaps as a first step toward political democratization. However much liberal economics may be associated with liberal politics in some other nations, let us pause to reflect on the particular implications of liberalization in the Spanish system.

In fact, liberalization was designed to restore centralized control over economic policy. Over the years, definitive control had slipped from the hands of central authorities. There were problems of public sector coordination, and critical branches of private enterprise could pretty well dictate public policy as it affected their own concerns. Despite the word *liberalization,* what the *Opus Dei* ministers were promising Franco was not a restoration of economic liberty but of economic order, a prime value of the authoritarian regime, and of the centralization of authority, a historic Spanish political propensity.

Direct controls no longer guaranteed responsiveness to central authority. But monetary and fiscal instruments, manipulated from above, could produce a regimented and predictable response throughout the system. It is significant that the *Opus Dei* technocrats often described the process of removing controls as one of subjecting Spanish industry to the "discipline" of the market. Hence, paradoxically, the liberal program advocated by the new ministers would produce greater order and stability than when the state had tried more rigorously to control events. This squares, of course, with the emphasis of the economic ministers on careful public budgeting and planning. Control and management were the essence of their economic philosophy.

In fact, the stabilization program was a conservative move. It was designed to promote the realization of persistent political values, rather than to change them. The prime policy objectives —growth with economic stability, improved foreign trade, and effective and centralized political order in society—remained consistent. It was the instruments that had changed, and the means to achieve these goals. In foreign trade, the emphasis was supposed to shift from import substitution to export expansion; domestically, from direct controls to market effects.

The Implementation of Stabilization

The most immediate and effective measures were the monetary instruments. The stabilization and devaluation of the peseta contributed to the expansion of exports, the decline of imports, and the restoration of balance-of-payments equilibrium within the first six months of the program.

The liberalization of foreign commerce was also implemented swiftly, though accomplishments leveled off after initial policy changes. By the end of the first year, most of the state trading agencies, other than those in wheat, had been terminated. However, the share of imports accounted for by state trading really changed but little into the 1960s. The elimination of quantitative restrictions on imports was more gradual. Within two years, five successive biennial lists of liberalized imports were published, and by the end of 1961, 43 percent of imports were from the new liberalized categories.[11] However, even for controlled imports, quotas were raised each year by 10 percent or more, and sometimes licenses were issued for more than the quotas. In many areas of nonliberalized trade, what was devised was something of a transitional measure of gradual elimination of the protection these controls had afforded. Though this was an important achievement that helped reduce raw materials bottlenecks, it was far from the 90 percent liberalization objective set in negotiations with OEEC. Into 1963, about 40 percent of Spanish imports were still subject to these restrictions.

In January 1960, a new policy toward foreign investment went into effect. The new system permitted free investments by foreigners of up to 50 percent ownership in Spanish firms, and investment above 50 percent could be authorized by the government. Transfer of currency, machinery, and parts was facilitated and dividends were exportable up to 6 percent of annual investment.

In May 1960, the new tariff was enacted. The task of drafting this law had begun in May 1957, and thus it antedates stabilization, though the revision of the antequated 1929 customs was a major component of the stabilization program. The new tariff used the Brussels standardized nomenclature, *ad valorum* charges, and in other ways brought Spanish practice into line with other Western nations. The tariff rates were quite protectionist. Though the "average duty" is of course a very rough comparative measure, some estimates showed that Spain now would levy a 24.5 percent average duty, compared to 18 to 19 percent for France and Italy, with the United States and Britain a bit higher and Benelux and Germany a good deal lower.[12] Thus, the major purpose of stabilization was to replace direct controls with tariff measures, but not to forego high levels of protection, despite some of the formal arguments of the liberals. In this area, at least, what was sought was acceptance of Spain by Europe, by adopting the policy equipment advocated by OEEC and eliminating bureaucratic regulations, rather than opening Spain to international market forces.

Though implementation of the stabilization program's measures concerning international commerce was relatively swift and effective, the measures proposed for the domestic economy were quite another matter. OECD, the successor organization to OEEC, would report eighteen months after stabilization that "in the course of 1961, not a single decisive measure was taken to hasten the suppression, agreed to in principle, of the vast network of direct controls over industrial investment, employment, etc." However, it was noted that regulations were being applied more liberally, and sometimes overlooked altogether.[13]

In fact, little action was taken in this area until early 1963 when, under new international (World Bank) and domestic pressures, some 66 different instruments of intervention were eliminated, for the most part price controls, and a pledge was made to raise annual global import quotas to 20 percent. The same series of actions, from November 1962 to April 1963, also eliminated the requirement of approval for foreign investments over 50 percent, provided for private activity in state controlled exports if the difference from support price were paid by the private trader and provided that national enterprises begin to issue reports and financial statements.[14]

During this period the policy-makers seem to have had their share of the perennial Spanish difficulty in achieving control over the public sector itself. The investment plan of 1959 was to be a key instrument of public austerity. While irrigation and other capital works were severely cut, housing and INI expenses went over the ceilings proposed for them. Though the authorities claimed that INI investments were held to the estimates, this really included only direct investments. Apparently, the authorities had considerable difficulty in persuading INI to reveal full information of its activities.[15] An order of July 26, 1958, requiring program budgeting, was not fully implemented in 1963.[16] One supposes that bureaucratic protectiveness also had something to do with the slow rate of domestic decontrol.

Other major projects anticipated by stabilization came to fruition slowly. In these cases, the more deliberate pace is understandable, for in the enactment of new banking, antimonopoly, and taxation legislation we are dealing with complex, politically sensitive issues, where the design of measures must take some time.

In April 1962, the Bank of Spain was nationalized. Monetary policy and supervision of the banking system were centralized in this institution. Again the motive was to modernize the instruments of monetary control in the hands of central authorities by imitating European central bank practice. The limited power of the

Central Bank at the time of stabilization had made it necessary to use such relatively crude instruments of monetary control as decreed ceilings on the amount of credit to be made available. Now the reorganized Bank of Spain would be capable of engaging in open market operations, setting reserve requirements for member banks, and so on.[17]

Not until July 1963 was a weak antimonopoly law passed, and the taxation reform anticipated in the stabilization program did not come into effect until June 1964.

Tamames's discussion of the evolution of the antimonopoly law is an excellent dissection of the Spanish policy-making process in this period, and provides some explanation of the long lead times required for the design and implementation of such measures. The stabilization program pledged Spain to take "appropriate measures to combat monopolistic practices and other activities contrary to commercial normality and economic flexibility." The Technical Secretary General of the Ministry of Commerce drafted such an instrument by mid-1960, using the Italian law as his basic model. However, here the matter rested. Sheer inertia, the press of other urgent policy-making, and the controversial character of the proposed measures (which would affect INI as well as powerful private firms) account for the low priority assigned this measure. Furthermore, the World Bank report of 1962 did not find it an important matter, and this report perhaps "tranquilized" the policy-makers on this issue.

After two years, in July 1962, the corps of economic technicians of the Commerce Ministry, on their own initiative, held a seminar in the ancient university town of Alcalá de Henares to deal with restrictive commercial practices. Visiting foreign experts described the experience of their own nations and apparently discussed a draft proposal for Spain.

At about the same time, Spanish policy-makers were once again concerned with rising prices, and Minister of Commerce Ullastres was beginning to focus more and more on the disparity between wholesale and retail price indexes as a little discussed factor in price pressures. Ullastres saw this matter as one particularly within the competence of his ministry, and he began to assemble a set of instruments to deal with the matter. Government support for supermarkets, cooperatives, and a network of refrigerator plants was on the agenda, and apparently he added the promised antimonopoly law to this package. The cabinet, focusing on the new inflationary problem, accepted the program, although they might not have been impressed with the antimonopoly measure in isolation. In October 1962, Ullastres received a mandate from the cabinet to draft the measure.

Between December 1962 and February 1963, a committee within the Commerce Ministry, advised by economists and lawyers, went through 110 different drafts before deciding on a plan to be submitted to the *Cortés*, where some 48 amendments were proposed by the commerce committee. In this forum, a high official of INI proposed that the operations of the industrial institute were a more effective way to keep the market open than restrictive practices legislation. Though this did not succeed, pressure from the syndicates led to the creation of a consultative committee to oversee the administration of the law. The committee had strong syndical representation. The law passed the *Cortés* and went into effect with enabling regulations on July 23.

The strategy of the law was to define and condemn a wide variety of restrictive practices and to set up a procedure for determining exemptions. Hence, "agreements, decisions or actions that are consciously parallel" and that tend to "impede, falsify or limit" competition were prohibited. However, "all situations of privilege created by the government" were excluded, as were most agricultural activities, consonant with European practice. Furthermore, other practices might be adjudged acceptable by the Council for the Defense of Competition (thus giving both the government and the syndicates independent capacity to override the law).[18]

Reflection on this process reveals something of the forces at work and the procedural limitations of Spanish policy-makers at this time. The role of rather junior economic experts in keeping the issue alive from within the bureaucracy is notable. We observe their Europeanizing drive and their interest in providing Spain with the policy equipment of Western states. Various foreign models formed the basis of expertise on this question, and the eventual outcome was a combination of German principles and British administrative practice.

That there were powerful pressures opposed to the technocrats is evident, and that they found in the legislature a useful forum for their actions is interesting, given the usual easy dismissal of the *Cortés's* relevance in policy-making. It is evident that there was insufficient power to support the antimonopoly law in its own right, but under inflationary pressures, cabinet and *Cortés* were willing to let Ullastres have his measure, primarily as a tool to be used against middlemen. This would be its real purpose; for the rest, there was sufficient scope for exemption that it would be no more than a symbolic gesture toward the commitment to antimonopoly legislation.

The taxation reform of 1964 was again largely a matter of streamlining and adjusting measures to correspond to European patterns, rather than a basic shift of tax burdens. Direct taxes were made somewhat more progressive by raising the minimum exemption from 25,000 to 60,000 pesetas per annum and increasing the progressivity of the tax above that. Preferential treatment was given investment income. The indirect taxation system was cleaned up by the elimination of minor taxes, which were reduced from thirty to five basic types.[19]

The lead times of two, three, and four years respectively for the banking, monopoly, and taxation projects is quite long by any comparative standard. True, each was a controversial measure, yet none connoted radical change in advantages in the system or in the balance of public and private power. In any event, it is clear that swiftness in execution characterized only the monetary parts of the stabilization program and that other projects waited long between proposal and implementation. The basic explanations for delay probably involve both the potential political saliency of the latter measures and the prudential approach of the Spanish policy-makers, who wished to take no more actions than were necessary to achieve desired results. The sheer capacity of the decision system to absorb such a heroic agenda may also have accounted for the long lead times.

It is evident that the program was basically a changeover in equipment, from that of economic nationalism to the policy instruments of neo-liberalism in Europe. Seldom did the policies connote shifts in structure, advantages, and burdens.

Spain seldom consulted her own experience or prior policies for guidance in devising these new measures. This was not adaptive tinkering with established and legitimate tools, which we have suggested as the most normal form of policy engineering. Rather, Spain engaged in wholesale borrowing from abroad. All the old machines were cleared from the shop and new ones put in their places. Few innovations on old models were attempted, nor was there much adaptation of the borrowed models to the new site.

Perhaps Cervantes was right about Spain, for in all of this one sees a mixture of innocent idealism and pragmatic cynicism. On the one hand, the policy-makers apparently sincerely believed that Spain could emulate the economic successes of Europe by using the policy machinery of these other lands. On the other hand, the policy-makers knew that such measures were the price Spain must pay to prove itself an acceptable partner in the developing integration of Europe, and so she must have them, whether they actually affected economic structures or not.

Impact and Evaluation

By the time Spain received it, stabilization was almost a packaged solution to a certain configuration of political economic problems. The advice of international economists was based on an analogy between the economic difficulties of France and certain Latin American nations and those of Spain. There was no way to anticipate what the actual consequences of such a program would be when applied to Spain.

The immediate results were very good and won the applause

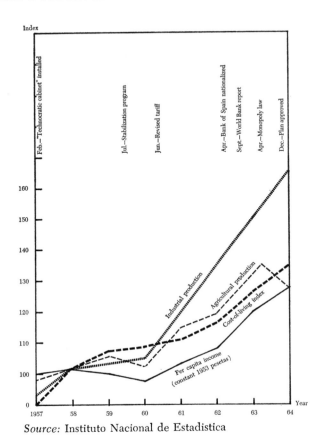

Source: Instituto Nacional de Estadistica

FIGURE 3. MAJOR ECONOMIC INDICATORS DURING
THE STABILIZATION PERIOD

of the participating international agencies. The credit limits, public austerity, and devaluation seemed to meet effectively the critical problems of inflation and balance of payments. Imports fell from $612 million to $477 million for the first nine months of the program, while exports rose from $305 to $405 million. More important, reserves, virtually exhaused at the beginning, had grown to $463 million after one year.[20] During the same period, prices rose by 2 percent. The stability of the price index probably

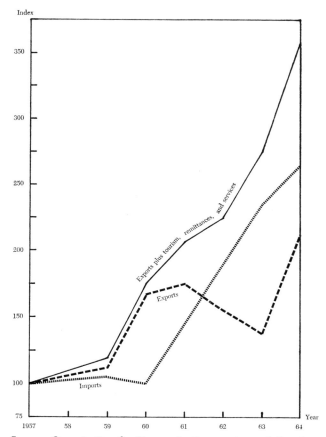

Source: Organization for Economic Cooperation and Development

FIGURE 4. SPANISH FOREIGN TRADE DURING THE STABILIZATION PERIOD

had something to do with selling off inventories built up in earlier inflationary periods. While this affected the production decline of 1959–60, it also led to restrained import demand.

Current private investment and consumer spending, particularly for durables and luxury items, also were immediately affected. The combination of these forces had an impact on income and employment. While there were few layoffs, overtime and other "wage drift" bonuses sharply decreased, meaning up to 50 percent reductions in real wages for many workers. One consequence was a rapid increase in emigration as workers now found comparatively more attractive positions in France and Germany. The number of emigrants, which averaged about 50,000 a year in the 1950s, suddenly rose to 79,700 in 1960, 146,200 in 1961, and reached a high of 186,000 in 1962. More important, the direction of emigration shifted from Latin America, the dominant direction in the 1950s, to Western Europe, which received 72 percent of the emigrants from 1958 to 1963.[21]

The interesting point about the quick effect of the stabilization measures is that the reaction was apparently more psychological than economic. Investment waned long before ceilings on available credit were reached and, in fact, the full supply of credit available to the private sector was never used. Some argued that this was because the great banks first attended to firms in their groups or held credit in reserve for them.[22] However, this is not a satisfactory explanation for the failure of Spanish industry to invest up to the level permitted or expected under the austerity plan. The more compelling point is that the private sector was responding to policy as "signal" rather than constraint.

It is clear from the design of the program that the policy-makers were anticipating a somewhat different economic reaction than they received. Their monetary policies were to create a slowdown in the rate of expansion, rather than the absolute decline experienced, for the ceiling on credit was not actually less than in prior years. The authorities also had expected much more difficulty in curbing inflation than they experienced. Furthermore, it was anticipated that the combined stabilization and liberalization measures would create an intense demand for decontrolled imports. To cushion this expected effect, Spain had contracted for a $420 million stabilization loan package. However, the nation hardly touched these credits. The pressure on imports did not materialize. By May 1961, repayment on the 1959 loan was completed ahead of schedule, and additional standby arrangements were canceled, while substantial reserves had accumulated.[23]

A number of situational factors account for some of these unexpected results. Remittances from emigrants and the burgeoning tourist trade brought unexpected foreign exchange earnings. A steel strike in the United States increased demand for Spanish steel, and a good harvest year lessened requirements for food imports. However, the basic fact was that the economy had reacted much more sharply than expected, and that instead of exerting pressure to restrain continued expansionist pressure, the problem soon became one of lifting Spain from a recession deeper and more prolonged than foreseen.[24]

Most commentators agree that the basic cause of the unforeseen economic stagnation was the response of the Spanish business, entrepreneurial, and investing community. Instead of sustaining expansionist pressure that the authorities would control, they withdrew from new activity, adoped a passive "wait and see" attitude, contracted operations, and sold off inventories where they could. Their dominant attitude was said to be uncertainty about the longer course of policy, and they were unwilling to make commitments until receiving clearer guidance on what the authorities had in mind.

Of course, Spanish industry, particularly the new industries founded since World War II, was closely responsive to public policy. These entrepreneurs had lived in an environment guided, controlled, and stimulated by the public sector. Furthermore, their skill and style of operation were geared to an inflationary economy, pushed by public investment. As Tamames writes, the stabilization plan, for most businessmen, represented "a very brusque change in their habits of twenty years of economic life."[25]

To be sure, there were good reasons for Spanish businessmen to be concerned about the course of things to come. The rhetoric, if not always the actions, of stabilization suggested that they were to be deprived of the public supports previously relied on, that they would have to compete with European manufactures in Spanish markets on even terms.

One can create a number of hypotheses about which sectors of Spanish business would have reacted most strongly to this situation. One could argue that the newer, larger firms, most closely tied to government incentives, most dependent on banking capital for expansion, most concerned with long range investment strategies, would change their plans more precipitously. Conversely, one might suggest that this was the sector that had sought a neoliberal policy most strenuously. Now they were assured policies favorable to their interests, the first steps had been taken toward integration with Europe and new markets for expansion of Spanish industry, and such firms no doubt understood the finer point that they were not immediately to be deprived of accustomed advantages and probably had informal assurance to that effect. Such an argument would suppose that the smaller, more traditional firms would feel most threatened and act most conservatively in the circumstances.

Apparently neither hypothesis singles out the sector that reacted to stabilization most strongly. Linz and de Miguel, in their study of Spanish entrepreneurs, found no meaningful relationship between size of firm and the judgment of businessmen on whether or not stabilization had affected their plans for innovation or expansion (see Table 9).

However, production indexes show that it was the most modern, most privileged sectors of Spanish industry, basic metals, particularly steel, and chemicals, as well as electricity and paper, that maintained a high rate of production during the stabilization period, while consumers goods such as foods and, more tradition-

TABLE 9. IMPACT OF STABILIZATION ON
PLANS OF SPANISH ENTREPRENEURS

	Large firms (over 500 employees)		Average firms (up to 500 employees)	
	%	N	%	N
Stabilization favored plans	2	4	2	6
Has not affected plans	27	38	35	111
Affected plans	48	70	49	154
No answer	23	33	14	44
Total	100	145	100	315

Source: Linz and de Miguel, *Los empresarios ante el poder público*, p. 99.

TABLE 10. Impact of Stabilization on Production
by Industrial Sector
(1958 = 100)

	1959	1960	1961
Food	96	105	98
Drink	94	95	115
Tobacco	99	99	106
Wood and cork	93	90	106
Paper	102	107	114
Leather	90	94	97
Chemicals	109	118	122
Glass and ceramics	89	86	92
Basic metals	118	111	126
Metal manufacture	80	68	79
Textiles	95	99	106
Coal	92	91	93
Minerals	98	99	118
Coal and oil derivatives	105	108	109
Cement	109	118	123
Electricity	109	118	128

Source: "La industria española en 1961," Estudios económicos 2 (December 1961).

ally, organized manufactures, including textiles and leather goods, were more listless (see Table 10).

In any event, Spanish businessmen simply reacted more sharply to the new policy than was foreseen in the model of their behavior which had been implicitly assumed in the stabilization plan. Earlier I suggested that we review the procedure of decision-making when a policy is attended by such unanticipated consequences, Would a more adequate procedural system have enabled the policy-makers to foresee and account for this reaction in the design of the original measures? Did relevant information exist that was not accounted for in the formulation of the first program?

It is hard to identify a potential instrument of policy initiation, formulation, or consultation germane to the Spanish setting that might have served to perfect this policy process. The surprise reaction to stabilization was in the business and industrial sector from which policy-makers received the most complete advice and information before making their decision. Furthermore, the information received from this sector enthusiastically supported the policy-makers' intentions. It might be argued that the decision process overrepresented the opinions and judgments of the larger, more modern firms and that syndical consultations were not an adequate mechanism to tap the reservations of smaller, less efficient enterprises. One might suggest that only a legislative process based on broad and decentralized constituency representation—one in which local commercial elites are quite influential, as is the case in the United States House of Representatives—could have been adequate to bring out this probable reaction to the program from the fuller range of commercial and industrial opinion.

However, it is not so much in the anticipatory mechanisms as in the processes of ongoing consultation, coordination, and feedback that the problem would seem to lie. Consultation with business interests was largely a one-shot process, and no techniques were created to involve the entrepreneurial community in the program as it unfolded. True to their persuasion as economic technicians, the key policy-makers relied primarily on the macroindicators of economic performance as their critical source of feedback from the business society. This enabled them to identify the overreaction quite quickly. However, it did not provide them with means to do much about it.

The problem by late 1960 was no longer one of stabilization, but of reactivation of a most hesitant economy. The prime means employed by the policy-makers was a reversal of the signals originally dispatched. In late 1961 and 1962 private sector credits were expanded and public spending and investment increased.

The policy-makers were aware of the psychological dimensions of the problem, but they were unable to find in the procedural format appropriate means of coordination, instruments of detailed consultation with the entrepreneurial community on the intensions of policy, or a forum for the synchronization of private and public efforts.

The critical role of ongoing procedural equipment in the success of stabilization becomes quite clear when we compare the Spanish case with two parallel programs of about the same time, those in France and Argentina. The French, as we shall see in more detail a little later on, had developed workable instruments for planning the relationships of private and public sectors for economic growth. The French stabilization effort of 1958 did set the stage for a subsequent program of development and expansion. The poststabilization setback of Spain was avoided. Only by imitating in exact detail the procedural technology of the French did the Spaniards eventually turn their program in the desired direction.

In both France and Spain, the stabilization phase of the program worked successfully. Inflation was controlled, balance-of-payments deficits corrected, and the currency stabilized immediately and effectively. This was not the case in Argentina, where a similar program failed to take hold. What seems to set the Argentine case apart is the relationship of labor to the decision process. Whatever the weaknesses of their respective systems, France and Spain had integrated labor into their economic policy-making processes. Formal labor leadership was willing to accept the neoliberal set of decision rules, including the important premise that inflationary wage pressures were in no one's best interest. In one way or another, labor was involved in policy-making negotiations in France and Spain, a process supplemented in Spain by suppression of dissenting labor leaders. In Argentina, on the other hand, organized Peronist and other labor unions saw themselves as opponents of, rather than participants in, the decision process. Despite Arturo Frondizi's best efforts, wage pressures and the failure of business to hold the line on prices led to the continuation of the crisis that stabilization had been designed to resolve and, eventually, to the collapse of the government.

Certainly, the means by which Spain accounted for labor's response to stabilization do not delight the liberal imagination. And it is clear from the experience of the rest of Europe that labor discipline and labor accord in a neo-liberal policy framework need not require labor coercion.

It may well be that only the outlet of emigration saved Spain from more volatile and unexpected effects of stabilization. The policy-makers had engaged in only the most rudimentary consultations with labor in designing their program and really had only the most impressionistic rule-of-thumb notions concerning labor interests and potential reactions. Generally, it would seem that they had assumed that the regime of order would satisfactorily account for labor reactions. Even the effect of emigration was something of a surprise, particularly in its magnitude, though it was generally interpreted as a fortuitous side effect of the policy and was officially encouraged.

It is true that Spanish labor paid part of the cost of stabilization, though its burden was probably not disproportionate to that of other sectors. The Office of Economic Coordination and Programming estimated that wages paid by industry increased 10 percent between 1958 and 1961 which, taking into account price rises, implied a diminution of about 1 percent in real wages. During the same period, the industrial index rose 15 percent; so salaries did not keep pace with productivity increases.[26] However, over a longer time span, the effect on labor does not appear quite so harsh. One estimate puts salaries in 1962–63 at 30 to 35 percent above 1958 levels, while prices were by that time 24 to 30 percent above the 1958 index.[27]

In overview, one must conclude that the technical competence demonstrated in the Spanish stabilization program was greater in the area of policy than of procedural equipment, and that the primary deficiencies, as measured by the gauge of unanticipated consequences, came in the area of structuring the collaboration and coordination of private and public sectors in the program in progress.

By 1961–62 the issue of stabilization had changed to the issue of reactivation, and a more effective dialogue with Spanish economic forces was recognized as a necessary means to that end. At this point, the policy-making process begins again; the unanticipated consequences of a solution generate a new problem requiring once more the design of procedural and policy measures to attain new objectives.

Chapter 6

PLANNING AS A PROCEDURAL INSTRUMENT

ECONOMIC STAGNATION, THE UNEXPECTED BY-PRODUCT of the stabilization program, brought a swift response from interested publics. Of course, the basic macroeconomic indicators signaled these effects to policy-makers. What is more significant is that the signals were recognized by a variety of groups and converted into political demands. At a number of points in the system, a criticism of public policy arose, totally in contrast to the generally positive tone of opinion a year earlier. A search for the causes of the economic doldrums was initiated, and suggestions of possible policy remedies came forth.

It was in early 1960 that the mood changed. For the first six months of stabilization, public support was steady. For example, the journal *Actualidad Económica* made no demands for new programs in its year-end editorial. Rather it struck an optimistic note and called for concerted efforts to fulfill the stabilization objectives.[1] However, by the end of February, it commented that "one need not believe that stabilization is like Lot's wife. Stabilization is something that must move."[2] The top leaders of the Syndical Movement issued a declaration of principles in early

February, strongly urging the reactivation of the economy and more complete information of the government's intentions.[3] Academic economists added their voices to the demand for growth-inducing policies, and at conferences held in April and May of 1960 they issued a forceful call for reactivation measures.[4]

In early 1960, the Spanish public authorities were faced with a new problem-solving situation. Though the indicated course of action was evident to many significant groups, the policy-makers were apparently far less certain. International agencies, the IMF and OECD, pressed Spain hard not to retreat from its commitments to stabilization and urged the policy-makers to follow through on the remaining agenda. Furthermore, the neo-liberals were convinced that with orthodox policies the economy would to a large extent heal itself.[5]

The new context of policy-making in 1960 still lacked clear definition. Faced with ambiguity, the policy leaders extemporized. Against the advice of the OECD, they did adjust the more flexible policy instruments in early 1960, opening up private sector credit supplies, lowering interest rates, and increasing public sector spending somewhat. On the whole, however, the policy-makers refrained from decisive action. There were few new policy initiatives in the 1960–61 period. Tamames felt that the policy-makers were resting on their laurels.[6] Another explanation is that the policy-makers did not expect the effects of stabilization to take hold so quickly, and Ullastres himself evinced surprise at the speed of stabilization effects. In a few months goals were achieved that should have taken the better part of a year to reach.[7]

Perhaps the system was simply not geared for further action when the public thought Spain was ready for it. Despite these possibilities, the major factor accounting for the policy pause in the early 1960s might be found in the cross-pressures on the policy-makers and the unexpected situation that they confronted. Unclear as to the indicated course of further action, they simply refrained from taking any decisive steps.

The Problem of Uncertainty

Despite the heterodoxy of the advice and diagnoses received by policy-makers in this period, there was virtual unanimity of opinion that entrepreneurial uncertainty about policy intentions or their potential effects on the economy was a critical dimension of the poststabilization problem. Gradually, from the diverse materials churned up in the poststabilization debate, this theme came to be selected by the policy leaders as a major item on the agenda of public action. Though other aspects of the problem were being processed simultaneously and public actions formulated, we shall follow this theme, for it led to the major policy initiative of the 1960s. This, then, becomes the second problem-solving situation in which to watch the Spanish policy-makers at work.

Many efforts were made to diagnose the unanticipated response of the Spanish entrepreneurs to stabilization. The OECD, in its 1960 report on Spain, reflected much of the conventional wisdom circulating in the Spanish capital:

Managerial attitudes of extreme caution and uncertainty have probably been replaced by larger expectations . . . after the shock of deflationary measures had been digested and the authorities had by a series of measures indicated their intention to maintain the level of economic activity. But private investment demand, which had certainly declined very considerably during the last two years, does not yet seem to have recovered sufficiently. A degree of uncertainty about the future "rules of the game" and an awaiting of a clear lead by the government could perhaps partly explain the persisting relative caution of private management.[8]

Antonio Robert suggested an additional dimension of the problem. Spanish entrepreneurs, accustomed to limited growth prospects, were not attuned to rapid economic expansion. "Perhaps the major difficulty that exists in many branches of . . . industry is the lack of knowledge of future demand, that first retards initiatives and later leads to an inorganic and pressured development."[9]

The problem of the policy-maker was to induce private sector collaboration with the intentions of public policy. The "new economics" of Western Europe apparently had a different effect on the Spanish entrepreneur than on his counterpart elsewhere. Throughout the Nationalist period and to a large extent, as we have seen, even before, he tied his fortunes and expectations closely to public policy. Perhaps it could be argued that the Spanish entrepreneur was not such, at least not in the pure Schumpeterian sense. The premise of much of modern economics is that the entrepreneur initiates, seeking self-interest; the state guides, directs, controls this original thrust of action. However, Spanish business and industry was long accustomed to acting as a consequence of public policies. The new policy format of 1959 was an act of state policy leadership. But the premises of this policy were liberal. The program adopted, the next move was up to the entrepreneur. The Spanish entrepreneur, apparently, was not yet ready to play the game. The consequence was a pause, while both private and public sectors waited for the other to take the next step.

A related factor probably was involved. The new economics rests largely on the assumption that the state can affect the decision-making environment of the entrepreneur by manipulating his resources through monetary and fiscal measures. The adjustment of such policies is also a form of communication, a special symbolic language, signaling government intentions for private activity. In Spain, for reasons we have noted, control of credit was used as the central policy device. However, a significant part of large Spanish industry, particularly the older firms of Catalonia, were largely self-capitalizing, did not use credit, and entertained a general hostility toward the banking system. One might expect that the messages involved in manipulating the supply of credit and the interest rate were largely lost on them. It was rather the newer industries, established in good measure during the Nationalist period, in the north and around Madrid, that would be most attuned to and influenced by credit-policy actions.[10] And it was precisely these industries, established and carefully nurtured under public sector guidance, that one suspects would be most hesitant to act without clear signals from the authorities.

The problem of uncertainty reduction transcended the use of purely economic policy instruments. Though marginal efforts to make credit available and to expand sector spending were useful (and apparently the rhythm of growth had been restored in many critical sectors by mid-1960), there was need to add political or procedural tools to the mix of programs in order to move stabilization toward development. As a procedural system, stabilization presumed that certain responses to policy would be automatically forthcoming on the classic model of entrepreneurship. They were not, and to the extent that they were not, the policy of stabilization was imperfect. What was required was instruments of information, communication, and collaboration between public and private sectors. Such, at least, was the diagnosis that the Spanish policy-makers made in the early 1960s.

Their first response was to stimulate a dialogue (their term) between the policy-makers and the entrepreneurs. The economic ministers took the stump, explaining and elaborating their philosophy at business meetings, industrial fairs, and conferences throughout Spain. The most prominent and articulate was the former economics professor, Alberto Ullastres. One prominent Catalan industrialist who was exposed to the persuasions of Ullastres held some reservations about the minister's habit of two-hour speeches, his tendency to talk down to businessmen, but nonetheless agreed that he cast a spell. "Cicero said that to convince it is necessary to be convinced. Ullastres is. And thus he was able to convince his audience and put the Barcelona businessmen in orbit."[11]

However, the more central response to the problem of uncertainty was found, probably more through serendipity than conscious search, in the unfinished agenda of the stabilization program. There was a process of discovering programs relevant to newly apparent problems that the policy-makers used throughout the poststabilization period. The accumulation of projects, pledged in the stabilization program but not immediately enacted, was always in the background of the policy-makers' consciousness. International agencies and domestic pressure groups continued to urge their implementation. Occasionally, the policy-makers would draw on these available policy instruments to find a remedy for a specific problem that arose in the poststabilization period. We have already noted that Ullastres used the pledge of an antimonopoly law to cope with commercial bottlenecks when price pressures set in after 1963. One killed two birds with one stone in this way, fulfilling the stabilization program and finding an instrument to deal with a current crisis. So as the policy-makers pondered the problem of generating energy and confidence in the Spanish entrepreneurial community, they came to see that the pledge to establish a long-range economic development and investment plan might be a tool relevant to this purpose.

Planning as a Procedural Instrument

In the stabilization program, the Spanish policy-makers had committed themselves to undertake long-range economic planning. Even before stabilization, a beginning had been made with efforts to coordinate public sector investments. The programs of investment regulation (*ordenación de inversiones*) of 1959 and 1960 really were one-year development plans. Theoretically they included definitive investment guidelines for the public sector and indicative projections of private investment. Though the 1959 program simply lumped private and public investment, with little effort at analysis, the 1960 effort involved real, though rudimentary, planning. Investment projections in agriculture, for example, were based on the targets of halving the volume of food imports in five years, while meeting related irrigation, parcel concentration, and other objectives. Similar projections were included for industry, housing, and public works.[12] During October 1960, the government invited the World Bank to make a developmental study of the Spanish economy, as a basis for more elaborate long-range planning.

The planning instrument was readily available to Spanish policy-makers in the poststabilization period. Their actions in moving from budgetary tools to public sector planning, and from these to long-range planning, were a matter of gradually enlarging upon accepted mechanisms. Planning was neither a dirty word nor a piece of policy exotica in Spanish policy debate. The question of the legitimacy of planning as an instrument of state action was only a minor byplay in the policy-making process. Though the policy-makers rehearsed the arguments, then much in vogue in Western discourse on economic affairs, concerning the distinction between central control planning of the type characteristic of the communist nations and those forms of planning compatible with democratic capitalism, this was but a minor aside in the process, probably designed to reassure quite specific and not too intensely concerned audiences. In fact, planning had been a central symbol in the rhetoric of economic reform groups of all kinds after 1955. The syndicates, as well as the neo-liberal groups, had warmly and insistently called for public planning in their statements of policy demands. The interest had led to a rather large-scale inquiry into the applicability of foreign planning models to Spain in 1956,[13] and a similar inquiry by the *Instituto de Economía de la Empresa* of Barcelona was carried out in 1957.[14] In that same year, Spain also participated in the United Nation's Food and Agriculture Organization's Mediterranean Project. And the government had used the concept of planning with favorable connotations in the Nationalist period, as in the irrigation and housing plans of the early 1950s.

Apparently the relationship between the problem of uncertainty and planning was perceived quite early. By December 19, 1960, in an address to the *Cortés, Hacienda* Minister Navarro Rubio elaborated at length on the idea of planning, describing it "as a means of reviving our creative tensions" and of "revitalizing the economy."[15] By March 1961, with Franco's statement to the First Syndical Congress, "We have come out of stabilization, we are about to enter the plan of development," it was clear that the policy-makers had opted for planning as the central instrument of economic development.[16]

Long-range planning would provide businessmen with some assurances concerning the future parameters of government policy—what credit and tariff protection they could expect, what the rhythm of public investment would be—thus partially clarifying some major factors in investment decision. Furthermore, planning could provide guidelines for the relative roles of the public and private sectors in the development process. Both the level of future government control and the extent of public enterprise were sources of the entrepreneurial hesitancy noted in the feedback period.[17] Finally, for the policy-makers to bring the Spanish entrepreneurs into a clearer understanding of what was expected of them in the new liberal policy format, persuasion and education were needed. For Ullastres this implied the use of the planning instrument to extend and systematize his dialogue with the business community. He sought the participation of the entrepreneurs in the formulation of a development plan for Spain.[18]

The Adoption of the French Planning Technique

The way the policy-makers established a procedural system to formulate a development plan for Spain was rather remarkable: they simply borrowed French planning procedure wholesale and in detail. The basic institutions and processes were imported intact. Even the titles of institutions and offices were retained, merely being translated from French into Spanish.

All political scientists and economists suspect the transference of institutions between cultures. It is a process fraught with pitfalls. The postwar experience of political and economic development has taught, if it has taught anything, that institutions and processes are apt to act in rather unpredictable ways when transplanted to cultures other than those from which they emerged. In the decision of the policy-makers to adopt the French technique of planning, we confront a classic case of the borrowing of procedural equipment between nations. We will want to evaluate the adequacy of this decision, the extent to which the French machinery operated in Spain in a manner analogous to the French experience, and the extent to which it led to unanticipated consequences.

The idea of adopting French planning techniques was not an implausible one for the Spanish decision-makers to make. They saw Western Europe as the center of a progressive and effective economic doctrine, embedded in specific policy machinery. They understood the European Common Market as both a threat and a promise to Spain's economic future, and they hoped that adoption of the political economics of the West would make Spain an acceptable future partner. The stabilization program, borrowed directly from the French and with the advice of international experts, had worked. The shortcomings of the program might have resulted from the failure to borrow wholeheartedly enough. Perhaps the French success was due to the relationship between stabilization and planning.

In addition, France was the current economic success story of the early 1960s, and the French policy format was much admired elsewhere. Britain's National Economic Development Council was established in 1962 after careful scrutiny of the French experience.[19] Walter Heller tells the story of President Kennedy's ordering him not to return from a Paris conference until he had discovered the secret of France's growth.[20]

And progressive opinion in Spain historically had been attuned to French policy initiatives. France's Latin culture seemed particularly compatible with that of Spain. Over the years, Spain had borrowed from France models of bureaucracy and administrative organization, parliamentary institutions, and welfare and military systems.

Furthermore, on the face of it, French planning seemed, of all available models, uniquely appropriate to Spanish conditions and to the problem Spain was attempting to solve. French planning had evolved almost as a process of conspiracy, of intimate contact and negotiation between the government and a small number of key industrial leaders and firms. French planners believed that their technique was possible only when at least 80 percent of production was in the hands of 20 percent of the firms, and that a 60-40 ratio would be unmanageable.[21] Furthermore, it was useful to have a substantial ratio of production and commerce in the public sector.

In principle, Spain met these conditions. Production was disproportionately concentrated in larger firms, many of which had developed with close links to public policy. Though the extent of public investment was not nearly so large as in France, the INI industries and the public role in transport, agriculture, and other fields represented a similar set of institutional arrangements.

The key to French planning was its indicative character. In the language of the period, this represented a middle way between nonplanning, or simple economic projection for informational purposes, and the centralized, control economies of the communist world. The long-range plan projected investment growth rates and related macroeconomic objectives with optimal policy mixes called for by the targets. The policy projections were mandatory for the public sector, but only indicative or suggestive for the private sector. The plan was developed through an elaborate series of meetings in which various groups in the economy were represented, including business leaders, public officials, experts, and representatives of labor organizations.* The committees of the plan, taking cognizance of official growth targets and macroeconomic projections, along with public policy expectations, then developed plans for their specific economic sectors.

Primary functions of indicative planning were to coordinate private and public growth and to provide business with full information on public intentions. The Spanish authorities were fully aware of this feature of the French system. In his first press conference after assuming the office of Commissioner (*Comisario*) of Spanish planning, Laureano López Ródo spoke as follows:

* However, the largest French trade organization, the *Confédération Genérale du Travail,* boycotted the planning activities after 1952.

The development plan will not try to put private enterprise in a rigid mold, but offer it a picture of the general future evolution of the economy and let it know the measures that the government is proposing to adopt immediately or gradually. In this way it facilitates the decisions of the entrepreneurs and diminishes the margin of error that is implied in every entrepreneurial decision. Thus, the great importance of an indicative plan is as the "great reducer of uncertainty" as in the well-chosen phrase of the French Director of Planning Mssr. Pierre Massé. . . .[22]

Though to borrow foreign policy equipment is an act of decision less normal than the adaptation of existing institutional equipment to new purposes, the Spanish policy-makers had good reasons for thinking that the imported French planning model would fit Spanish conditions and needs.

The Political Tension Between the Plan and the Syndicates

There were other reasons, rooted in Spanish politics, for the economic leaders to be attracted to the French planning technique. The established and legitimate instrument for contact between the policy-makers and the business community was the syndical organization. In principle, this organization could easily have been adapted to the purposes of economic communication and coordination and long-range planning. Twice during the period of the new economics in Spain, first with the analysis of the Ninth Economic Plenum and then in 1961 with the First Syndical Congress, the syndicates proved themselves capable of generating a statement of national economic objectives and programs. As we have noted, these statements showed a definite sympathy toward liberalization policies. If what was desired was an instrument of collaboration with the private sector, it would seem that it should have been quite natural to work through this existing machinery. Why then did the policy-makers decide to create an entirely new set of institutions for communication with the economic sectors?

We have already noted the low levels of participation and confidence in the syndical structures, particularly among the larger Spanish firms. The industrial giants had no real need for the brokerage services of the syndicates, and the managers of the major firms were apt to see the leaders of the syndical bureaucracy as a rather disreputable lot. It was the medium-sized and smaller firms that depended on the syndicates for representation and lobbying activities. However, to the policy-makers the key to planning, to exports, and to enhanced development lay with the larger firms. Hence, they needed to go around the syndicates, to fashion instruments of economic collaboration which would over-represent the interests of larger enterprise.

Furthermore, something of a power struggle was going on between the leadership of the syndicates and the economic policy-makers. The syndical leaders saw themselves squeezed out of their preeminent position in policy-making, virtually ignored by the new economic team. The *Opus Dei* ministers and the syndical leaders frequently were simply different human types. The technocrats often saw the syndical leaders as petty politicians, given to demagogic appeals for mass support, crude, a carry-over from an earlier phase of Spain's development, much perhaps as a successful executive sees a political boss in the United States. The syndical leaders, in turn, saw the new economic leaders as cold, mechanical, ruthless, and autocratic. The antagonism between these two elites had smoldered from the beginning, and it broke into flame on several occasions in the 1960s. Within the cabinet, clashes between the older *Falange* ministers and the *Opus* technocrats were continuing. The feud between Navarro Rubio and the Falangist housing minister José Luis Arrese became so acute that Franco replaced Arrese in March 1960.[23]

In February 1964, José Solís Ruiz, the head of the Syndicates, lashed out at the *Opus* technocrats, condemning them for "playing politics, following political directives, and holding political offices while hypocritically claiming not to be politicians" and of "conspiring against the unity of Spain with state funds." Emilio Romero, editor of the syndical paper *Pueblo*, was also suspicious. In an editorial on February 5, 1964, he asked why so many *Opus* members were to be found in important posts in business, industry, culture, and administration.[24]

This matter of personal and political conflict should be considered in explaining the planning structure devised for Spain. Through the participatory institutions of planning, the new economic leaders established a base for support by the prime economic factors, offsetting the organizational monopoly of the syndicates. In point of fact, the neo-liberal ministers had virtually no base of power within the syndicates, and to use them as a link to the private sector would have implied relinquishing control over the entire process of incorporating this sector in policy formation. Conversely, the planning process placed the syndicates in a role quite subservient to that of the economic ministers, in a struggle for predominance in economic affairs that had been going on since the rise of the *Opus* ministers. With the establishment of the procedural machinery of the plan, the syndicates were definitively outmaneuvered.

The Formulation of the Plan

From February 1962, when López Ródo was appointed Commissioner of the Plan, to December 1963, the date of ratification by the *Cortés,* it took a little less than two years to formulate Spain's first economic development plan.*

The generation of the institutional apparatus occupied most of 1962. During that year the central planning agency was set up

---

* A fairer estimate of the time-lag would include the year 1961, for the World Bank was invited to prepare a report on Spanish development in late 1960, and this was the time when Franco pronounced his watershed remark about "entering the Plan of Development." However, little was done to follow up the intention to plan until the appointment of López Ródo. Some charged that the whole process of Spanish planning had been delayed while "waiting for the Bank" to make its report. However, the normal lag in cabinet agenda and the fact that the full utility of planning as a problem-solving device had not yet been recognized probably are equally important in explaining the lapse of a full year between firm intention and implementation,

and most of the *ponencias* and *comisiones,* the participant committees, were established, though their membership was far from complete. Macroprojections of economic and social growth were prepared. And in August 1962, the study of the International Bank for Reconstruction and Development was presented.[25]

The IBRD study was a reputable and on the whole craftsmanlike piece of work. Though it contained few surprises—much of its analysis covered matters well known in Spain—the sections on transport and irrigation, particularly, included useful analysis. The report stressed planning and sound, efficient fiscal and monetary administration. Most striking was the note of dedicated economic orthodoxy that ran throughout. IBRD generally recommended that price mechanisms discipline economic growth, that Spain remove distortions inhibiting the proper function of the market, and so on. Competition was to be encouraged and monopolies discouraged by "progressive exposure to foreign competitors."[26]

Thus, the IBRD report further undergirded the policies of the neo-liberals. It stressed policy priorities in a number of fields, and many of these were taken seriously in the policy deliberations that preceded the plan. However, it is possible that the prime utility of the report was its becoming a focus and target of a critical public debate on Spanish economic policy. We will come to this matter a bit later on.

In November 1962, a series of directives and preliminary norms for the plan was issued. These actions cleared the way and announced the public sector's role in the planning effort. Some considered these measures more significant than the plan itself. First, all restrictive measures on internal commerce and production were abolished, except those specifically requested by a ministry. This clever approach to clearing away the deadwood of ministry inertia had the effect of forcing action on those responsible for the supervision of economic restrictions.

Second, national enterprises were required to publish an annual investment program, and their economic role was delimited.

Each ministry was to propose the sectors that could be exempted from the requirement that foreign capital not exceed 50 percent of investments. Modifications were to be made in the Law of National Interest Industries, the early autarchic policy that provided substantial incentives to selected industries. A policy was created to limit the maximum and minimum sizes of projected enterprises, in both industry and agriculture, that would be permitted free installation, expansion, or movement. Legislation on restrictive trade practices would be proposed by the Commerce Ministry. A Foreign Trade Institute was established. A program to improve scientific and technical education was to be devised.[27]

This battery of new policy measures seems to have had two purposes. First, it was a cabinet agreement to fulfill some of the uncompleted agenda of stabilization. Second, and of more interest, it was a process of dusting off and updating much of the policy equipment of economic nationalism for use in new ways. The old Law of National Interest Industries was to be used as a technique of the new economics. Direct controls would be available to prevent the establishment of firms too small to be efficient or too large to be competitive. The series of measures represented an interesting example of the adaptation of policy equipment to new purposes. The basic tools of nationalist economics were to be coordinated with the borrowed devices of stabilization and indicative planning in a policy package for the mid-1960s.

The Organization of Planning

The procedural system foreseen by the policy-makers in designing Spain's development plan was approximately as follows: The Planning Commission's staff economists specified the "targets," the macroeconomic projections for a four-year period, which were basically a 5 percent growth rate and the requirements for full employment. The program specified, in the preliminary directives and norms provided, the public sector actions to be anticipated for the period of the plan. These two factors would be the primary inputs or givens that would be used by the *ponencias* and *comisiones* in formulating a four-year program for specific sectors of the economy.

The *ponencias* corresponded to the French "horizontal" committees and considered general factors that would condition the plan, such as commerce, finance, economic flexibility, labor, productivity, and geographic location, and human and social factors. The *comisiones*, like the French "vertical" committees, each represented a specific economic sector, roughly corresponding to the syndical organizations.*

These committees would carry out studies and provide such information as the Planning Commission required. They would also design the program for their specific sector. They could propose objectives and the means to reach them, presumably in this way adding to or revising the public sector agenda. They were to report on the execution of the plan for their sector.[28]

The members of the *ponencias* and *comisiones* were appointed by the relevant ministry, the commission of planning and the syndical organizations, representing the public bureaucracy, private enterprise, and the syndicates, respectively. Over 400 members were eventually appointed, of which 250 were private entrepreneurs.[29] The presidents of these committees were named by the ministers. Most were the technical secretaries general or undersecretaries of the ministries. Only a few came from the private sector. Each committee was furnished with economic and statistical advisers from the Planning Commission. The work of the committees was overseen by four subsecretaries of the Planning Commission, one for the *ponencias* and regional committees, one for the eight industrial committees, one for the service and public sector groups, and one for the four committees on agriculture and transport.

---

* Agriculture; fishing; irrigation; energy; steel and iron; nonferrous metals; construction material; chemicals, fertilizer and paper; construction machinery; food industries; diverse and artesan industries; textiles; education; transport; telecommunications; information services; health and social assistance; interior commerce; scientific and technical research; Canary Islands; Equatorial Guinea.

The link between planning and the state involved primarily a putting together of pieces of ongoing institutional machinery. Historically, the *Presidencia del Gobierno* had the function of elaborating plans of economic development. Now the Planning Commission was created as an agency of the presidency. The OCYPE, created just before the cabinet turnover of 1957, now became a staff agency of the plan, to serve primarily as an organ of interministerial coordination. The National Statistical Institute also was made an agency of the plan. The post of Secretary General for Socio-Economic Coordination, created in 1946, became Secretary General of the Planning Commission.[30] The unfulfilled objective of economic coordination was still on the agenda of the Spanish state. With the new effort of planning, there was also an effort to draw together the various experiments at policy-planning that had been tried and had failed. Ultimately, the Planning Commission reported to the Delegate Economic Committee and through it to the full cabinet.

Planning as a Procedural Instrument

It is time to recall that we are interested both in the use of a procedural instrument, as intended by the policy-makers who designed it for the process of public problem-solving, and in what actually happens in the work of such agencies. The participants in such an arrangement may not play the roles foreseen for them, or they may seek to perform policy-making functions other than those anticipated.

It appears that the policy-makers intended their participatory apparatus primarily for coordination and, in a secondary sense, consultation. This is clear from López Ródo's many statements about the structure of planning. He saw the primary mission of the plan to be that of disciplining public investment, coordinating the political economy, and offering complete information to the private sector on the evolution of the economy. In addition he also expected information from the committees on the probable private reaction to proposed policy formats and growth targets.[31]

A certain aggregational effect was expected from planning. López Ródo stressed the political goals of development. Since articulation and integration are goals of planning, development is a "true national enterprise of solidarity."[32] However, he took pains to point out that planning was not to be seen "as a new instance of the right of petition" or as a vehicle for lobbying. The committees must respond fully to the directives of the government. They must retain a long-range and macro-economic vision. One must "cut off at the roots" all tendency toward "cantonalism."[33]

Although other statements of the power and functions of the committees lead one to expect an initiatory or formulatory role, proposing public projects or perhaps opening aspects of the developmental problem not anticipated by the planners, it seems certain from policy leaders' tones that the committees were not really expected to function in this way. They had an hierarchical and instrumental view of the process of participation in planning. They made it clear that they were not opening a new dimension of the political process.

On the whole, these procedural instruments acted about as expected. The decision-makers were able to control the instruments they had set in motion and to confine them to their specific purposes.* Naturally, there was considerable diversity in the experi-

* At this point, a word must be said about the character and quality of the evidence I am using. I was able to obtain relatively thorough documentation on the internal deliberations of only three committees for the first plan, and only one for the second, which was in the process of formulation when this research was carried out. In all cases, I received the documentation without official sanction, and I was asked not to quote it directly. Hence, I must generalize these findings and I cannot identify the committees involved, though three of the more controversial committees were represented. This imperfect process was not due to lack of cooperation on the part of the Planning Commission, whose officials tried diligently to help, but they did not themselves have copies of the minutes of the committee meetings. These sources were supplemented by interviews with members of as many committees as possible. Since these interviews were carried out at the time the second plan was in preparation, there was a natural and unavoidable tendency on the part of the respondents to generalize their impressions or experiences in formulating both plans. These sources were supplemented with public documents and publications and the archives of the Planning Commission.

ence of different committees. In some cases, the economic advisers and public officials who were officers of the committees prepared the sectoral plans with only rudimentary participation by committee members. In other cases, the committees of the plan represented a continuation of established patterns of negotiation between industrial leaders and their public sector counterparts, a transference to a new arena of a type of interchange that had long existed in policy-making. This was particularly apparent in the larger, more important industrial sectors. In a minority of cases, a healthy and persistent dialogue was joined between groups with differing interests and points of view. This interchange, sometimes quite heated, was normally resisted by the leaders of the committees, who saw it as disruptive of the purpose of formulating a sectoral plan in a limited period of time. However, it may have served the useful purpose of introducing individuals and groups to the different perspectives of other participants in a common economic activity.

For the more active and effective committees, the pattern of work was similar. Plenary sessions were held, as often as once a week, between mid-1962 and mid-1963, with some committees reporting over fifty such sessions. Attendance was high in those committees for which I have records, averaging 80 to 90 percent of the membership at each meeting. (In the first plan, per diem fees were provided for members outside Madrid, but there was no compensation for residents of the city.) Normally the committee broke down into working subgroups which reported to the committee as a whole. The agriculture committee had the most complex structure, eighteen working groups in all. Most committees had from three to eight subgroups.[34] In addition, some individual members spent considerable time collecting and analyzing information from a variety of sources. Syndical representatives often provided extensive materials from that organization for working papers.

In some committees a tension was evident between the leadership, which sought to get on with the work expected by the Planning Commission, and those members who preferred to raise major issues of policy debate or to question the premises of the planning effort itself. I have the impression that those not in the inner circle who could phrase their interests in the quantitative and projective language of the planners were more apt to have their particular demands included and sent on to the Planning Commission than those who merely raised a point of philosophy or criticism.

Though there were conflicts in most committees, the specific objectives and deadlines specified by the Planning Commission dominated the work in the long run. To a certain extent, the participants became errand boys who served as a convenient way to collect information on the state of the economy. Given the paucity of statistical information collected both officially and unofficially in Spain, this was a necessary function. The fact that the participants themselves discovered the frustrations of data collection probably forestalled future criticism of the planners on grounds of the quality of materials used. Thus the committee on information services evinced some shock at the lack of data available on the economic aspects of the press, radio-TV, and cinema.[35]

However, policy debate in the committees was not futile. In at least two significant areas the criticisms of participants in the planning process, together with the more general environment of public debate in which the plan was formulated, led to changes in the overall approach of the plan.

Regional development was the more substantial initiative which emerged from the participatory phase of planning. Though the policy-makers were aware of the problem of regional inequalities in economic development, it was evident that they did not propose to do a great deal about them as they set about designing the priorities for the plan. In a press conference held in September 1962, López Ródo was asked whether the plan would take regional differences into account. He responded, "We're dealing with a national plan, though one doesn't leave aside problems of location, evident in every economy and especially our own."[36] The general context of deliberation in this preparticipation stage of planning suggests that this was a peripheral concern of the policy-leaders.

However, in the final presentation of the plan and, as we shall see, in its implementation, the establishment of decentralized poles of industrial development in the less prosperous sections of Spain became perhaps its most distinctive feature. Though the specific mechanism was again a French import, the priority given it appears to have been in part a contribution of the planning participants, perhaps most centrally of the syndical representatives.[37] The issue was also particularly pressed in the general public debate that went on in Spain during this participatory period of the plan's preparation.

One other impact of participation is quite evident in the evolution of the plan. From the syndical representatives and from some sectors of the press and expertocracy came the claim that the plan was not sufficiently social in its orientation and that in structure and format the process of planning overstated the claims of industry and the goals of productivity at the expense of necessary social services and structural reforms. This was a somewhat different perspective of the planning task from that of the policy-makers, who had been restricting their vision quite explicitly to economic matters, even to the point of including such sectors as education primarily so that technical and professional preparation could be accounted for among the factors of production. The response of the planners was largely to handle the problem of social content through symbolic rather than real changes in the content of the plan. The rhetoric of the planning documents carefully highlighted the social goals of development. The social byproducts assumed to come with a rise in standard of living were made explicit.

Although the plan was reshaped in some important directions not anticipated by the technicians, for the most part the policy leaders tightly controlled the formulation process. While the authorities tried to get some good public relations—both for domestic and foreign consumption—from the democratic character of planning, no one took this seriously. Of course, it was neither a representative nor a democratic process. The membership of the participatory instruments was not elected but appointed. The committees had no authority; they were advisory institutions. The members of these organs were not representative either in the sense of being selected by or recreating the composition of their constituencies. They were selected on the basis of their collaborative and coordinative capacities, as critical figures in effectively meshing public and private sector performances, not because of any confidence reposed in them by any specified group.

Debate in the Cortés

The reports of the *ponencias* and *comisiones* were added to other materials of the Planning Commission, and a first report on the plan was published in April 1963. In October, the government sent the plan, now more fully refined, to the National Economic Council, which approved it with minor modifications. The cabinet adopted it on November 8 and sent it on to the *Cortés* for consideration at its session late in December.

This step in the procedural process was expected by the policy leaders to be no more than a ratifying or enacting function. There was no desire to use either the cabinet or *Cortés* for further refinement of the plan. The planners used their leadership roles in both forums to minimize the temptation to revise by providing detailed explanations of the rationale of the plan in response to challenges and inquiries. (This tactic is one which, if used consistently by a leader to confront a forum, seems to imply, "You have the formal right to ask questions but we have answers to all of them, and we do not intend to take your questions into account in refining our proposals.") However, they never opened the door to new initiatives or criticisms that would have implied substantial revision. In the main, they were successful in controlling the procedural use of these forums. But when the plan reached the *Cortés,* some *procuradores* were not content to play the classic legitimatizing role assigned the parliament in Spanish policy-making.

The objections raised in the *Cortés* were both procedural and substantive. In early December debate began in the Budget Committee which, in the course of hearings on the biennial budget, raised questions about the relationship of the Planning Commission to the normal budgetary process. At issue was the power of the commission to judge changes in the public budget during the life of the plan. Some *procuradores* argued that this made a superministry of the commission and infringed on the powers of the *Cortés*. The opponents were capable of changing the government's proposal that the Planning Commission "report favorably" on proposed budget changes to language which specified merely that the commission make a "report" prior to such changes.[38]

The major substantive debate occurred in the Committee on Fundamental Laws and the Presidency. Here, in the session of December 17, a total amendment was proposed, urging reconsideration of the entire project by the government. It was argued that the plan did not make an "organic whole," that its social and agricultural aspects were too weak, that it was economically imperfect. Opponents claimed that it would triple the commercial deficit in four years and raise the entrance of foreign capital dangerously. Various criticisms of technical flaws in the projections and the criteria of planning were raised. Some argued that growth projections were probably faulty, since they were based on the unrepresentative experience of stabilization. Instead of linking wage policy to productivity, it was suggested that the appropriate test of wages was price stability and the prevention of emigration. Similar technical criticisms were made on investment, capital, tourism, and agricultural policies.[39] (Many of the consultative points raised in this hearing, by the way, were later proven correct.)

Additional amendments were proposed that would have required the government to submit a "law of Rural Organization" within eighteen months. The principle of socioeconomic parity for rural and urban areas was also introduced.

The policy leaders, including López Ródo (we recall that the

Cortés includes ministers) led the policy debate, attempting to prevent the committee from assuming an initiatory or formulatory function by explaining the rationale of planning and by sidetracking proposed amendments. Some symbolic concessions were made. The leaders did agree to underline the role of the syndicates as an "active collaborator" in drafting the plan. Highly laudatory statements on the developmental contribution of INI and its head, José Suanzes, were entered into the record for the benefit of those who felt that the wording of the plan appeared to censure nationalized industries.[40] At the end of the hearing, the several amendments were defeated, but four votes were cast for the proposal to recommit the entire project, and ten opposed the designation of the plan as one of economic and social development.

The revolt against the plan in the parliament got virtually nowhere. Yet the revolt did occur, and that is significant. Nonetheless, as a forum for criticism and consultation, the *Cortés* demonstrated its incapacity. Some of the criticisms raised were good ones. However, given the discipline of the great majority of the members of the body and the limited time and staff resources available to this part-time and largely honorific body, the minority was incapable of developing its arguments into plausible form. The opposition *procuradores* could pick impressionistically at selected aspects of the program and make their dissent public but little else, for they lacked ammunition to attack the counter-arguments of the authorities.

The *Cortés* opposition was hardly a cohesive group. The debates reflected the resistance of the syndical and Movement bureaucracies to the style and the power of the technocrats. Another dissent involved those concerned with the role of agriculture in the plan. Others feared "ideological osmosis," the unintentional importation of liberalism and foreign ways. And there were some economically oriented skeptics who doubted the validity of the plan. In the full session of December 27, the plan was approved with sixteen dissenting votes. On the same day, the budget was approved with only three negative votes and a reform of the social security system, with eleven.

Evaluation of the Procedure: Comparison
with the French Experience

In assessing the Spanish planning process as an aid to decision, comparison with the French experience would seem the most satisfactory standard of evaluation. In the first place, French planning was widely admired as the most interesting and substantial democratic approach to planning. Moreover, the Spanish explicitly fashioned their planning process after the French. If there were differences in the two experiences, they should be differences either in leadership or in the total political environment, the larger institutional context of the complete political systems in which planning was set, for the planning structures themselves were as identical as the transference of a system across boundaries could conceivably allow. We shall be particularly interested in the difference in environment, for French planning, until 1958 at least, took place within a republican system of government.

The French, like the Spanish, intended the participatory processes of planning primarily for purposes of collaboration. They sought to bring the economically powerful public sector, the national industrial sector, and the leading private firms into coordinated effort. The planning process in France was no more intended to be, nor did it succeed in becoming, an arena for the general debate or reassessment of economic policy than in Spain. The functions and purposes of the planning institutions were apparently as tightly controlled by the policy leaders in France as in Spain.

In participation and representativeness, there are probably more parallels than differences in the two cases. One is skeptical of the capacity of the syndical organization to provide full representation of the Spanish working force. However, the French unions took little if any part in drawing up the plans in that country. The communist trade unions boycotted the plan in the 1950s, and the Christian and socialist trade confederations were normally quite underrepresented in comparison to government or enterprise. As in Spain, smaller businesses were structurally underrepresented in the planning process.

Parliamentary consideration added little more than a ratifying effect to the formulation of the Spanish plan, but any effective criticism or control of the planning mechanism by the legislature was absent in France as well. The French parliament hardly debated the first three postwar plans of 1946, 1956, and 1959. In the case of the first, it was not consulted at all, and in the second, its formal ratificatory sanction came only after the plan had been in effect for two years. Though there was some debate of the fourth plan (1962), it marked but a slight change in the general tendency of French parliaments to assume little responsibility for scrutiny of the plan and no role in the process of formulation.[41] In fact, it seems not inappropriate to suggest that the *Cortés* took as active a role in the planning process as any French parliament.

Despite the fact that the institutions and processes of the French political system were structured in a more participative and representative fashion than those of Spain, particularly under the Fourth Republic, there was little significant difference in the way economic policy was formulated in the two nations. If anything, the participatory processes of planning were more vital in Spain than in France. The criticisms of economic policy-making processes on grounds of democratic practice and public accountability are substantially the same in the two societies. The limitations of participation in the fashioning of policy-making procedures seems to have had little to do with the distinct institutional equipment available in the two nations. If in Spain the basic political institutions and processes were imperfectly representative, in France the representative institutions were either unwilling or unable to exert any significant influence over the course of economic policy-making.

Chapter 7

THE GENERATION OF
A PUBLIC DEBATE

THE PROCESS OF PLANNING hardly constituted a political process in the full sense of the term, for this was not a system for the deliberation and reconciliation of diverse points of view on the economic future of the country. However, the total process of introducing the new approach to economic policy after 1957 did set in motion a lively and telling public debate on the issues of economic policy. Public debate is a residual category in our scheme for analyzing policy-making. It is a procedural instrument that may serve to assist the policy-maker in public problem-solving. Like the market mechanism in economics, which is its policy instrument equivalent, it appears autonomously and is not intentionally established by the public authorities. Yet as the authorities may use the market as a means of ordering economic processes, so they may use the public debate as a means of generating the materials of decision. And as policy-makers may structure and direct the workings of the market, so what public debate does and what it contains may be shaped by decision-makers through techniques ranging from censorship to the control of information on public affairs.

In Spain, politics in the normal, partisan, Western sense was excluded from the public debate. For years, it seemed that sports, religion, and the doings of the monarchy took the place of politics as outlets for men's normal propensity to gossip about, discuss, argue, and judge the affairs of the community.[1] After 1957 economics was added to the agenda of outlets. Economic policy was a technical matter, not subject to the political taboos of the system. Debate on economic affairs seemed to become a substitute for politics. The newspapers, magazines, the intelligentsia, and, soon, conversation in general, came to focus on the intricacies of the balance of payments and the developmental uses of fiscal and monetary policy. By the mid-1960s, many street vendors, waiters, and cabdrivers were prepared to pronounce their personal judgments on the probable effects of integration with Europe or on the impact of tourism on Spain's industrial prospects.

The generation of this public debate occurred with stabilization. Between 1958 and 1963, the quantum leap in newspaper and magazine coverage of economic affairs was quite remarkable. The names of the economic ministers became household words, and the leading Spanish economists—Tamames, Fuentes Quintana, Rojo Duque, Antonio Robert, and others—became public personalities, their opinions solicited and debated in the news media, their books achieving best-seller status among the reading public. By 1960 the editorialist of De Economía, the house organ of the Syndical economists, was commenting on the extent and involvement in the controversy on economic policy, noting that while professionals might be appalled by the misuse of economic concepts and theories, such public concern was to be applauded.[2] España económica wrote of the phenomenon as follows: "Economic problems never before attracted the attention they are receiving today in our country. . . . In the opinion of many sociologists, the activity that these problems have provoked, previously restricted to a clique of professionals . . . shows the political good health of the Spanish people."[3]

A number of explanations may be offered for the timing and

magnitude of the phenomenon. Spain was obviously changing in the 1950s, and the language of economic analysis provided a medium for understanding and discussing the new rhythms and patterns of national life. Stabilization was a major national event, leading to uncertainties for many groups and raising many questions about the future course of public life. Furthermore, public life in Spain in the 1950s was, frankly, rather dull. The Spaniards are not unlike other peoples in wishing to spice their public life with a certain amount of drama, interest, and activity. The economic policy events of the late 1950s and 1960s lent a certain zest and excitement to public affairs. Within the legitimate bounds of a technical argument, there was some latitude for dissent and controversy.

The debate focused on the philosophy and program of economic liberalism. At one level there was a direct attack on the policy-makers for concentrating on productivity, industrial incentives, and similar economic goals at the expense of social objectives. Within the syndicates, the Movement, the intellectual communities, and, increasingly in the 1960s, among reformist churchmen influenced by John XXIII and Vatican II, vigorous protest was raised against the preoccupation of the policy-makers with the health of the industrial sector. The economic ministers were accused of contriving a policy that only made the rich richer and of proposing no remedies for the condition of the great majority of the Spanish population, who continued to live a preindustrial way of life, and who were not included in the agenda of change even in terms of basic public services.

Though vigorous, this phase of the debate was also frequently bombastic. The mood was often one of ideological and rhetorical appeal, of protest without the specification of remedy. The policy-makers seldom engaged their critics but more frequently dismissed their "demagogic appeals." Nonetheless, the issue had an impact on the conditions of politics in the country. The syndicates representing the peasantry and the agricultural workers took on new life and vitality. The Movement and the syndicates found a new function, as did some sectors of the official press, as critics of the going concern. Catholic protest organizations and the underground labor movement spread widely, and this new activism and influence had to be taken into account by those charged with the formulation of policy.

Alternative Problem Contexts

At a different level of discourse, the intellectual community, and particularly the professional economists, took a leading role in the debate. I noted earlier that the structuralist school of economic analysis had joined in the near unanimous wave of assent to the stabilization program in the spring of 1959. The meeting of minds between the neo-liberals and the structuralists was short-lived. Within a year, the structuralists reasserted their position as critics of official policy. Throughout the 1960s, these economists provided the prime alternative to the problem-solving context offered by Ullastres, Navarro Rubio, and López Ródo.

For the structuralists, the monetary and fiscal solution offered by the neo-liberals were not sufficient to the economic transformation of Spain. While stabilization was essential, it must be followed by deep, basic changes in economic structure. No matter how vital industry might be, Spain could not permanently rectify her balance-of-payments crisis nor provide her rural population with a decent standard of living until archaic patterns of land ownership were eliminated or transformed into patterns that made for investment in agriculture and better productive technique. The centralization of economic power in the great banks and the concentration and noncompetitive nature of most industry were systematic limitations on Spain's capacity to achieve a competitive position in world industry. Commercial and trade structures provided a most old-fashioned distribution system, hardly compatible with the needs of a modern nation. In short, the institutional equipment of the economy, no matter how many incentives were provided, was simply inadequate to the total task of modernization. The job of public policy must be more tho-

roughgoing than the programs of the neo-liberals anticipated.[4]
The structuralists felt that they had been deceived by the luke-
warm antimonopoly, banking, and progressive taxation measures
eventually taken by the neo-liberals. Post-1959 policies could only
reinforce the inefficiencies of industry and agriculture and further
accentuate income inequalities. The policy-makers had not attempted a sweeping liberalization of trade. To do so would only
have destroyed Spain's foreign commerce, for the productive sectors were inherently inefficient as organized. Therefore, the policy-makers had been forced to retreat to de facto protection and
privilege not unlike that afforded in the Nationalist period.

Yet the structuralist economists should be seen as something of
a "loyal opposition." In large measure they were sympathetic with
the objectives of liberalization, though they sought a more decisive set of policy instruments than the policy-makers offered. Initially they agreed that liberalization and integration with Europe
would force Spanish entrepreneurs to become more efficient and
productive. Only by the mid-1960s did Tamames and a few others begin to doubt whether the effort at integration was worth the
candle. However, during the early 1960s, Tamames, like his colleagues, was a strong advocate of integration, liberalization, and
planning.[5]

The policy-makers themselves contributed to the debate among
professional economists. Ullastres, after all, was a member of the
fraternity, and as part of the dialogue he proposed on economic
development, the Commerce Minister developed his views in
terms of economic theory. In a much debated article in the *Opus
Dei* edited journal *Arbor,* he set forth a strategy of unbalanced
growth for Spain. Closely following the argument in A. O. Hirschman's *A Strategy of Economic Development,* Ullastres proposed that the state intentionally stimulate the sectors which
offered the greatest socioeconomic returns in terms of time of
investment, profitability, manpower use, multiplier effects, and so
on. The previous Spanish economy was unbalanced in the direction of import substitution. Now it was time to create an intentional

disequilibrium in the direction of exports. Later there would be time and resources to correct the imperfections of this initial thrust and to deal with agricultural development directly and other sectors.[6]

The *Arbor* article created considerable controversy, and the merits of unbalanced and balanced growth strategies were debated. Soon the terms lost whatever technical significance they might have held and became symbols representing various degrees of agreement with or dissent from Ullastres on whether Spain ought to stress incentives to more vital sectors or encourage the more underdeveloped areas of the nation's economic life. Thus Hugo Galiani, writing in *Pueblo,* consciously posed an alternative design of balanced growth, one based on criteria of "efficiency, equity and stability" through "changes in the agrarian structure, fiscal reform, and a better distribution of wealth and income."[7]

As in the 1950s, in the policy debate of the 1960s, alternative perspectives on the problem of growth were available to the Spanish public, against which they could judge the position of the public authorities. Though formal socialist or communist options were excluded, the range of *grand options* on economic policy and the temper of criticism of the going concern were not unlike those characteristic of other Western nations. Nor was the debate purely an academic one. To be sure the logic of these positions was first hammered out in learned journals, but the language and argument quickly filtered down to a broader public arena of discourse.

Toward the middle of the 1960s, two important additional critiques of the neo-liberal policy came from the professional economists. Higenio París Eguilaz reiterated his establishment Falange positions in *El Desarrollo Económico Español: 1906–1946.*[8] He saw stabilization and liberalization as a betrayal of the successful record of Nationalist economic policy. He argued that stabilization was unnecessary, for inflation was controlled by the time the program went into effect, and the stabilization measures only triggered a recession. The recommendations of international agencies that guided the program were neither technical nor expert. The foreign technicians simply imposed a standard stabilization model on Spain, without taking into account the specific situation of the country. "Equilibrium and stability" are not prime values for a developing nation, which must use credit resources to stimulate growth. Liberalization works to the interest of advanced nations, but paralyzes the development of underdeveloped ones.

More novel and provocative as a critique of neo-liberal policy was Manuel Funes Robert's *Un programa para la Economía Española*. Funes offered an alternative to the orthodox, equilibrium economics of "prudent Spain." According to Funes, Spain had been obsessed by the question of balance-of-payments equilibrium. "We cultivate wheat on poor land and raise the price of bread to save foreign exchange. We subsidize our cotton production and raise the price of clothes to save foreign exchange." Spain's stabilization program was designed for an exchange-poor nation. However, tourist revenues and a cautious fiscal program had transformed Spain into a nation with one of the soundest currencies in the world. By 1965 Spain had $1,500 million in reserves, about 15 percent of her national income, and was in eighth place in the world in reserves. Yet she continued to follow a program designed for a period of exchange scarcity.[9]

To Funes, Spain's accumulated reserves were a potential but neglected instrument of growth. The dead weight of unused reserves might win international acclaim for financial respectability, but at the price of restricting her development potential. Funes recommended a psychology of abundance rather than one of scarcity. Spain was no longer a desperately poor nation, though it continued to phrase policies as though it were. The dependable bonanza of tourism had changed all that. Now Spain could actually invest abundance in imports to build a high-level technological society. Spain could create its own internal Marshall Plan, investing perhaps $1,000 million of reserves in growth. This sum would represent about 50 percent of the amount European nations received from the original Marshall Plan. Invested in industry, agriculture, educational and social change, such a program could make Spain a capable competitor in Europe. However, want of imagination, excessive caution, dedication to economic orthodoxy, and the myth of Spanish poverty had prevented this from coming about.

The raw materials of skepticism were available to the Spanish elites in judging the policies of their government in the 1960s. This was not a closed society in the normal sense of the term, in which the only handle on reality is the prevailing orthodoxy. In fact, the terms of reference of the economic argument had changed significantly from the 1950s. Now neo-liberalism was the established position that formed the target of criticism, and Nationalist orthodoxy, the policies of the 1950s, was running a poor third in influence on the public mind.

European Integration

A prime objective of liberalization was the integration of Spain with Europe. From the fluid point of view on this subject in 1957, before Gaullist policies led to a stabilization of structures and communities around the Six and the Seven, it appeared that Spain was about to be excluded from a great continental adventure unless drastic action was taken. Liberalization was first to make Spain an acceptable partner in the European experiment, and, second, to prepare the nation for the new competitive circumstances that would come with a common market.

The degree of original and sustained support for a European policy was really quite remarkable. In fact, it seems fair to say that a primary source of support for the program of the neo-liberals was the threat and promise of the common market. Industry and commerce could forgive sharp policy changes, in which they were to a certain extent the losers, on the basis that such steps were an essential prologue to entry into Europe. Reformers could ride along with a policy not precisely cut to their specifications in view of the long-range transformation of society that could be expected to come with integration.

With the possible exception of the stand-patters of the Movement, who saw integration as a threat to Spain's special system, the feedback received by the policy-makers from the vital forces in the political economy was almost exclusively affirmative. The syndicates regularly went on record enthusiastically at their meetings and conventions. Entrepreneurial attitudes, especially among the larger firms and the banks, was positive.[10] With the exception of París Eguilaz, spokesman for the establishment *Falange* position, all leading Spanish economists advocated integration by 1963.[11]

The apparent support for integration in Spain was really not particularly surprising. Public opinion throughout Europe in the same period was highly integrationist. Simultaneous opinion polls taken in the Six in February and March of 1963 record overwhelming majorities "very much for" or "more or less for" integration, and only minute minorities opposed. Though we do not have fully comparable evidence for Spain, the available data seem to indicate a similar level of enthusiasm for integration. One study found 58 percent of Spanish students in favor of integration and 27 percent opposed; 30 percent of farmers were for and 14 percent against; 41 percent of workers favored integration and 22 percent opposed. Asked whether it would be better for Spain to integrate with Europe or Latin America, the students preferred ties with Europe by 53 to 39 percent; the farmers voted for integration with Latin America by 42 to 26 percent; and the workers were almost evenly divided, 40 percent favoring integration with Europe and 37 percent with Latin America. (The high proportion of "don't know" responses is evident from the totals.) As we noted earlier, about 60 percent of Spanish entrepreneurs favored integration with Europe in the early 1960's.[12]

Spain made application to the European Common Market on February 9, 1962, after considerable stock-taking and weighing of the move by the public authorities. Welles reports that fifteen successive cabinet meetings were devoted to the question before application was made. The risks of a rebuff were great, and the move was viewed as a calculated adventure.[13] No action was taken on Spain's application until the autumn of 1964, when it was shelved.

Though some economic motives were involved, such as Italian competition in citrus products, it seems clear that political considerations were predominant in the rejection of Spain by the Six. The public authorities were conscious of this problem. At the Munich meeting of June 8, 1962, West European statesmen demanded Spanish exclusion from the ECM until democratic reforms were accomplished. On June 11, Franco dismissed two cabinet ministers, one being Gabriel Arias Salgado, the Spanish censor for more than a quarter of a century, and strengthened the role of the technocrats in the cabinet. However, the strong objections of European democrats, especially social democrats, and the feeling that the Spanish system was incompatible with the new European design were not satisfied by Franco's gestures. Feeling against Spain was particularly strong in the Low Countries where the memory of the Hapsburg empire is still politically vivid.

Though the policy-makers acknowledged the primacy of political factors in the rejection of Spain's application, the system's boundaries of legitimacy prevented this from becoming a public issue. In fact the regime probably lost little support because of this ill-fated initiative. Those who were ill disposed toward the ECM were reinforced in their opinion. Those for whom integration was more salient than the integrity of the corporate state—including the more prominent technocrats—did receive an additional measure of leverage to press for political reforms. However, the dominant response was quite like that which occurred in Spain at the time of the postwar boycott. The ECM's action was interpreted as a rejection of the nation, not of the government, and potentially divisive effects were minimized. The dominant groups largely supported the policy-makers in a "wait and see" attitude concerning Spain's relations to Europe after the fall of 1964. The main impact of the rejection appears merely to have reduced the saliency of that objective among the goals of dominant political economic groups.

Other factors contributed to this outcome. By 1965 the context of the question had changed. No longer did it appear that Spain was to be excluded from the great European adventure. After de Gaulle's famous "non" and the implicit settlement of the Six for the "smaller Europe" alternative, it was not just Spain but Britain and other nations that stood outside the great experiment. Furthermore, the boom in Spanish tourism of the 1960s, the dramatic increase in foreign investment, and the Spanish presence in the OECD and related international economic arrangements indicated that even without formal membership in the ECM, Spain was not going to be peculiarly isolated from the economic activities of the advanced industrial community. It could easily appear, in this tentative transitional period, that Spain, fortuitously and unintentionally, had achieved the best of both worlds. She was involved in the prosperity and dynamism of Europe without taking the great risks attached to exposing her economy to the fuller effects of European competition.

Nonetheless, through the middle and late 1960s, there was little direct criticism in the public forum of an eventual integrationist destiny for Spain. By 1965 and 1966 only a few of the structuralist economists were willing to suggest that the aspiration itself might be inappropriate and undesirable. Salvador López de la Torre was willing to conclude by 1967 that the common market had not hurt Spain economically and that entry was not urgent.[14] Tamames pressed the point that European integration would not greatly aid Spain as it was organized, and until major changes in Spanish economic structure had taken place, it was just as well that Spain stood outside. Citing some current thinking on regional economics, Tamames suggested that Spain's integration with Europe would only increase the development of the more industrialized powers and that the competitive capacity of the Germans and French would enable them to dominate the Spanish market. The center of industrial gravity would simply move closer to the Ruhr and to Paris, farther from Madrid and Barcelona.[15]

Planning as a National Pastime

Through the late 1950s and early 1960s, there was a growing public awareness of economic issues and events in Spain and an increasing confidence in discussing the implications of economic policy choices. Public debate reached something of a high point from 1961 to 1967. The First Economic and Social Development Plan was probably less significant as a policy instrument in Spain than as a focus and symbol in this more general public discussion.

The process began with the presentation of the IBRD report on the economic development of Spain.[16] Of the scores of similar comprehensive-development surveys carried out in the postwar period, probably none has received so much attention or interest in the recipient country. Normally such reports are politely received by government authorities, enjoy a brief flurry of examination by top level officials, and then are quietly put away to collect dust on archive shelves. For the public authorities, they often serve primarily as a required prologue to aid or credit negotiations. Compendious, technical, arid, often written in haste with little attention to stylistic grace, and then imperfectly translated, they are not the sort of document that invites a mass reading public. Though the report on Spain was much like the rest in style and format, its reception was completely different.

For six months prior to the publication of the report, an attitude of suspense and anticipation was noticeable in the Spanish press. As Tamames puts it, "The publication of the study, awaited by many like the New Testament of the Spanish economy, served as the point of departure for a lively polemic over its theses and recommendations, a polemic in which as many defenders and supporters as skeptics, detractors, or severe critics took part."[17] From its publication in October 1962 until the end of the year, over 20,000 copies of the report were sold. During the same period, over 200 articles on the report were published in Spanish newspapers or in the specialized economic press.[18]

López Ródo, the Planning Commissioner, and Fraga Iribarne, the Minister for Information, invited the Spanish press to examine fully and to criticize the World Bank volume.[19] Generally speaking, the leading papers, the economic journals, the larger banks, and the interest groups representing larger firms took a supportative position on the report. *Actualidad Económica* cited the prudence, sensibility, and concreteness of the recommendations, though it also wondered whether the World Bank had not been a bit too orthodox in its approach.[20] *La Vanguardia Español*, of Barcelona, noted that "on the whole, it seems altogether plausible and reasonable."[21] *España económica* was supportive, but less enthusiastic, noting that most of the problems and recommendations cited in the report were already known.[22]

Criticism came primarily from the structuralist economists and their allies in the syndicates, the Movement, and the more reformist sectors of the church intelligentsia. In general, objections focused on the fiscal and monetary orthodoxy, the neo-liberal economic approach, and the neglect of basic structural changes. Tamames criticizes the "excessive benevolence" toward the taxation system, the "blind confidence in a market economy that permeates the entire text."[23] Emilio Figueroa stated that "to argue that free market forces bring with them economic rationality is to ignore the entire economic history of the last two centuries." The establishment Falangist París Eguilaz argued that "it does not have the minimum technical-scientific character that would be required for it to be taken into account in preparing a development plan."[24]

The critics cited the World Bank's neglect of agriculture, particularly the social questions of the quality of rural life in terms of education and services. The World Bank seemed unaware of the problem of regional inequalities in income and wealth. However, in general the critics did not condemn the entire report. On the whole their approach was one of supporting the overall recommendations while pointing to specific aspects or problems that they felt were neglected. The tone of criticism was not polemic but on the whole constructive and reasonable.[25]

The World Bank report provided an interesting vehicle for extending the debate on economic policy. Coming from an international agency rather than from the public authorities, it provided a politically neutral target for criticism and dissent. The invitation of the authorities to debate the report further legitimatized the discussion.

The process of formulating the plan was accompanied by a similar pattern of public debate. In a sense, whatever participation in the planning process was accomplished through the *comisiones* and *ponencias* was extended by this rather spontaneous process of public commentary. Very much aware of the public relations component of their task—particularly after initial criticisms of the Planning Commission on this point—the planning authorities became active participants in the general debate through press releases, conferences, public speeches, and participation in meetings and seminars.

The intensity of such activities may be indicated by events in one two-week period of 1963, one which does not seem particularly unusual in terms of the amount of public discussion of planning. On May 6, Ullastres opened a series of lectures on economic development at the University of Salamanca, while the secretary general of the Planning Commission spoke on the plan in Barcelona. On May 7, Antonio de Miguel addressed the Institute of Hispanic Culture on "What the Man in the Street Expects from Economic Development." On May 8, the Marqués de la Vega Inclán spoke to the Marian Congregations on "Economic Development and European Integration." On May 14, a conference on planning was held at the naval academy. During these two weeks, two major conferences on economic policy were in progress, along with a variety of addresses and other activities.[26]

The Effectiveness of the Public Debate as a Procedural Instrument

For policy-making, the public debate serves a purpose similar to the market in economic analysis. It is an autonomous process, not formally structured, although it is influenced and directed by public authorities. As the market may serve as an alternative instrument of economic policy, so the public debate may be viewed as a procedural instrument on which policy-makers rely, to greater or lesser extent, in the formulation of public policy.

The economic policy transformation in Spain was accompanied by a remarkable expansion of the scope and intensity of public commentary on this issue. How did this public debate change the environment of decision-making from what it had been in 1957? At the time of stabilization, commentary on economic policy was somewhat constrained and largely limited to professional and elite groups. Did the broader public forum of the 1960s significantly affect the conditions of decision-making in Spain?

There is no doubt that the considerations entering into policy-making and the options available to policy-makers are richer and more various in the 1960s. There is a greater diversity of points of view on the purposes of policy. Interest group activity becomes more differentiated. The clarity and simplicity of the policy framework of 1958 is no longer possible by 1965, and policy becomes more ambiguous and heterodox. Many factors contribute to this change of atmosphere, but the public debate is certainly one of them.

Spanish decision-makers proved to be reasonably aware of the materials generated in this debate, which is not to say that they were equally responsive to all the new claims put upon them. If we consider the processes of initiation and consultation, the introduction of new problems, objectives, or techniques into the process and the criticism of earlier initiatives, it is evident that planning itself was accelerated as a component of public action by the feedback from stabilization, the general and diffuse demand for reactivation that began in early 1960. Considering that many of the critical economic indicators were showing satisfactory recovery at about the time that the public clamor for decisive action was most acute, and that international agencies were not pressing for such action, it might be that the generic demand had quite a bit to do with this addition to Spain's policy format.

The most concrete instance of the effect of pluralist process on public decision is probably the regional development strategy incorporated into the plan in early 1963. We have noted that one of the more effective and imaginative programs of the planning process was the system of development poles designed to lure industry into the more underdeveloped parts of Spain. It seems evident that regional development was not a high priority for the public authorities as they entered the planning process. However, by March 1963, this was a central objective. The increased importance of regional development probably owes much to the syndical and more general reformist interest in such a program. The syndical efforts no doubt derived from local level development studies of the late 1950s which were for them, among other things, a way of fulfilling representative responsibilities and adding to their credibility as major participants in economic policymaking. For the structuralist economists, regional development was a way of incorporating a redistributionist component in the neo-liberal development strategy.

It is interesting to note that regional development was a peculiarly legitimate way of pursuing reform in Nationalist Spain. Analysis of class-based inequities in income or wealth was ideologically suspect. The presumption of the regime was that class conflict was an inappropriate mode of analysis in the corporate state. However, for a nationalistic government, preoccupied with the unity of Spain, to point to disparities in development between sections of the country was quite acceptable as a form of policy criticism. Furthermore, Spanish statistics was organized in such a way that information could be generated on geographically based distinctions in income, but not on class-based disparities.

The structuralist critique was not, of course, a product of the 1960s; it had begun to take shape much earlier. However, this position, largely an academic matter in the 1950s, was popularized and diffused as a result of the heightened vitality and interest in economic policy analysis in the later period. The policy leaders did take into account this alternative problem context, though they did so largely at the symbolic level. Thus, in response to the criticism that it had been too narrowly "economic," the nomenclature and rhetoric of the plan changed to give a better account of its social justifications and its impact on the agrarian sector. Promises were made to emphasize agriculture in the second plan.

One should consider also the possible effect of the public debate in the implementation of public policy. Though its consequences are not precisely identifiable, one suspects that the environment of interest in economic policy generated in the 1960s had some impact on the developmental enthusiasm of Spanish entrepreneurs. In fact one is entitled to ask whether the specific programs of the state or the bonanza atmosphere of the time had more to do with the real growth achievements recorded in that period, and there are not a few commentators on Spanish affairs who suspect that the latter was largely the case.

The question of whether the plan or planning—the concrete public measures or the atmosphere generated as a byproduct of policy deliberation—had more to do with Spanish growth in the 1960s is a difficult one to answer. In fact the period of rapid economic expansion antedates any possible programmatic effects of the plan, and probably it was largely a combined result of the longer range effects of stabilization, together with a more optimistic psychology.

Evidence from four separate studies made during the first two years of the plan seems to indicate that the planning process itself had something to do with generating a more positive response from entrepreneurs. Moreover, the evidence suggests that the policy-makers were on target in their design for stimulating enthusiasm, specifically among the entrepreneurs, for the economic elites seemed much more optimistic about the course of economic policy than other groups in the population.

In a study by Miguel Siguán at the beginning of the plan period and apparently involving a general population sample, 61 percent of the respondents believed that the plan would have a positive influence on growth, and only 2 percent, a negative impact. "Moderate progress" under the plan, with growth rates around 5 percent, was expected by 74 percent; but only 8 percent expected growth to exceed 6 percent. While 65 percent believed that Spain could achieve adequate growth without integration with Europe, only 19 percent thought this impossible.[27]

After one year of the plan's operation, the Spanish Institute of Public Opinion conducted a thorough inquiry on knowledge of the plan and expectations concerning it. A national sample of 13,500 was used, which somewhat overrepresented the large cities. Of the 30 percent of the respondents who had knowledge of the plan and believed that the economy had improved during the past year, 78 percent believed that such growth was due to the plan and 13 percent felt that conditions would have improved anyway. Of those with knowledge of the plan, 7 percent expected the results of the plan to be "very good," 71 percent "good," 2 percent "average," 3 percent "bad," and 17 percent did not reply. Less than 1 percent thought the results would be "very bad." Among managers and professionals, however, 11 percent expected "very good" results, 65 percent "good results," 1 percent "average," 6 percent "bad," 1 percent "very bad," and 6 percent did not reply.

The fact that 43 percent of the sample indicated no knowledge of the plan suggests that all the agitation, debate, and controversy surrounding this effort was confined to a relatively small part of the population. However, only 3 percent of managers, 1 percent of those with a university education, admitted to having no information on the plan. Again it appears that the intention of the policy-makers, to engage the elites without particular concern for more general public attitudes, was successful.[28]

A similar report of cautious but general optimism concerning the plan is found in a survey of minutes and reports of stockholders' meetings of Spanish corporations in 1964.[29] On the other hand a membership poll by the Syndical Organization in 1965 found a majority of all its members (managers, technical workers, etc.) pessimistic about the plan. Generally this survey found that managers and technical personnel were "most pessimistic" about the plan, workers the "most optimistic." This seems to contradict directly the inference derived from the other surveys. However, the criticisms most frequently cited were the plan's neglect of regional development and the problems of small and medium-sized enterprise. Also noteworthy is the fact that much of the discontent with regional development can be explained by the reactions of regions that received no specific stimulus from the program. It seems rather likely that the syndical survey tapped a body of opinion on the plan not otherwise apparent, the smaller and more provincial business and industrial groups identified by Linz and de Miguel as closely associated with the syndical program.[30]

If the inferences we have drawn from these data are anywhere near the mark, it would appear that the vehicle of the public debate had an impact on economic change in Spain that was quite congruent with the intentions of the policy-makers and the restricted participatory structure of the plan itself. The policy-makers sought the active collaboration of the most modern, most powerful entrepreneurs in their policy design of providing Spain with a developmental impulse parallel to that which had taken place elsewhere in Europe. Whether this was the most adequate procedure of participation and involvement in economic advance is quite another question altogether.

Of course none of the evidence cited clearly differentiates between attitudes toward the plan and the more general public interest in economic growth in which it was embedded. If anything, this evidence, given the good-natured skepticism which Spaniards hold toward any public effort, probably understates the developmental mood of the nation at this time.

Finally, the international effects of the public debate should be considered. Western interest in Spanish planning, policy, and development was heightened during the 1960s. Spain became more respectable in international political economic circles as the poli-cy-makers quite intentionally cultivated good relations with cen-tral bankers, foreign investers, governments, and the press. News-papermen abroad quickly coined the phrase "the Spanish mira-cle," after the previous German and Italian "miracles," to describe the increasing dynamism of the Spanish economy.

However, once this all has been said, one must specify the limi-tations and boundaries of the procedural instrument of public de-bate in Spanish policy-making in the 1960s. Those who partici-pated in the discussion of economic policy, or more directly in the actual formulation of the plan, represented but a narrow stratum of the entire population. The effective participants were those at the top of public and syndical bureaucracies, those with recognized places in the hierarchy of corporations and banking, a handful of intellectuals, and private entrepreneurs with long-established ac-cess to public authorities. Few new participants in the policy-making process were created. Particularly neglected were the small farmers and businessmen, who had few opportunities to in-corporate their interests and perspectives into the new "environ-ment" of policy-making.

Finally, there was no mechanism by which policy leaders were required to seek public opinion in the formulation of policy. The public debate and other mechanisms of participation could affect the environment of information in which the policy-makers acted but not their environment of power. There was politics in the process, in the sense that events occurred and participants acted for purposes at odds with those in authority, but in all cases the policy-makers ultimately could control the drift and direction of the procedural system they had created. The policy-makers ad-justed to the initiative and demands generated in the public fo-rums, it is true, but they adjusted in terms of their own volition and not at the will of the participants.

Chapter 8

THE ECONOMIC AND SOCIAL DEVELOPMENT PLAN

AT FIRST GLANCE, THE FINAL PRODUCT of this planning effort appears terribly complex and prodigiously detailed. In fact, the essential structure of the plan is remarkably simple. The first Spanish Development Plan was designed for a four-year period, 1964 to 1967 inclusive. The fundamental goal was a 6 percent annual growth rate throughout the period. This figure seems to have been derived as a cautious increase over the 4.5 percent growth rate of 1954–62, and it was a goal comparable to the achievements of other Western countries. Most of the writing on development in Spain during the preceding public debate also postulated growth rates of about 5 or 6 percent. Although this projection quite underestimated the actual growth that was to be achieved during the first years of the plan, it would seem a reasonable goal, a cautious estimate of how growth might be accelerated under planning.

Only a few additional macromagnitudes were calculated to form the plan's outline. A projection of the active working force and its distribution by sectors anticipated a slight decrease in the employed population, primarily a result of an increase in the school-leaving age, offset partially by an expected growth in female employment and a decline of emigration. Labor mobility from agriculture to industry and commerce was expected to increase by 2 to 3 percent for the period. Labor productivity was to grow by 4.5 percent per year. The planners estimated that exports would grow by 9 percent and imports by 10 percent annually. Public sector spending would increase at a rate of 5 percent while gross capital formation was projected at 9 percent. Again the bases for these projections seem to have been extrapolation from trends in the 1954–62 period, checked against European experience and against such target criteria as balance-of-payments equilibrium, economic stability, and full employment.

These general projections were followed by specific targets for the various sectors. A detailed plan of public investments determined the extent and role of the state in growth, specifying investments to be made by the central government, the autonomous institutions, local governments, and the private sector. In the light of these projections, each of the committees or *ponencias* then reported a growth plan for its specific sector of the economy.[1]

From a purely technical point of view, there was a certain haphazard quality to the plan. The statement of proposed objectives included virtually every goal that one could think of. No growth model was proposed to relate these objectives systematically one to another, and many were stated in such a way that it would be absolutely impossible to measure progress or strike optimum balances between them. Clearly the objectives of the plan were hortatory and symbolic, designed less as an instrument of decision and preference than as a political gesture to satisfy the diverse demands of different sectors and interests. The real priorities assigned by the planning process—to export industry in particular— were implicit in the intended assignment of resources and had little to do with the formal statements of the plan. Even the major macromagnitudes were not bound tightly together into a general developmental model. For example, there was no indication of how the estimated intersectoral pattern of labor mobility was to be related to investment.

Nor was a rigorous effort made to relate sectoral plans to the general goals and projections. In the fields of housing and transport, the planners simply incorporated existing long-range programs, despite the fact that they had been calculated on different assumptions. The housing and transport projects were based on 5 percent growth estimates and presumed an investment rate of 21.20 rather than the 22.47 percent specified by the plan.[2] Similarly, projections in electric energy and in basic industries, particularly steel, metals, and chemicals, did not seem to mesh, and shortages in these industries could be predicted if investment proceeded as anticipated.

Criticisms similar to these on specialized technical grounds were forthcoming from domestic and foreign economists.[3] Nearly all pointed out that more sophisticated techniques were available than those employed by the Spanish planners. The absence of an explicit formula for relating objectives and projections was cited. Others noted that the planners had failed to consider such major policy possibilities as entrance into the common market or taxation reform. Hence all the committees involved in the plan operated on the premise of a constant fiscal system and a constant pattern of international markets.[4]

However, it may be that such technical judgments miss the point of the planning enterprise. Spanish planners were frankly less concerned with optimizing the use of resources than with encouraging the private sector to expanded productivity. The planning document was less an exercise in technical economics than a testament to a contract between the state and the private sector. The language of development planning was used to assure the private sector that public investment would not compete with private enterprise, that public spending would be suitably restrained, and that specific public incentives would be offered to private effort. For their part of the bargain, the private sector set goals of growth and expansion. The plan was predominately a political instrument, serving collaborative purposes, rather than a device for assigning priorities and allocating resources. As such, the assumptions and standards of technical planning doctrine simply did not apply.

Furthermore, the Spanish planners were quite pragmatic about their efforts. They were skeptical of Spanish statistics and doubted their capacity to build trend lines back more than a few years. They realized that there were many imponderables in their analysis—the effect of the common market, the response of the private sector, and so on. They chose the role of Sancho rather than Quixote and insisted that the plan must be flexible, tentative, and subject to revision as they went along. If their economics were primitive rather than elegant, it was not because Spanish economists lacked facility in sophisticated technique, but that they chose, probably wisely, not to indulge in it.[5]

The Plan as a Policy Instrument

We have been considering two dimensions of public problem-solving throughout this study. The first task of the policy-maker is one of procedural instrumentation—the selection and arrangement of institutions and processes to define public purposes and the means to their achievement. The decision-maker structures an environment of choice. The second task is policy instrumentation—the selection, from the equipment of the state, of means appropriate to the achievement of public purposes.

Viewed as a public program, as a set of policy instruments, the Spanish Development Plan is remarkably parsimonious. There were few policy innovations in the plan. Five or six novel instruments of considerable importance were contrived and set in motion as a package. However, in general the plan reconfirmed continuity with the policy format established in the late 1950s. In a sense, the plan denied certain instruments to policy-makers, as in the agreement to restrict public enterprise, particularly INI investment.

The internal logic of the plan, the method of its construction, was basically a process of weaving together a set of objectives, problems, and instruments in different ways depending on the sector or issue under consideration. Much of the exercise was a matter of making explicit the obvious linkages of various instruments, long in the agenda of the state, to specific problems. For example, let us examine the way the problem of export stimulation was analyzed in the plan (see Table 11).

The public investment program also revealed more continuity than change. In those programs associated with the Nationalist strategy, public works in particular, no marked change in the earlier format of the state's role was visible. In housing, transport, and irrigation, modest increases of about 15 to 30 percent for the four-year period were the rule. Public investment in agriculture was no more than a holding operation at best. Only in education was a definitive change in the magnitude of public investment visible. Public expenditures in this field were more than doubled over the four-year period. Here, and in the specific goals set for educational advance, one sees a decisive change from earlier public policy.

The major novelties introduced by the planners were three coordinated packages of policy instruments.

CONCERTED ACTION

A group of enterprises in a priority sector could devise a program of investment and growth, including attention to labor and welfare factors, and solicit specific public incentives in fulfillment of the program. The underlying principle was that full public and private capabilities would be concentrated on a specific project. Public incentives might include special access to credit, particular taxation or tariff advantages, public works related to investment (perhaps public housing close to a new plant), and so on. France had adopted a similar program in 1958, and it is generally felt that the Spanish program was borrowed from that source. However, it is worth noting that there is a substantial resemblance be-

TABLE 11. THE PROBLEM OF EXPORTS AS ANALYZED IN THE
FIRST DEVELOPMENT PLAN

Objective	Problems	Relevant Instruments
Export stimulation. (A high level of imports requires expanded exportation to achieve balance-of-payments equilibrium. Commercial policy is not sufficient to this end. Structural change is required in the most promising export industries.)	1. Economies of scale —fragmentation of enterprise	1. "Concerted action" involving associations of firms, tax and other incentives to such associations 2. Cooperatives, and marketing cooperation by small firms 3. Syndical action 4. Laws of "minimum economic size"
	2. Constraints on investment and expansion such as lack of exchange and savings	1. Tariff reform 2. Foreign investment 3. "Liberalization"
	3. Competition of public enterprises	1. Restraints on INI
	4. Inflation: deferring needed investments	1. Stabilization
	5. Taxation policy	1. Investment incentives in fiscal structure
	6. Inflexibility of labor market	1. Reform in labor law and welfare system
	7. Lack of entrepreneurial attitudes and "uncertainty" as to public policy	1. Planning 2. Market effects of foreign competition and liberalization 3. Research on export agriculture

Source: Presidencia del Gobierno, Comisaría del Plan de Desarrollo Económico, *Plan de desarrollo económico y social para el periódo 1964–1967* (Madrid: Imprenta del Boletín Oficial, 1964).

tween concerted action and the old law of National Interest Industries. From one perspective, concerted action was no more than an updated adaptation of a technique long in the repertoire.

MINIMUM ECONOMIC DIMENSIONS

Spanish economists had long seen the small scale of much enterprise as a critical bottleneck to development.[6] Through the plan, a variety of state capabilities were to be used to assure that new or expanded enterprises met minimum standards of scale. The Ministry of Industry was empowered to establish criteria of efficient size for various types of enterprise and to enforce these criteria by refusing authorization to projects that did not meet the standards. State incentives and assistance were to be provided to authorized projects for grouping small firms, which did not imply merely consolidation, but preferably various production and marketing agreements. State incentives, including credit and taxation, were to be used to encourage activities of an economical size.

POLES OF DEVELOPMENT

However, the most dramatic and distinctive innovation of the plan was the program of regional development, which centered in the creation of seven regional poles for industrial growth. Ironically, as we have noted, emphasis on regional development was not an original priority of the policy leaders, nor of the IBRD report, but was added to the plan in the process of its formulation, under pressure from more reformist constituencies. The basic idea was to coordinate and concentrate state incentives in seven industrial parks located in the more underdeveloped areas to encourage new industrial location there. Approved industrial projects would receive priority access to credit and generous taxation incentives. They could receive forced expropriation of desired sites. Public services, housing, and transport investments were to be coordinated at the poles. Again, this policy innovation involved some borrowing from both French and Italian precedents, though there was also a deep continuity with Spanish experience. The great irrigation projects of the Nationalist period had involved a similar coordinated deployment of state capabilities. Furthermore, in 1959–60 zones of industrial deconcentration had been created at Aranda del Duero, Campo de Crintana, and Guadalajara in an effort to relieve pressure on the Madrid metropolitan area.[7]

In Chapter 1, I suggested that public problem-solving is more often an adaptive than an innovative art. In adding new components to the stock of equipment of the state, it is true that the Spanish decision-makers borrowed heavily from suggestive foreign experience. The development poles and concerted action, like the stabilization program and the plan itself, were taken from the hypothetically more advanced policy technology of neighboring states. Yet it is also apparent that these borrowings were made in the context of the longer continuities of Spanish policy experience, or, at least, that they were compatible with it. In their wholesale use of foreign policy instruments, the policy-makers were also tinkering with an ongoing system, perfecting and adapting the policy equipment that was their legacy from the past. And it is worth noting that pure creativity, experimentation with totally new approaches to the public developmental role, was not characteristic of the prudent and practical Spanish economic leaders in the 1960s.

The Implementation of the Plan

To a very great extent, the implementation of the plan depended on the initiatives of others than the policy-makers. The public investment program required the will and ability of several key agencies to get projects moving. The private sector program would need the responsiveness of firms to the packages of incentives offered and their capacity to generate relevant programs. Once the plan was ratified, the role of the policy-makers was to await response. The position of the public authorities was largely to be one of coordination and control.

For example, the program of concerted action depended on the capacity of groups of firms to generate programs that met the standards of the planning officials. By the end of 1965, five such programs were in effect, in steel, coal, hides, cattle, and vegetable canning, selected from numerous inquiries and requests.

How were these sectors singled out for special treatment? The Planning Commission noted that there had been some feedback of dissatisfaction from industries not selected, and it sought to make the ground rules perfectly clear. Proposals must represent a "true program" for the sector and must represent a substantial part of the productive capacity in that field. Hence, it was admitted, it was easier to apply the program in sectors where production was concentrated in a few firms than where organization was fragmentized. Proposals had to specify social goals, such as wage increases related to productivity, programs of creating new jobs, housing, and so on.[8] As the commission noted, "The common factor in the bases of concerted action has been . . . knowledge of their projects by the administration, thus constituting through their presentation and discussion a technical guarantee of their efficiency and the possibility of fulfilling the agreements made."[9]

In other words, preferential treatment was available to those industries whose leaders shared the planners' conceptions of modern management and economic technique. Substantially, these were also the sectors that had been closely involved in planning and public policy processes for some time and had established access in the system. However, the point must not be exaggerated. For one reason or another, the sectors selected for preferential treatment were critical to overall development, or, as in the case of coal, critical industries badly in need of help. They were also sectors that had the capacity to compact for a common program. Beyond this, it is hard to say what combination of expertise and established access was decisive when the final narrowing-down occurred.

The Case of the Development Poles

The way the policy-makers worked out the implications of their strategy of regional development is perhaps the most significant illustration of the ongoing decision processes involved in the plan.

The decision to base the regional development program on the concept of the development poles was itself a choice from among several alternatives. The structuralists had argued for a general attack on the problem of agrarian poverty which was, for them, equivalent to the problem of underdeveloped Spain. The regionally unequal distribution of wealth was largely a difference between the industrialized and agricultural parts of the country. Furthermore, the problem was particularly acute in such regions as Andalucia, where archaic land tenure and agricultural labor arrangements accentuated class differences and hampered the realization of the region's productive potential. The structuralists argued for agrarian reform and on-site improvements in rural life. They tried to create a standard of parity between urban and rural areas in such public services as education, transport, and the like.

On the other hand, the syndical leaders had always conceived of a regional development strategy based on the existing provincial units. From the late 1950s, they had drafted and lobbied for development programs for each of the provinces. Of course the provinces were the base of power for both the adherents of the Movement and the local leaders of the syndicates. Local civil government was largely the preserve of the older partisan bureaucracy, or at least it can be said to have had more strength here than at any other point in the system.

The concept of the development poles was in part a way to avoid the implications of these alternative strategies. The planners saw massive social investment in the marginal agricultural regions as both uneconomic and politically unfeasible. However, they could not ignore the claims for deconcentration of the development process. Hence they acted to encourage industrial investment in selected centers within the low income regions. Labor migration out of submarginal agriculture was the preferred technique for improving the rural way of life, since migration made rural labor more expensive on the *hacienda* and reduced population density on poorly endowed lands. Now the migration would be to provincial cities rather than to Madrid or Barcelona exclusively.

At the same time, the seven development poles created new regional units in Spain, superimposed on the existing provincial organization. The planners bypassed the local government bureaucracies and did not need to deal with them directly in their own domains. This point was subsequently somewhat misunderstood by liberal Spaniards. Many criticized the poles for their lack of local autonomy and because power over their management remained effectively in the hands of Madrid. However, in evaluating this point, it is worth noting that under existing conditions, decentralization generally would have implied diverting authority to the militant and faithful in local partisan and syndical bureaucracies. It may be that these officials who were bypassed had something of value to contribute to the administration of the program. However, the alternative to centralized, technocratic control was not democracy and local autonomy.

The program adopted, the first problem of implementation was the location of the poles. In making these decisions, it appears that internal, technical considerations predominated over consultation and discussion with interested parties. The procedures of site selection reveal virtually no structured instruments of participation outside the planning hierarchy and only limited informal consideration of interests and perspectives outside this group.

In early 1963, López Ródo suggested that six general zones were under consideration, the Northeast, eastern Andalucia, Aragón and Rioja, La Mancha, western Andalucia, and the Duero region. Eventually Galicia and the Northwest, zones not included in the initial consideration, would be chosen as the sites for two of the poles, western Andalucia would get two, and eastern Andalucia and La Mancha none.[10]

In April 1963, a team of Planning Commission specialists undertook a survey of thirty Spanish provinces below the national average in income, based in large part on the syndical studies of the Spanish provinces done in the late 1950s and early 1960s.[11] The first decision rule of location, income below the average, was basic. Other factors making for potential industrial development were added, such as the presence of a dynamic urban center with existing potential for growth, transport, power, active population, and the like.

I asked many Spanish professionals outside the Planning Commission for their impressions of how site selection had been accomplished. Almost invariably, "political factors" or "local pressures" were prominent among their offhand explanations. In one case the presence of these factors is absolutely certain—the siting of an eighth development pole for foreign policy reasons just across the border from British Gibralter. Certainly a great deal of lobbying from a number of cities and provinces surrounded the selection process. However, it does not appear that such efforts had any decisive impact on the location of the poles.

An independent study, made by J. González Paz at about the same time as the site selection, used a variety of measures (income, active population, economic concentration, etc.) to rank the regions of Spain in terms of relative backwardness.[12] The author also recommended sites for poles. Reading in order from poorest to richest, his ranking of the regions and related development centers was as follows:

1. Extremadura   Merida
2. Northeast   Coruña, Vigo
3. Duero   Valladolid
4. Andalucia   Sevilla
5. Aragón   Zaragoza
6. Canary Islands   Santa Cruz
7. Levant   Murcia-Almería
8. Center
9. Cantabria
10. Northeast

His order shows a close correspondence to the eventual location of the seven original poles at Burgos, Huelva, La Coruña, Sevilla, Valladolid, Vigo (Pontevedra), and Zaragoza. Actually, the planners located all the poles in the five poorest regions, eliminating the Canaries and the Levant (southeastern) coast as proposed by González. No pole was located in Extremadura, the assumption being that the two poles in Andalucia (Huelva and Sevilla) and Duero (Valladolid and Burgos) would sufficiently affect that region. One notes that the planners followed no principle of geographic balance. Instead, except for Zaragoza, all the sites are paired in the western part of Spain: La Coruña and Vigo in the far northwest, Huelva and Sevilla in the southwest, Valladolid and Burgos in Old Castille. The clearest criterion of selection appears to have been the potential redistributive effects, though there were other apparent factors, such as the resources of Huelva and the strategic geographic position of Zaragoza.

Had political factors been significant, other plausible sites might have been selected. Almería on the Levant coast has a long history of effective lobbying by the local syndical organizations, which led, in 1956, to a coordinated program by INI and the Ministries of Public Works and Agriculture.[13] The city fathers of Avilá, in the Duero region, tried forcefully to promote a development pole for their area.[14]

One rough measure of potential pressure by local syndical organizations to promote their own regions may be found in the number of syndical organization studies and publications on the development of each province from 1940 to 1965. These studies may reflect some dimensions of the relative consistency of interest by syndical authorities in the development of various regions. I have subtracted studies dealing specifically with the poles from the totals. It is apparent that regions on which the syndical organization concentrated its research efforts were not necessarily selected as locations for poles (see Table 12).

There was little consultation with local officials or interests concerning the selection of sites. In fact, the selection of Zaragoza was vigorously protested by the civil governor, the President of the Provincial Assembly, the mayor of the city, the chamber of commerce, and the Syndical Organization. All argued that the

TABLE 12. SYNDICAL PUBLICATIONS ON DEVELOPMENT OF EACH PROVINCE
1940–65: AN INDEX OF POTENTIAL PRESSURE FOR DEVELOPMENT
POLE SITE SELECTION

Site	Number	Site	Number	Site	Number
Alava	30	Granada	13	Las Palmas	9
Albacete	9	Guadalajara	13	Pontevedra°	10
Alicante	13	Guipuzcoa	30	Salamanca	5
Almería	11	Huelva°	11	Santa Cruz	22
Avilá	10	Huesca	12	Santander	14
Badajoz	16	Jaén	30	Segovia	8
Baleares	9	León	7	Sevilla°	14
Barcelona	16	Lerida	7	Soria	3
Burgos°	11	Logroño	4	Tarragona	5
Caceres	5	Lugo	5	Teruel	18
Cadiz	17	Madrid	8	Toledo	8
Castellón	12	Malaga	6	Valencia	34
Ciudad Real	4	Murcia	8	Valladolid°	8
Cordoba	14	Navarra	6	Vizcaya	5
Coruña°	38	Orense	6	Zaragoza°	0
Cuenca	5	Oveido	9		
Gerona	18	Palencia	5		

Source: Consejo Económico Sindical, Catalogue: 1940–1965 (Madrid:
Consejo Sindical Nacional, 1966). Provinces for which no studies were made
are not listed, with the exception of Zaragoza. Provinces in which poles were
located are starred.

city was growing at a sufficiently rapid rate, and that the Aragón
region would have benefited more had the program's advantages
been distributed among lesser cities of the province. The decision
procedure seemed to involve amazingly little structured consultation with the interests potentially affected by the choice. There
was neither a system of program initiation, of the presentation of
applications by interested communities, nor of analysis of the program in communities tentatively under consideration. There was
apparently no consultation with local officials, not even to determine the territorial bounds of the zones.[15]

The administrative arrangements for establishing and running the poles reflect a similar minimal concern for involving local interests. For each pole a manager was appointed who was to act as the representative of the Planning Commission in the area. He possessed broad powers. In a sense he was something of a city manager for the zone, coordinating public and private services, stimulating private enterprise, proposing relevant public works, and so on. The first seven managers were drawn from the technical branches of the public service. All had professional backgrounds as engineers or attorneys.[16]

A Provincial Commission of Technical Services was established in each pole; it was presided over by the civil governor and included the pole manager, the mayors of the affected communities, and seven syndical representatives. This body possessed some important powers. It coordinated public services in the zone; it received requests for public benefits from private firms and prepared a ranked list of such proposals for submission to Madrid.[17]

Despite the presence of the Provincial Commission, most of the important decisions regarding the poles were made in Madrid with little local consultation. Criticism of this procedure appeared at the time that the second plan was formulated, and after 1967 some hesitant efforts were made to decentralize some small portion of authority over the management of the poles.

As in concerted action, the essential initiative for implementing the program came from the private sector. Industries bid for the incentives offered for locating in the new sites. Industry proposed projects to meet the economic and social criteria set by the planners (scale, export possibilities, social improvements, viability, etc.). Industries that applied were ranked in four categories and different incentives were offered each group. In 1965, the plan's second year, 344 industries applied for such advantages, 233 were offered incentives, and all but 23 accepted.[18] Groups A and B, the highest, received subsidies of from 5 to 20 percent of investment. Priorities for official credit, reduced tariffs on necessary imports, low taxes on corporate formation and profit, and free amortization for five years were offered all approved firms.

Despite problems of local participation and of initial difficulties in coordinating private investment with expanded public services, the development-poles scheme may fairly be regarded as the most distinctive and successful policy accomplishment of the Spanish plan. As early as 1964 one editorial asks, "Will it be possible to affect all Spain with the take-off atmosphere coursing through the development poles today?"[19] Industrial parks did blossom quickly and bring prosperity to some of the more impoverished regions of Spain. The program was big enough and its impact fast enough to affect noticeably the location, structure, and direction of industrial development in the nation as a whole.

An example illustrates the effect of the poles on one city. At Zaragoza, the United States air base had gone on standby status at about the same time that the city was designated as a development pole. There was some fear of unemployment—about 10 percent of the population worked on the base—and of housing underoccupancy. However, no visible unemployment occurred. Many former employees of the base were absorbed by new industry, and at higher wages. There was full occupancy of the expensive housing built for United States servicemen despite the lifting of rent controls. Spanish engineers and businessmen took over the deluxe apartments, often paying twice as much as the Americans had.

The Impact of the Plan

The presence of the plan and of exceptional economic growth together, in the mid-1960s, posed an interesting chicken and egg riddle for thoughtful Spaniards. Had the one much to do with the other? Would Spain have grown just as swiftly without the plan?

In fact, the timing of rapid economic expansion was such as to preclude any possible direct impact from the plan. For the five years, 1961 to 1966, Spain's gross national product grew at a rate of 8 to 9 percent, far ahead of the prudent 6 percent estimate of the plan. This record was matched by only Japan and Greece among OECD member nations. Per capita income went from $446 in 1963 to $660 in 1966, and thus passed the $600 sum often used by development economists to distinguish an underdeveloped from a developed nation. During the same period, annual industrial growth averaged 11.4 percent. Spain's historically perverse balance of payments was righted, reserves accumulated, and the peseta became the world's eighth strongest currency.

To a large extent, this record of development was probably not due to the plan itself but to the longer range effects of stabilization, combined with an exceptionally fortuitous set of trends in the Western economies as a whole. Spanish devaluation coincided with a wave of prosperity on the Continent, and holidays on the peninsula could be had at bargain rates. Receipts from tourism came to represent a major component of export earnings and contributed greatly to the favorable balance of trade enjoyed in the early 1960s. The number of tourists entering Spain rose from 3.5 million in 1958 to 6 million in 1960, 8.6 million in 1962, and 14.1 million by 1964. Annual earnings from tourism reached $1 billion in 1965, almost doubling the 1962 and 1963 income. Tourism, emigrant remittances, and a new surge of foreign investment, made possible again by new legislation well timed to match the extroverted mood of European and North American investors, constituted the lion's share of foreign currency earnings, though Spanish merchandise exports also improved in this period, for the first time since the Korean War.

In its first years, the plan probably served primarily to maintain and enhance the growth rhythms started earlier. The plan contained few policy innovations that in themselves could have accounted for such change. The mechanisms of the plan probably helped concentrate growth in specific sectors, affected its physical location, and did result in a marked upswing in public sector investment and spending, when compared to the stabilization years. The plan's main effect was probably the creation of an atmosphere congenial to growth both at home and abroad. Of course, this was one of the prime intended objectives of the planners. They wanted to put Spaniards, and particularly the business community, in an expansive mood. In this they succeeded, perhaps too well.

Prices rose rapidly in the plan period. The cost-of-living index rose 7 percent in 1964, 13 percent in 1965, and over 6 percent in 1966 and 1967. The precipitous climb in all price indexes began in the second half of 1964, coinciding with a round of wage increases in 1963 and 1964. Under pressure from newly aggressive labor leaders and organizations, and anxious to preserve social peace within the prevailing system, the government granted across-the-board increases and collective contracts in specific industries that exceeded productivity expansion. Industrial wages went up 16 percent in 1964, 15 percent in 1965, 9 percent in 1966, and about 14 percent in 1967.[20]

The pattern appeared to be a fine case of demand-push inflation. In the expansive atmosphere of the 1960s, Spanish consumers, particularly the middle classes and the industrial workers, apparently decided to achieve European standards of living quickly. Consumer's durables sold well. The change in the dietary pattern of Spaniards, with an increasing consumption of protein-rich animal products in place of historic reliance on grains, was totally unanticipated by the agricultural planners. Such consumer demands put pressure on imports. After 1965, Spain began to import more agricultural products than were exported. Imports of consumers manufactures increased faster than that of either raw materials or capital goods from 1963 to 1967. In 1965, Spain began to register deficits in total trade and started to expend its preciously accumulated reserves.

The management of a modern economy in a period of rapid growth is always a complex task. The coordination of all the factors is never free from difficulty, and some of the indicators of economic health are bound to be pointing the wrong way. However, it is apparent that these wage and demand pressures were among the unanticipated consequences, the imperfections in the design for change formulated by policy-makers in the early 1960s. They did not expect, nor could they control, the pressures that resulted from the economic bonanza they had helped create.

The policy-makers seemed to assume that they had solved the

problem of economic stability through the policy paraphernalia adopted at the time of stabilization. The plan itself took relatively little notice of this problem. It was almost exclusively a design for expansion. It was presumed that the interaction between the programs of stabilization and the plan would provide for stability with optimum growth. Wage and import expansion rates that would be compatible with stable growth had been projected. However, little attention was paid to the devices through which these goals would be achieved. The planners assumed that the prevailing institutional order would continue to provide effective means of economic control.

What changed, curiously enough, was the capacity of the state to exercise effective economic control in a political economic system that prided itself on just that point. Wage increases in excess of productivity gains were opposed to the assumptions of the plan. Apparently, the planners assumed that the prevailing system of labor relations could be considered a constant in their projections: it could not. In the 1960s, strikes, both legal and illegal, increased at a rapid rate. Defection from the official corporate system of labor organization became increasingly apparent. To maintain the syndical system under pressure implied rewards in the form of wages and benefits, since to grant further autonomy for labor organizations lay outside the premises of the system. Ironically, the rationale for this boundary condition on permissible innovation in organizational matters was the presumption that order and stability were only possible for Spain within the corporate order.

The overall strategy of the policy-leaders did include programs to permit greater latitude to labor organization. Collective bargaining, a limited right to strike, and the election of leaders were privileges granted in the post-1958 period. However, there were strict upper limits as to how far such reforms could go. What these reforms themselves probably accomplished was to raise expectations in the labor movement and to provide new capabilities to its leaders. Unwilling to move further in the direction of structural change, economic rewards were the only instruments left to the government as responses to increasingly effective demands. Of course, whether greater permissiveness in the labor field might have caused even more disruptive demands is an open question.

Labor policy was not the only area in which the Spanish political economic program failed to match intention with effect. The most important deviation from the plan was public sector spending itself, since the state was unable to keep its own house in order. In each year of the plan, public spending exceeded budget estimates, and estimated expenditures in 1968 were budgeted 40 percent ahead of those for 1966. A rapid expansion of public investment and public credit to the private sector marked the first years of the plan. The rate of housing completions doubled. Public service wages rose faster than those in the private sector. Government current consumption expenditure was projected to rise 21.5 percent, but it actually increased 120 percent during the plan period.

Hence, a critical difference between the intention and impact of the plan is the incapacity of the policy-makers to control the public sector itself. Spain's historic problem of managing the state, which had led to the appointment of the new group of economic policy-makers in the first place, proved to be one they could not adequately resolve. The policy-makers had not provided themselves, or could not provide themselves, with adequate instruments to control their own domain.

Despite recurrent efforts within the cabinet to upgrade the role of the planners, and particularly by López Ródo, by the mid-1960s imperative demands on the system and the weight of the inherited economic policy machinery were reducing the Planning Commission's capacity to play a central coordinating policy role. Ramón Tamames wrote:

In sum . . . one concludes that the ministerial departments and certain public agencies [INI] . . . function today with an autonomy almost as great as that which existed before the preparation and application of the Development Plan. In fact, the plan is hardly a point of reference for the decisions of the administration. In each administrative compartment it is often felt that the aspirations of the plan are "too ambitious" or perhaps "theoretical," and consequently, "one does what one can."[21]

The policy-makers' overall strategy of growth itself contributed to the stresses of the plan period. The approach advocated by the technocrats involved heavy stress on industrialization and relative neglect of agriculture. By the end of the plan period, the one-third of the labor force engaged in agriculture was producing less than one-fifth of the national product. From mid-1964 to the end of the plan, Spain was importing more agricultural products than were exported, adding to the strains both on the balance of payments and on the price structure.

Though accumulated foreign exchange enabled Spain to weather this period far better than it had the crisis of the late 1950s, the issues at the end of the plan period were remarkably similar to those that had led to the stabilization revolution itself. The policy manipulations of the neo-liberals had been insufficient to deal with the basic problems of the political economic management of the nation.

The response of the policy-makers to the unanticipated consequences of the plan was to deploy the arsenal of monetary and fiscal techniques which were their chosen instruments. By the end of 1964, sweeping measures were taken to control inflation, including the reduction of housing construction, food importation, and efforts to tie further wage increases to productivity. In 1965 more vigorous steps were taken. Maximum salary increases were fixed at 8 percent, treasury operations apart from the budget were prohibited, and public sector expenses were held to the previous year's levels. In monetary policy, banks and savings and loan associations were limited to a 17 percent increase in credit, and public sector credit was limited to PTS 28,500 million.[22] In November 1967, Spain took the occasion of the devaluation of the pound to devalue the peseta by a similar amount, establishing a new .70 to $1.00 parity. This also gave policy-makers the opportunity to impose severe controls on prices and wages, to cut public expenditures further, and to raise consumption taxes.[23]

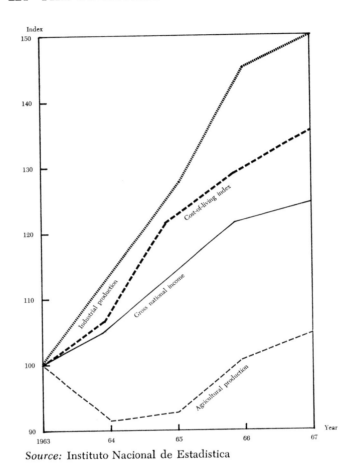

Source: Instituto Nacional de Estadistica

FIGURE 5. MAJOR ECONOMIC INDICATORS DURING
THE PERIOD OF THE DEVELOPMENT PLAN

As in France in the same period, monetary and fiscal policy su-
perceded the plan as the critical lever of public economic action.
The new austerity measures, coupled with a slowdown in the
growth rate in Europe generally, led to a slackening of Spain's
rapid pace of expansion. Industrial growth dropped to 4 percent
in 1967 compared to 11.4 percent for the previous five years[24] (see
Figures 5 and 6).

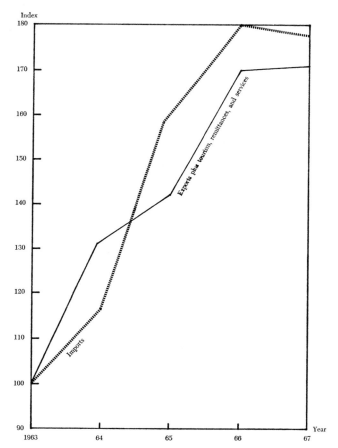

Source: Organization for Economic Cooperation and Development

FIGURE 6. SPANISH FOREIGN TRADE DURING THE PERIOD
OF THE DEVELOPMENT PLAN

Feedback and Plan II

Early in 1967, a Spanish essayist, José María Pemán, reflected on the changed style of Spanish policy-making. Where once the dominant form of public information on the policy-making process had been the cataloguing of past economic achievements, now the emphasis was on the future, on planning. In making promises of future accomplishment, the policy-maker created a standard for criticism of his stewardship: "Now to be administrator of public affairs involves an act of self-condemnation four or five years and one day in the future."[25]

These new standards for evaluating the performance of the state and the nation did have an effect on the ongoing process of problem-solving in Spain. The targets of the plan structured the pattern of criticism, and plan projections provided a built-in agenda of the unanticipated consequences to be looked for.

Public debate and criticism of the programmed performance began in earnest in the second year of the plan. Generally speaking, the first year, 1964, was one of relative satisfaction with the accuracy of the plan's projections. Here the planners' conservatism was probably a tactical advantage, for with growth above the prudent goals of the program, it appeared that the plan was working exceedingly well.

The inflationary pressures and the poor agricultural performance of the second year triggered a more critical public response. In early 1966, when preparations for the formulation of the second plan began, public examination and criticism of the direction of economic policy became even more intense and probing.

In the agricultural sector, the planners had very bad luck. The 1964 harvest was the worst in a decade, which not only threw off many of the assumptions of the plan but also provided a conspicuous disparity between its expectations and achievements by the end of the first year. The failure to meet agricultural production targets was the signal that the time had come to revive the argument that the planners had encouraged industrialization at the price of neglecting agriculture.

The leading economic journals and professional economists took up this theme.[26] Under the leadership of the dynamic Luis Mombriedro de la Torre, the official Brotherhood of Agricultural Workers and Cattlemen became an increasingly effective interest group. Mombriedro suggested that the plan should be reoriented toward "the man that lives in the country, and consequently, the agricultural infrastructure."[27] Persistent representations were made in a variety of forums. In the *Cortés,* the matter came to something of a head, in April 1967, when Robina Domínguez, a representative of the agricultural syndicates, so forcefully interrogated the Minister of Commerce concerning the impact of liberalization on agriculture that the President of the *Cortés* cut short his strong series of embarrassing questions.[28]

The question of agricultural policy was closely linked to that of the social content of the plan. As the process of developing a second plan began, *Pueblo,* the voice of the syndicates, published a series of seven editorials strongly critical of the exclusively economic orientation of the first plan.[29]

As they had at the time of stabilization ten years earlier, the policy-leaders consulted critical groups in the formulation of a new plan, through the instrument of a questionnaire, and requested comments on an outline proposed by the Planning Commission for the further direction of planning. The responses provide a good notion of the lines of cleavage on political economic policy that had developed by this time.

The spokesmen for the banking system and the business elites (the Bank of Spain, the National Economic Council, Superior Banking Council, and the Savings and Loan Associations) in their reports stressed the need for economic stability. They regarded extensive social or agrarian reform as visionary.

Other agencies stressed the social and agrarian aspects of the plan. Of these, the document provided by the Syndical Organization was the most remarkable. The expertocracy within this institution had learned much from its first encounter with the planners. Symbolic demands would be met with symbolic responses. Now they tried to phrase demands in the language of the new policy-making style, and efforts were made to develop concrete proposals and to make social goals operational.

The Syndical Organization proposed profit-sharing, stock ownership, and management participation by workers. The assumption that wages should be tied to productivity was finally challenged, and an argument was made for a "national wages policy" linked to both productivity and the price level. The Syndical Organization sought to introduce macrosocial indicators into the planning process, including projections of population, consumption, and income distribution. They tried to establish a parity principle for assessing the relative returns from industry and agriculture. They argued for an educational policy based on full-scale manpower planning. They proposed that the planners analyze the sectoral distribution of income, social services, access to property, and habitat development—a key concept used frequently—as a guide to the distribution of the returns from development.[30]

The argument and the effort were much like that mounted by Daniel Bell and others in their proposal for a social report paralleling the president's economic message in the United States. By the mid-1960s, the syndical experts, together with Spanish sociologists, many of them associated with and encouraged by the independent *Fundación FOESSA*, seem to have begun to create a climate of opinion on the social aspects of development not unlike that generated by the economic experts in the late 1950s.

The drafters of the second development plan showed an acute sensitivity to the political and economic adjustments that should be made in the strategy of the first; so they focused directly on the stresses and distortions that had become apparent in the execution of Plan I. Moreover, they were responsive to the criticisms and pressures generated in their political environment.

Plan II did not go into effect on schedule. The international monetary problems of late 1967, including the devaluations of the pound and the peseta, threw off some of the critical calculations on which Plan II had been drafted. Given the uncertainties of the moment, it was decided to delay the enactment of the plan. Hence Plan II, designed to run from 1968 through 1971, did not actually go into effect until February 1969.

The contrast in the style and approach of the two plans is striking. The first was comprehensive in scope and dedicated primarily to macroeconomic issues of productivity generation. The second was selective and was directed explicitly at the bottlenecks that had become apparent in the planning period and at the criticisms of the lack of social content which had been leveled against the first plan. The first plan emphasized sheer economic growth, the second the distribution of the proceeds of development.

The central priorities of the second plan were agriculture and education, with more limited attention to public housing, urban planning, public health, and revisions in the social security system. The emphases of the first plan, incentives to industry and growth, were subordinated to these concerns. They appear as background issues, primarily a matter of maintaining and further rationalizing the going concern.

Responsiveness to the political environment is much in evidence. The process of information gathering that preceded Plan II revealed a fairly clear cleavage between the advocates of social reform, primarily in the syndical organization and the intellectual groups, and those who stressed sound economic management, primarily the spokesmen for financial and industrial institutions. Plan II was clearly contrived to reconcile these demands, and massive efforts in the agrarian and educational fields have been mounted, but within the context of economic stability.

The advocates of social reform won important victories in the drafting of Plan II. Income policy was tied both to cost of living and productivity, more concretely to the former with a commitment to revise minimum wages annually against this index. Many of the programs suggested by the syndicates, such as profit-sharing, at least won mention among the programs of the plan. The demand for the inclusion of social indicators had an impact on the design of Plan II. Projections of income distribution, in terms of the composition of national income, by regions and occupational categories, occupied a more prominent place in the planning effort.

Similarly, the planners were sensitive to the criticism that economic policy-making had become overcentralized. A new concept of regional development was introduced, stressing the potential role of municipal and provincial governments in effecting the works of the plan. Essentially, what the planners seem to have had in mind was that local corporations, syndical groups, and other institutions might take the initiative and solicit contracts to undertake programs subsumed by the plan in their jurisdictions.

The choice of instruments for fulfilling the plan's social reform mandate showed interesting continuities with the persistent policy-making style of dusting off, redeploying, and reemphasizing capabilities and programs in the established repertoire. In none of the priority fields—agriculture, education, social welfare, and decentralization—was the emphasis on striking policy innovations. The central strategy of the planners seemed instead to have been to shift the emphasis from the economic tactics in vogue in the 1960's to the ongoing commitments in social fields, commitments which had been in the background of policy during this same period.

Thus in agricultural policy the central reformist goal of creating economically viable units was to be achieved primarily through a renewed emphasis on the Nationalist program of concentrating land parcels into units of a more economical size and by a more forceful application of the *Ordenación Rural* law which required investment in underutilized landholdings. Reforms in tenancy and rental legislation were promised. The program to increase agricultural production was largely a matter of selecting the specific sectors (cattle, fruits, etc.) for the concentration of credit, relevant incentives, and public services, along the lines of the concerted action policy of Plan I, and of generally expanding and emphasizing established public programs of interest to agriculture.

Similarly, the educational program was most notable for its goal to universalize education between the ages of six and fourteen. There were few new concepts for policies, and the emphasis was on expanding the existing educational system of the nation, creating new universities, providing greater scholarship funds, and promoting research. In social welfare policy, too, with the exception of the state's commitment to fund part of the social security system, the plan largely represented a reaffirmation and perfection of ongoing programs.

The emphasis, then, was on the expansion of existing public sector responsibilities. In public investments, expenditures for education and research would increase from 6 percent to 12 percent of the total projected public sector program. However, it is interesting to note that, despite the hortatory emphasis on public sector agricultural development commitments, public investment in agriculture (exclusive of irrigation and rural betterment projects) would be only about 6 percent of total investment in each plan.[31]

In Plan II there is a certain symbolic quality to the emphasis on the social factors in development. The language of the plan points to a more striking reassessment of priorities than the actual distribution of resources. However, this shift probably is more than just a matter of providing symbolic satisfactions to concerned constituencies. Given the plan's commitments for all sectors of Spanish policy-making, the planners seem certainly to be using their instrument of influence to require a readjustment of priorities on the policy-making agenda throughout the system.

There is an interesting similarity of approach in both the first and second plans. The first spotlighted the Spanish enterpreneur, hoping to arouse his enthusiasm by making him a central figure in the development effort, provided economic incentives, and coordinated administrative and legal mechanisms at stategic points on his behalf. The second plan focused on the public administration as the critical actor. The means chosen to stimulate the public administration are much the same as those used earlier to spur on the entrepreneurial community. The language of the plan is packed with references to "stimulating" agricultural research and to "fomenting" the role of municipal and provincial bodies in regional development. In a sense, what we have is a strategy of incentives, coordination, and engagement applied to the public sector and the social side of development. Come the end of the second plan, it will be interesting to compare the relative success of such a strategy when applied, respectively, to the private and public sectors.

Chapter 9

CONCLUSIONS

THIS STUDY WAS DESIGNED so that in the end we could render a judgment, both on the problem-solving capabilities of the Spanish political economic system and on the skill with which these capabilities were used by Spain's leaders. We have measured these men and this system by a number of standards. It is now time to take stock of their overall performance.

When the time came, in the late 1950s, to make major choices in the field of economic policy, how well prepared was Spain for the task of reassessing the existing program, how capable of charting a wise course of action for the period to come?

A naive model of Spanish authoritarianism might have predicted that the regime would find it most difficult to appraise honestly the deficiencies of the established design for action, to generate a range of potential alternatives, and then to choose a course that implied a significant departure from prior policy. Nationalist Spain, after all, had proscribed competitive politics and had established a definitive truth about the nature and purposes of the political order. The coalition of forces that supported the regime had benefited extensively from the policies of the previous period. Vested interests had been created that owed their existence and continued influence and prosperity quite directly to the program of the Nationalist economics. The regime took substantial pride in the accomplishments of the first twenty years of its rule, and there was a considerable psychic investment in what had gone before.

However, when the moment of decision was upon her, the Spanish regime, in this realm of economic policy at least, demonstrated a flexibility and openness to change quite as great as that of most Western nations. While political innovation might be severely circumscribed by the rigorous imperatives of the political order, there were few overall prescriptions for the economic thrust of the system. The objectives of autarchy were hardly sacrosanct. Whether Spain should pursue self-sufficiency or seek engagement with the larger economic relationships at work in Europe and the West was an open question.

While liberalism, like communism, was officially a pernicious doctrine, the system proved capable of generating a well-articulated version of current liberal thinking on economic policy for the appraisal of top policy-makers. Furthermore, this was not the only critique of the going concern available in the system. Although the structuralist argument did not reach full flower until the 1960s, the reformist imperatives of Falangist thought were at least incipient in the policy debate of the mid-1950s. The function of interest aggregation, the simplification and synthesis of heterodox demands and perspectives into major patterns that the policy-maker can cope with and choose between, did not go unfulfilled in Nationalist Spain. Although the absence of parties and a pluralistic pattern of interest organization eliminated the possibility that the citizenry would play any vital role in the choice among major alternatives, for Franco and the elites of the system a range of possibilities was open. To the extent that the available problem contexts overlapped those of the Western milieu generally (for the neo-liberal position was directly comparable to the modern capitalist options elsewhere, and the structuralist critique reflected a position quite compatible with that of the Western social democrats, though adapted to the specific heritage and circumstances of Spain), one might conclude that political authoritarianism had not seriously narrowed the range of general approaches to the political economy that decision-makers were able to consider.

In some good measure, the capacity for change present in the Spanish system in the late 1950s must be attributed to the leadership style of Francisco Franco. To the extent that one man can be presumed to be the central architect of a political system, and to the extent that he is the dominant decision-maker, then it is appropriate to judge his skills of statecraft by whether or not he boxes himself in, by whether his actions in one period hamper him in making more adequate choices later on. The persistent characteristics of Franco's leadership were prudence, caution, and an avoidance of making more lasting commitments in the economic realm than were absolutely necessary. The fact that the Spanish system was open to the reconsideration of policy and the formulation of change at a crucial point in its political economic evolution is critical in an overall evaluation of his rule.

However, there was more to the capacity of the Nationalist system to make choices than can fairly be attributed to Franco's style of leadership alone. The richness of the policy and procedural equipment of the system must also be considered. We can assess the system disembodied from its builders, and see the environment of choice of the leader as ultimately conditioned by the system which he played a leading role in creating. The very complexity of the coalition that supported the regime, contained both the great banks and enterprises and the populist reformers of the *Falange*, implied, in principle at least, a considerable breadth of possibilities.

It was the presumption of the organic state that the appropriate channels of problem recognition, advice, and participation in policy-making were to be specified in advance and accomplished through a delimited set of institutions. If taken seriously, this rigid structuring of decision processes should have severely circumscribed the capacity of policy-makers to acknowledge and cope with changes in social and economic reality. However, the formal structures of the organic state were not taken that seriously. While the syndical organization was formally supposed to be the definitive link between polity and economy, the recognition of new economic problems in the 1950s and the drawing of necessary inferences from them was accomplished largely outside the syndical system and by economic elites that had established, though informal, access to the decision process.

Successful authoritarianism also requires that when the leader has chosen a new course of action, the prime forces will rally to its support. Despite the fact that vital groups were either politically or materially disadvantaged by the choice of the neo-liberal option in 1957, support for the new system was not jeopardized by the new course selected, nor was implementation of the new design seriously hampered by dissidence among the elites directly connected with the maintenance of the regime.

A healthy political economic system requires an effective compromise between richness of possibilities and efficiency in coming to conclusions. It is desirable that the system should portray for the decision-maker the heterogeneity, the complexity, and the many possibilities in the society with which he works. On the other hand, the system cannot be so full of possibilities that decision is paralyzed. Yet, maximum decisiveness may imply foolishness, when action leads to disastrous consequences that could have been foreseen had the decision-makers been forced to grapple with a more perplexing problem than the one that a streamlined environment of choice portrayed for them.

In the field of economic policy, the Spanish decision-making environment in the mid-1950s brought to policy-makers' consideration a range of goals and potential measures fairly comparable to that of Western Europe generally. Similarly, the elapsed time from problem recognition to the enactment of measures for the major choices we have considered was well within the range of similar European experience. The balance between richness and efficiency in the system, one concludes, was not inappropriate by the comparative measure.

When he selected the *Opus Dei* team of cabinet ministers in 1957, Franco implicitly chose also neo-liberalism as the guiding framework for policy choice for the years to come. As I have noted, it is difficult to assess exactly what Franco intended. It is perhaps more plausible to assume that he sought a general improvement in the efficiency and coordination of policy than that he was intentionally opting for a new economic policy strategy. In any event, the transformation in the direction of Spanish policy was perhaps not so great as has generally been assumed. From Franco's point of view, the program of the new economic team was less of a policy revolution and more an incremental step along a course compatible with the intentions and values of the regime. Economic affairs had from the beginning been somewhat insulated from the regime's unique political orthodoxies. By the mid-1940s, most economist ministers were political independents and not ideologues. Gradual steps to decontrol the economy had been in process since the late 1940s and early 1950s.

Furthermore, the selection of the new policy format did not imply a reconsideration of the long-run objectives of the regime, but rather the means by which these goals would be accomplished. The technocrats promised a formula that would strengthen central control and restore order and discipline to economic affairs. The paradox of economic liberalization in Spain is that it was intended to make the economy more responsive to governmental direction rather than less so.

The leadership provided by the economic policy-making team that came to power in 1957 meets many of the tests of successful statecraft. The stewardship of the decision-making process was marked by a rational matching of objectives and measures, and clarity of purpose was balanced by care and prudence in taking action. Before the stabilization program, the economic policy-makers proceeded cautiously for awhile, tinkering with the prevailing policy equipment. They searched widely for an agenda of policy actions and carefully evaluated alternative possibilities. Within the framework of their intentions, they provided themselves with the most competent advice and information available, and they took this advice quite seriously. Once persuaded that all was in order, they acted decisively and effectively. However, they paced their actions well, taking no more steps than were necessary to achieve their immediate goals and leaving many options open and available for the adjustment and elaboration of their program in the light of its consequences. Their design for action sought immediate effects, but it looked also beyond them to middle-range intentions, and they did not confuse the two. The policy-makers took into account the realities and limitations of the situation they were dealing with but did not deny themselves the possibility of imaginative innovation and rather thoroughgoing change. They had the vision to direct their energies toward a long-range goal, yet they were realistic enough to understand development as a process, not as a state of affairs to be established by fiat.

Furthermore, their leadership meets the pragmatic test; it worked. Spain, economically beleaguered in the mid-1950s and verging on national bankruptcy, becomes in the 1960s a nation with one of the soundest currencies in the world, enjoying one of the fastest rates of economic growth.

Yet, once all of this has been said, when one looks back on the accomplishments of the Spanish technocrats from the perspective of a decade and more, a certain paradoxical quality becomes apparent. They were successful, but virtually nothing worked out as they had expected. They believed that a sweeping reform of policy equipment was necessary for Spain's integration with Europe, but Spain was not permitted to join any common market arrangements. The nation's balance-of-payments problem was resolved, but the technocrats had thought this would be accomplished through export industry. The possibility that this resolution would come through the windfall of tourism and emigrant remittances had not been foreseen at all. To combat inflation, they stressed firm control and sound management of public sector spending and this they failed conspicuously to achieve. The technocrats had instituted a system of planning that was supposed to be prescriptive for the government and suggestive for private enterprise, and its end result was almost the other way around. They had thought to liberalize the economy, to reduce the extent of public control, and to increase the scope of competition and market forces, and they achieved a system of centralized policy direction perhaps more thoroughgoing than the one that had existed before. By 1962 they had concluded that expansion and not stability was the major unresolved problem, and by 1966 inflation was their dominant problem once more.

One measure of the adequacy of a policy-making process is the relationship between intention and outcome. The fewer the unanticipated consequences, the more adequate the procedure of choice. Yet, it is hard to imagine how the policy-makers might have structured an alternative environment of decision for themselves, particularly given the procedural equipment of the regime, that would have enabled them to foresee these outcomes. Given the situation of the late 1950s, Spanish diplomacy was not at fault for not guessing that Europe would consolidate smaller units of integration and that Spain would be excluded from them. To my knowledge, no one in Europe anticipated the extent of the tourist boom. Perhaps the policy-makers were not realistic in their assessment of the competitive potential of Spanish enterprise, but at the time they formulated their program, this appeared not as a projection but rather as a desperate imperative. Had they, through more perfectly representative institutions, been able to probe deeper into the real attitudes and expectations of the vital forces in the Spanish economy, they might have uncovered the latent hesitancy, skepticism, and potential unresponsiveness to the overall design for change that appear to have been lurking there. And had they known this, they might only have set their growth targets lower than they did, and the targets they did set understated the pace of change that was to occur.

However, one does not measure the effectiveness of policy-making by the avoidance of unanticipated consequences alone, but also by the capacity of decision-makers to adapt to the way things work out. Were the policy-makers capable of capitalizing on these unexpected results of their actions? Were they flexible enough to see alternative possibilities in the surprising by-products of the process they had set in motion? Funes Robert and others believe that they were not. Their opinion is that the decision leaders were so committed to their initial promises that they neither saw nor comprehended new opportunities. So committed were they to the doctrine that Spain had a chronic balance-of-payment problem, and so sure were they that the only remedy lay in building an economy like that of France or Germany, that they could not see in tourism and the accumulation of reserves an opportunity for new undertakings and an alternative route to development.

However, in Plan II the policy-makers had largely committed themselves to the objectives of their prime critics. The countervailing forces that had developed in the 1960s had argued for forceful national effort in the fields of agrarian reform, education policy, social welfare, and the decentralization of decision-making. These were the predominant themes of the development strategy proposed for the period after 1968. The future will determine whether this was primarily a symbolic gesture, meant to deter dissent, or whether it implied a real redeployment of the developmental resources of the Spanish state. In either event, Plan II does suggest that the Spanish policy-makers were attentive to feedback, that they had not come to treat the policy format developed in the earlier period as dogma, and that they were capable of adapting to the implications of prior choices.

The process of economic policy-making in Spain in the 1960s must be explained in terms of the impact of something strongly resembling pluralist politics. At the beginning of their period in power, all the decision-making procedures contrived by the *Opus Dei* team of economic leaders were designed to render policy-making more efficient, coordinated, and effective. At the same time, they made more homogeneous the range of considerations that would enter into choice. Their appeal was that economic policy should be primarily a matter of expert judgment, that political considerations should not interfere with technical issues. From the very beginning, they sought to concentrate decision-making on economic affairs, and they did this by narrowing the range of those involved in economic choice. Among their first actions was the establishment of the delegate committee on economic affairs, thus removing economic policy debate from the full cabinet and centralizing it in the hands of the economic ministers. Instead of emphasizing the role of the syndical organizations in economic affairs, which was a potential option, the *Opus Dei* leaders systematically de-emphasized it. While the capacity of the syndicates increased in the 1960s, their influence atrophied. Though the economic leaders' planning technique did add new participants to the policy-making process, the range of interests effectively represented was from a relatively narrow spectrum of the potentially concerned.

In the first half of the 1960s, Spain traded a certain flexibility present in the old order for more rigorous techniques of making choices in economic affairs. Paradoxically, the liberals were far more doctrinaire than the nationalists in defining the range of considerations that might appropriately enter into economic policy-making. In a serious sense, Spain was less pluralistic in this field immediately after liberalization than it had been before.

It may be that this diminished impact of pluralism on policy was due to unexpected consequences of the procedural systems devised by the policy-makers. At the outset, it appears, the economic policy leaders defined their mandate quite narrowly and severely. I think they presumed that their sphere of activity was to be confined to management of the macroeconomy. They saw a division of labor in policy-making, and felt, it would appear, that educational, labor, social, and agricultural choices would be made elsewhere in the system. Though they sought to influence these choices, they did so in forums other than those created for the management of economic affairs, in the full cabinet for example.

However, the drama and effectiveness of the policy-makers' work caught the public eye, and their actions had implications for virtually all aspects of public policy. Furthermore, they quite consciously sought public debate on their program. No matter how they might have defined their own role, the institutions and procedures created for economic management came to represent a paramount focus of policy-making for many sectors. Demands were made on them, and criticisms rendered on their performance, for activities which they defined as outside their own sphere of competence. Being attuned to the political context of their work, they sought to adjust their performance accordingly. Under pressure, they redefined the plan as having not only economic but social implications as well. While this may have seemed no more than a symbolic gesture at the time, it also served to broaden the general understanding of their mandate.

Here is a clear case of the activation of politics within a procedural system. The policy-makers apparently had a relatively delimited view of the range of issues that would be entertained in the decision-making process they had established. But interested groups thought these institutions and processes ought to consider other problems, that the policy-makers ought to assume responsibility for a broader range of actions. The result was substantial tension and misunderstanding about the functions of this policy-making apparatus.

The policy-makers tried to maintain the integrity of their expertise, which was their stock in trade. In their problem context, in the decision rules they employed, there was simply no convenient way to measure the comparative value of improved living conditions in small Spanish towns against growth in gross national product. As other Western nations were also to learn, neo-

Keynesianism could not provide the same persuasive guidance for the full range of policy issues affecting the modern state that it could in the field of fiscal and monetary management.

However, by late 1966 and early 1967, the policy-makers began to bend before the countervailing pressures that they themselves, to some extent, had generated. The argument that the initial strategy of development had been too one-sidedly economic was widely supported by significant sectors of opinion. The Spanish social science community and the syndical organization leaders, particularly their technical cadres, became increasingly effective proponents of a sophisticated policy strategy of social development. Furthermore, the signals that Spain received from the Western world were changing. The Kennedy-Johnson "Great Society" program in the United States and the new vocabulary and concerns of protest throughout the West suggested additional dimensions to the policy format of a modern nation. While the policy-makers themselves may not have been attuned to these signals, they were quickly picked up by their more effective and influential critics.

Plan II bears the markings of that style of accommodation that characterizes, at least partially, pluralist politics. That the policy-makers were capable of such accommodative politics had much to do with their own understanding of the policy-making process and with the problem context they adopted. They saw themselves from the beginning practicing a strategy of unbalanced growth that would require adjustment for distortions and imbalances as they went along. Hence, they were not hampered by assumptions of doctrinal orthodoxy concerning the objectives they had pursued and the instruments they had used in the first period. Furthermore, the feedback regarding bottlenecks in the execution of the first plan, particularly in the agricultural sector, was compatible with the demands of their critics. However, it is most important to note that they themselves did not generate the alternative strategies and programs contained in Plan II. These initiatives were a product of the process, of the procedural equipment of economic policy-making which had been designed in the early 1960s. Hence, by the time of Plan II, the procedures of participation in planning, and the generalized public debate, they were capable of genuine initiation of policy-making alternatives, in addition to their earlier coordinative role.

In the conventional taxonomies of political system, Spanish authoritarianism and Western liberal democracy appear as categorically different types. If a comparison of economic policymaking in Spain and in the rest of the West suggests anything, it is that the absolute distinctiveness of the rival systems, in this field at least, is far from self-evident. In Spain, as elsewhere, economic policy-making in the postwar period did not involve widespread political participation. The Movement and the *Cortés* played relatively peripheral roles in the process in Spain, but this was the range of options effectively open to electoral choice very (The exception is the United States, where Congress retains a major economic policy role.) Certainly, we have noted, there is the critical difference that in Spain the principle of "one man, one vote" applied to only one man. In most Western democracies, the fundamental choice between alternative total approaches to economic policy was in the hands of the electorate, while in Spain the *Caudillo* performed that function. But nowhere in Europe was the range of options effectively open to electoral choice very wide, and most Western nations did not change the general contours of their total policy design during the postwar period. The public debate on these options that occurred in Spain, particularly in the 1960s, was at least as lively and meaningful as that which took place elsewhere. In Spain, as in the rest of the West, economic decision was normally a matter that involved a relatively limited part of the society. Labor organization adapted itself to a design prepared by others in Spain, but this was true in most of Europe and North America as well.

We have, of course, commented on the very real structural differences in the two systems. The policy-makers of Spain responded to demands churned up in the political process, but they did so on their own terms, at their own volition. The structure of power did not require them to bend their designs to the will of interested publics, as it would in procedural systems designed on the basis of democratic assumptions. But again, this difference in structure connoted few differences in policy formulation or impact.

This blurring of the distinctiveness of the two systems will have different implications for different readers, largely depending on their ideological predispositions. For some, it will imply that Spain was not so different from the Western norm after all, that Spain was a far more open society than they had assumed. Others will draw a completely opposite conclusion from this study and assert that the Western liberal democracies were less liberal than we have permitted ourselves to believe. The observer seems to be free to argue that the similarities between the policy process in Spain and the rest of the Western world were not due to the fact that Spain was less authoritarian than conventionally believed, but that the Western democracies were more so.

It seems evident that Spain's distinctive political system was quite compatible with the practice of neo-Keynesian economics. In comparing the Spanish experience with modern economics to that of the Western liberal democracies, it does not appear that these different contexts for politics provided markedly distinctive problem-solving capabilities in this area of public choice and action.

However, it may be that the implications of these two forms of political system are least apparent in the field of public policy that we have been considering. The compatibility of the problem-solving styles associated with each may have been temporary and somewhat fortuitous. The period we have been considering, from the mid-1950s to the mid-1960s, was, one recalls, a time marked by a certain sterility of reformist thought and of policy innovation in both East and West. Needless to say, many problems appearing on the agenda for action in complex industrial society were missing from the problem-solving program both in

Spain and in other modern nations. It is not altogether clear that the political system of Spain will prove as adequate to the policy tasks of the 1970s as it did to those of the 1960s.

Among these problems, the most apparent are: the distribution and use of the products of economic growth; the critique of the impersonality and quality of life provided by modern complex society, and of participation in its decision-making processes; the problem of cultural pluralism and the role of ethnic or cultural minorities; and the mass intelligentsia's challenging and criticizing the norms and values of the middle class, whose way of life and values become dominant standards for modern political economy. Each of these problems is salient in Spain, as they are in all modern societies, both East and West.

It is completely possible that the procedural and policy equipment of Nationalist Spain is as capable of mounting a concerted program of redistribution and social reform as that of other Western nations. A shift in the balance within the coalition of elites in Spain—toward the syndical organization, the reformist intellectual and social science community, and the relevant agencies of the bureaucracy—could provide the same procedural equipment that the entrepreneurial community, the interest groups, the banks, and the economic technicians did in the case of economic growth. The state is probably as well equipped with the policy instruments essential in the fields of education and welfare as it was in the mid-1950s for economic development. A comparison of the achievements of Plan II with, for instance, the "Great Society" program in the United States, bearing in mind the contextual differences between the two nations, will be a relevant test of the respective capacities of the two systems to mount centralized efforts, relying primarily on the resources and capabilities of the state, in this field.

However, were the signals from the rest of the West to become those of decentralization, increased citizen participation in public affairs, and perhaps greater autonomy for minorities and dissident groups to pursue life styles distinctive from majority standards, it is likely that we would discover the limitations in the problem-solving equipment of Spain. Programs of political reform were advanced in Spain during the past generation, but they encountered much greater resistance than efforts in either the economic or social fields. The orthodoxies of the organic state, which strictly delimited the channels of participation in policy-making and the range of demands that could appropriately be brought to the agenda of decision-making, were probably least influential in the fields of substantive policy. In both economic and social affairs, we have noted, critics of the going concern could generally find channels of access and influence in the decision-making process. However, regional minorities, disadvantaged interests, and intellectual dissidents were in quite another position. The irregular groups and movements they fashioned to press their claims were more often than not declared inappropriate to the procedural system. Given the centralizing tradition of Spain, reinforced by Nationalist politics, the capacity of the system to engage in an effective program of decentralization and local initiative would seem to be most limited. The meager suggestions contained in Plan II perhaps indicate the limited instruments available to decision-makers for this purpose. (They may, of course, also indicate the limited intention of policy-makers to proceed in this direction.)

In most of those fields where specific interests and groups wished to differentiate themselves from the going concern, or express criticism of some larger trends in the society as a whole, suppression of dissidence rather than consideration of problems was the more characteristic response. Certainly, here the record of the liberal democracies may show as many compatibilities as differences from Spanish practice. Student dissent, for example, was increasingly met be similar forms of resistance in Spain and in the rest of the West in the late 1960s. The electoral processes of liberal democracies, in fact, may provide a stronger basis for the imposition of majority standards through state powers than the "gentle anarchy" that characterizes Spanish public mores in many fields of personal eccentricity.

However, the basic procedural commitments of liberal democracy and authoritarianism should make some eventual difference in the way each treats the new issues of politicization arising in the Western world in the late 1960s. The earlier commitment of the Nationalist regime is to procedural orthodoxy: political activity must be expressed through licensed channels. It has been the case in Spain that the preferred response to illegal movements is suppression, and that the possibility of recognizing new problems or considering new demands is reserved as a residual category, a way of restoring peace if all else fails. The basic procedural commitments and, indeed, the reflex response to most forms of dissidence in the liberal democracies are usually the other way around. The distinction is often a fine one, to be sure, and in some areas it may disappear altogether. It would take a much more extensive analysis than mine to establish the exact areas in which these basic procedural commitments of the two types of system apply, and where they do not.

When one looks back on it all, perhaps the most striking fact is that the Spanish policy transformation was almost exclusively imitative and was not in the least an experimental or creative approach to public problem-solving. If the Spanish experience contributed anything to the wisdom of how to conduct modern government, it was the more or less successful transfer of the policy equipment of one culture to another. Spain herself opened few new roads and seldom tried bold or unique approaches to the problems of our time.

In the design of the stabilization program, and later in the apparatus of planning, Spain simply took over, complete and in detail, the most recent programs of other European nations. Even the projects of social concern represented by Plan II show striking parallels to initiatives taken in Western Europe or in the United States, when they are not incremental adjustments in the ongoing program of the Spanish state. The Spaniards rarely consulted their own national heritage for the design of measures. Politically the policy-makers were, especially in the economic realm, far more responsive to the demands and interests of critical groups and institutions beyond the nation's borders than they were to the political forces within.

This would seem most surprising for a proud nation, in a period of world history when nationalism is in the ascendency and the assertion of cultural uniqueness a general trend. Of course, since the Enlightenment, there has been a persistent tendency for the most modern in both Spain and Spanish America to deplore their own cultural heritage and to identify more closely with the philosophies and institutions of other lands. Perhaps all that we have witnessed is another episode in a continuing pattern of Hispanic civilization.

However, it may be that this curious characteristic of Spanish public policy has something to do with the conditions of public problem-solving in an authoritarian system. It may be that policy innovation is more apt to be associated with pluralist politics, which, of course, is not precisely the same thing as contemporary Western practice. Public policy-making, like scientific procedure, is a matter of satisfactorily accounting for the factors that must be reconciled to yield a solution to a problem. In politics, the variables to be considered are the diverse interests, demands, and perspectives generated by the body politic.

In authoritarian systems of the Spanish type, the range and type of interests that may be brought to bear on the policy-making process are to some extent specified in advance by the legitimation of specific forms of interest representation. The orthodox corporate structure of political institutions serves to define and reduce the number of factors that must be accounted for in policy-making. The norms of political tranquility, the interlocking of elites in the system, provide considerable constraints in the presentation of demands that are awkward to reconcile with other interests in the system. Unconventional or novel interests, expressed outside the sanctioned channels of representation, may be deemed inappropriate to the policy-making agenda. The policy-maker in such a system works with a fairly clean problem, one in which the factors to be considered in the equation of policy are to a large extent stabilized and in which controls exist to prevent the introduction of factors that are difficult to reconcile.

In fully pluralist politics, the presumption is that no predetermination of the forms of interest appropriate to public problem-solving will be made and that every potential interest has a right to be considered in the process of policy-making when it is presented according to procedures that are generic to all. The policy-maker is required to account for a more fluid and complex problem. The political structure provides less assurance that the factors to be considered in policy choice will be compatible with one another.

At its worst, policy-making in a pluralistic environment of choice may lead to confusion, uncertainty, and the dissipation of resources, as the condition of Britain in the period we are considering illustrates. However, policy-makers may rise to the challenge of finding a design for action that fits the more knotty and apparently ambiguous problems of choice presented by a pluralistic system. If they succeed, they may have made a contribution to the capacity of man to cope with the problems of governance, their nations will be denoted the more advanced, and less fortunate lands will seek their advice and counsel or emulate their ways.

Policy-makers in stabilized, legitimate authoritarian systems do not tend to devise innovative approaches to policy primarily because they do not encourage their citizens to present unique or unprecedented problems or proposals for public action. The image of social reality received by the policy-maker will be less complex and problematic. For the system, the values of tranquility and the routinization of decision predominate over initiative and innovation. Political differentiation and novelty are not the sources of progress, but of potential conflict and crisis.

In a pluralistic system, there is probably an inevitable tendency to move toward corporatist styles of decision-making. The policy-maker does not seek the challenges of complexity; he wishes to streamline his environment of choice, to routinize the resolution of problems, and to delimit the factors and standards that have to be considered. It is precisely the faith of the pluralist that this tendency should be resisted, that the policy-maker should be forced by the structure of the system to take into account a more complex and problematic portrayal of social reality than would be his natural inclination. Only when the environment is perplexing is he apt to come up with creative responses or programs that fit the diverse aspirations and needs of the body politic. The purpose of pluralism, after all, is not to make policy-making easier, but to make it more adequate.

However, all relevant political values are not neatly arrayed on one side or the other of this argument. There is a need in every society for some degree of order, consistency, and stability in its public affairs. Most citizens hardly yearn for chronically creative politics. On the other hand, the human spirit is such that some portion of any population is constantly seeing things in new perspective, seeking new tasks, and redefining what it is about. The political system that cannot reflect these new possibilities in its decision-making process condemns its people to frustration and stagnation, and perhaps jeopardizes its own continuity. The technical problems of policy-making apparently still involve the eternal issue of the appropriate balance between liberty and authority in any political order.

REFERENCE MATTER

NOTES

Chapter 1

1 Juan Linz, "An Authoritarian Regime: Spain," in *Cleavages, Ideologies and Party Systems*, eds. Erik Allardt and Yujo Littunen, Transactions of the Westermarck Society (Helsinki: Academic Bookstore, 1964), 10:304.

2 On the formal political philosophy of Nationalist Spain, see Instituto de Estudios Políticos, *El nuevo estado español: 1936–1963*, 2 vols. (Madrid: Editora Nacional, 1963), 1, 2; Manuel Fraga y Iribarne, *Horizonte español* (Madrid: Editora Nacional, 1965), and his civics textbook, *Estructura política de España* (Madrid: Editorial Doncel, 1961); Jesus Fueyo Alvárez, *La época insegura* (Madrid: Ediciones Europa, 1962); José Antonio Maravall, *La teoría del estado en España en el siglo XVII* (Madrid: Instituto de Estudios Políticos, 1944); Servicio Informativo Español, *Referendum 1966: Nueva Constitución* (Madrid: Ministerio de Información y Turismo, 1967); Boletín Oficial del Estado, *Leyes Fundamentales* (Madrid: Boletín Oficial del Estado, 1966).

3 Andrew Shonfield, *Modern Capitalism* (New York: Oxford University Press, 1965).

4 Herbert March and James Simon, *Organizations* (New York: John Wiley & Sons, Inc., 1958), p. 191.

5 The concept of "problem solving capabilities" is borrowed from Albert O. Hirschman, who uses this notion in a similar sense in his *Journeys Toward Progress* (New York: Twentieth Century Fund, 1963).

6 Theodore Lowi has suggested a taxonomy based on the distributive, redistributive, or regulative effects of public actions. See his "American Business, Public Policy, Case Studies and Political Theory," *World Politics* 16 (July 1964):677–715, and his *At the Pleasure of the Mayor* (Glencoe, Ill.: The Free Press, 1964). I used a similar scheme for classifying the powers available to Latin American leaders, based on the "essential" characteristics of government. The capabilities of the state were classified as those deriving from its character as a monopoly of power (law), those deriving from its character as a focus of authority (ideology and persuasion), and those deriving from its economic characteristics—its power to derive resources from the society by taxation, and to spend for public purposes. See Charles W. Anderson, *Politics and Economic Change in Latin America* (Princeton, N.J.: D. Van Nostrand Co., Inc., 1967), pp. 5–6, 54–55. Gabriel Almond and G. Bingham Powell, Jr., *Comparative Politics: A Developmental Approach* (Boston: Little, Brown and Co., 1966), pp. 190–212, divide the "capabilities" of a political system into extractive, regulative, distributive, symbolic, and responsive categories. Perhaps the most sophisticated taxonomic technique is that developed by Robert Dahl and Charles Lindblom, *Politics, Economics and Welfare* (New York: Harper and Bros., 1953), pp. 6–17, which poses a number of complex continua of choices between public and private ownership, direct and indirect control, voluntary and compulsory association, and compulsion or information in the settlement of disputes. However, Dahl and Lindblom neither intended nor created a general taxonomy. Their scheme was devised merely to suggest the variety of possible policy instruments.

7 For full description of these objectives, see E. S. Kirschen et al., *Economic Policy in Our Time*, 3 vols. (Chicago: Rand, McNally and Co.), 1:9–15.

8 Various efforts to create a typology of stages have been made. See, among others, Harold Lasswell, *The Decision Process* (College Park: Bureau of Governmental Research, University of Maryland, 1956); Gabriel Almond and James Coleman, *The Politics of the Developing Areas* (Princeton, N.J.: Princeton University Press, 1960), pp. 14–16; Kirschen et al., *Economic Policy*, 1:265.

9 For a thorough review of this problem, see Morris Davis, "Some Aspects of Detroit's Decisional Profile," *Administrative Science Quarterly* 12 (September 1967):211–19.

10 One useful way of thinking about this problem is to assume that

the stress, time, and effort involved in reaching a decision is one cost of collective action. Hence, one might postulate a "margin" in the structuring of decision systems, where increased heterodoxy would be tolerated to that point where the costs or reconciling diverse interests would be greater than the gains expected from collective action. This is conceptually appealing, though I can imagine no way of operationalizing such a proposition. For a sophisticated development of the idea, see James M. Buchanan and Gordon Tullock, *The Calculus of Consent* (Ann Arbor: University of Michigan Press, 1962), p. 48.

11 Vilfredo Pareto, *The Mind and Society*, 10 vols. (New York: Harcourt, Brace and Co., 1935), 4:255.

12 An additional dimension of this problem is Robert Merton's identification of "unanticipated consequences" with the latent functions of a social system. See Robert Merton, "The Unanticipated Consequences of Purposive Social Action," *American Sociological Review* 34 (January 1936):894–904; see also his *Social Theory and Social Structure* (Glencoe, Ill.: The Free Press, 1957), p. 86 and passim.

13 Kirschen et al., *Economic Policy in Our Time*, 1:265–96.

14 Albert O. Hirschman, *Development Projects Observed* (Washington, D.C.: The Brookings Institution, 1967), p. 35 and passim.

15 Charles Lindblom, *The Intelligence of Democracy* (New York: The Free Press, 1965).

16 Karl Deutsch, *The Nerves of Government* (New York: The Free Press, 1966); and David Easton, *The Political System* (New York: Knopf, 1959).

Chapter 2

1 Francisco Franco, *Política económica nacional*, Documentación económica no. 7 (Madrid: Oficina de Coordinación y Programación Económica, 1959). See also Felipe Ferrer Cabetó, *Nacionalismo económico español* (Cadíz: Estudio Cerón, 1938).

2 Antonio Robert, *Perspectivas de la economía española* (Madrid: Ediciones Cultura Hispanica, 1954), p. 111.

3 A good critical commentary on the boycott policy can be found in Arthur Whitaker, *Spain and Defense of the West* (New York: Frederick A. Praeger, Inc., 1962), pp. 22–33.

4 International Commission of Jurists, *Spain and the Rule of Law* (Geneva: International Commission of Jurists, 1962), p. 6.

5 Stanley Payne, *Falange* (Stanford, Calif.: Stanford University

Press, 1961), pp. 78–79. On the conflict between the *Falange* and the business, banking, and industrial sectors, see particularly pp. 188–89.

6 For an excellent interpretation of this historic pattern, see Robert, *Perspectivas de la economía española*, pp. 31–79.

7 Juan Velarde Fuertes, *Política económica de la dictadura* (Madrid: Guadiana de Publicaciones, 1968), pp. 34–71.

8 "El arancel en la economía Española," *Información comercial española* 322 (June 1960).

9 T. E. Rogers, *Overseas Economic Surveys: Spain* (London: H. M. Stationery Office, 1957), p. 76.

10 On the Spanish use of licensing and bilateral agreements, see Rogers, *Economic Surveys: Spain*, pp. 91, 97; Ramón Tamames, *Estructura económica española*, 3d ed. (Madrid: Sociedad de Estudios y Publicaciones, 1965), pp. 551–64; Robert, *Perspectivas de la economía española*, pp. 97–108; Fondo Monetario Internacional, *Informe sobre España* (Madrid: Imprenta Nacional, 1965), pp. 12–44; Organization for Economic Cooperation and Development, *Economic Surveys: Spain, 1959* (Paris: OECD, 1960), pp. 6–11.

11 Wolfgang König, "Multiple Exchange Rate Policies in Latin America," *Journal of Inter-American Studies* 10 (January 1968): 35–52.

12 The literature on the Spanish use of multiple exchange rates is vast. Some useful sources are: "¿Qué causas determinan el cambio de la peseta?" *Información comercial española* 318 (February 1960): 18–22; and *Información comercial española* 284 (April 1957); Higenio París Eguilaz, *Diez años de política económica en España: 1939–1949* (Madrid: Sanchez Ocaña y Companía, 1949), pp. 79–96, 256–61; Tamames, *Estructura económica española*, pp. 551–64; Rogers, *Economic Surveys: Spain*, pp. 73–75; OECD, *Spain, 1959*, pp. 28–29.

13 París Eguilaz, *Diez años de política económica*, pp. 101–52.

14 See the law establishing INI, Ley de 25 Septiembre 1941, *Boletín oficial del estado* 280 (October 7, 1941). Probably the most objective assessment of INI's role in the Spanish economy is in Horst Hans Hergel, *Industrialisierungspolitik in Spanien Seit Ende des Burgerkrieges: Auswirkungen des Staatlichen Wirtschaftsinterventionismus auf das Wirtschaftswachstum* (Cologne: Westdeutscher Verlag, 1963).

15 Whitaker, *Spain and Defense of the West*, p. 223.

16 Rogers, *Economic Surveys: Spain*, p. 141.

17 However, the intimate relationship between INI, the great Spanish banks, and other elements of "monopoly capital" in mixed enterprise was not lost on either the left or the reformist Falangist critics of the regime. Manuel Tuñon de Lara, *Panorama actual de la economía española* (Paris: Librería Española, 1962); Ramón Tamames, *La lucha contra los monopolios* (Madrid: Editorial Tecnos, 1966).

18 M. Sánchez Gil, *Problemas de actualidad económico-social* (Madrid: Aguilar, 1962), pp. 119–20.

19 For an extended and unusually competent treatment of this entire problem, see Tamames, *Estructura económica española*, pp. 250–68, and his *La lucha contra los monopolios*, pp. 375–418.

20 See París Eguilaz, *El desarrollo económico español: 1906–1964* (Madrid: Sanchez Ocaña y Companía, 1965); and Juan Sardá, *El sistema financiero español* (Bilbao: Ediciones Duesto, 1964). Sardá notes that about 50 percent of the requirements for new financing in the private sector is provided by the private banking system.

21 Rogers, *Economic Surveys: Spain*, p. 76.

22 Ley de 25 Octubre 1939, "Protección y fomento de la industria nacional," *Boletín oficial del estado* 298; and Ley de 25 Noviembre 1939, "Ordenación y defensa de la industria nacional," *Boletín oficial del estado* 329.

23 Ministerio de Industria, direct information.

24 Tamames, *Estructura económica española*, p. 375.

25 Rogers, *Economic Surveys: Spain*, p. 154.

26 París Eguilaz, *Diez años de política económica*, p. 45.

27 Servicio Nacional de Trigo, *Veinte años de actuación* (Madrid: Ministerio de Agricultura, 1958).

28 For criticisms made by the FAO mission, see International Bank for Reconstruction and Development and Food and Agricultural Organization, *El desarrollo de la agricultura en España* (Madrid: Ministerio de Hacienda, 1966).

29 IBRD, *The Economic Development of Spain* (Baltimore: The Johns Hopkins University Press, 1963), p. 283.

30 Ibid., pp. 169–254.

31 Tamames, *Estructura económica española*, pp. 416–23, and direct information, *Instituto Nacional de Vivienda*.

32 Evidence of the perversions and imperfections of the system of direct controls is almost totally impressionistic, but the literature of the period contains numerous examples and illustrations. Several

illustrations at the level of the industrial and commercial elites appear in Salvador de Madariaga, *Spain: A Modern History* (New York: Frederick A. Praeger, Inc., 1965), pp. 632–33. An interesting example of the problems of enforcing controls at the local level is found in Julian A. Pitt-Rivers, *The People of the Sierra* (London: Weidenfield and Nicolson, 1955), pp. 19–21. See also Gerald Brenan, *South from Granada* (New York: Farrar and Rinehart, 1957), pp. 86 ff.

33 Rogers, *Economic Surveys: Spain*, p. 81.

34 The devices used for evading legal wages were complex and ingenious. One bank paid its workers seventeen months' wages a year. Masons and metallurgical workers were paid high bonuses for overtime they did not work. *Hispanic American Report* 12 (July 1959): 248. However, it should be noted that "wage drift," the tendency of market wages to exceed legal rates, was not unique to Spain, but characteristic of most European nations in this period. M. M. Postan, *An Economic History of Western Europe: 1945–1964* (London: Methuen and Co., Ltd., 1967), p. 82.

35 One estimate of the wage pattern in the steel industry is included in the article, "Los salarios durante los ultimos veinte años," *Moneda y crédito* 60 (March 1957):52–53.

WAGE INCREASES: STEEL INDUSTRY (Pesetas)

	Peon (daily)	Foreman (daily)	Engineer (annual)
Nov. 11, 1938	9.50	15	10,000
June 16, 1942 add 5% family bonus	9.50	15	12,000
Nov. 30, 1943 add 10% family bonus	10.50	17	12,000
July 28, 1945 add 15% family bonus	10.50	17	12,000
July 27, 1946 add 15% family bonus	14.00	22	23,184
April 21, 1950 add family and 25% cost of living	17.50	27.50	28,890
Oct. 30, 1952 add above and 20 days extra	18.50	29.10	30,670
Nov. 27, 1953 add family bonus of 75% to others	20.15	31.65	33,327
March 23, 1956 add special bonus of 20% to others	24.20	38	39,922
Oct. 26, 1956 add family bonus of 20% to others	36.00	47.50	40,200

36 This discussion is based largely on the following sources: Shonfield, *Modern Capitalism;* Kirschen et al., *Economic Policy in our Time,* vols. 2 and 3; Postan, *Economic History of Western Europe;* Organization for European Economic Cooperation, *Economic Progress and Problems of Western Europe* (Paris: OEEC, 1948–53); Murray Edelman and Robben W. Fleming, *The Politics of Wage-Price Decisions* (Urbana: University of Illinois Press, 1965).

Chapter 3

1 Madariaga, *Spain,* pp. 349–50. Stanley Payne clearly analyzes how José Antonio Primo de Rivera, the founder and in some sense the ideologist of the *Falange* was defending the legacy of his father in his support for this type of national reconstruction. See his *Falange,* ch. 2.

2 These include two "bills of rights," the *Fuero de los Españoles* of July 17, 1945, covering civil and political matters, and the *Fuero de Trabajo,* March 9, 1938, dealing with social and economic rights. The *Ley de las Cortés,* July 17, 1942, structures that body; the *Ley de Sucesión,* July 26, 1947, establishes the role of the Chief of State and the technique of succession, as well as basing the regime on the principle of monarchical legitimacy. The *Ley de Referendum,* October 22, 1945, creates an optional referendum procedure for legislation while the *Principios del Movimiento,* May 17, 1958, states the philosophic postulates underlying the organic state. The *Ley Organica* of 1966 reformed the structural system in a number of areas. Since we are considering the equipment of the system in the mid-1950s, we will be concerned primarily with the structure before these changes. Boletín Oficial del Estado, *Leyes Fundamentales* (Madrid: Boletín Oficial del Estado, 1966).

3 *Ley de 30 Enero 1938* (specifying the legislative power of the Chief of State) and *Ley de 26 Julio 1957* (on the structure of the public administration). *Leyes Fundamentales,* pp. 41–48, 153–94.

4 Manuel Fraga y Iribarne, *El reglamento de las Cortés españolas* (Madrid: Imprenta Pueblo, 1959), pp. 171–74.

5 Two good short summaries on Spanish constitutional institutions are: International Commission of Jurists, *Spain and the Rule of Law;* and Manuel Fraga y Iribarne, *How Spain Is Governed* (Madrid: Editora Nacional, 1967). For the details, see Instituto de Estudios Políticos, *El nuevo estado español* 1, 2.

6 Fred Witney, *Labor Policies and Practices in Spain* (New York: Frederick A. Praeger, Inc., 1967), p. 14.

7 Ibid., pp. 15–16.

8 *Official Bulletin: International Labour Office* 47, suppl. 2 (July 1964); *Hispanic American Report* 12 (June 1959):188; Witney, *Labor Policies and Practices.*

9 Amando de Miguel and Juan Linz, *Los empresarios ante el poder público* (Madrid: Instituto de Estudios Políticos, 1966).

10 Ibid., pp. 163–64, 166–67, ch. 8 passim.

11 Ibid., pp. 43–48, 54–57, 75–103.

12 Ibid., p. 120.

13 Benjamin Welles, *Spain: The Gentle Anarchy* (New York: Frederick A. Praeger, Inc., 1965), p. 33.

14 Manuel de Torres Martínez, *La coordinación en la política económica de España* (Madrid: Instituto Social Leon XIII, 1953), pp. 11–20.

15 Fraga y Iribarne, *El reglamento de las Cortés españolas.*

16 Juan Velarde Fuertes, "Algunas problemas de la estructura y desarrollo de la economía española," *Sobre la decadencia económica de España* (Madrid: Editorial Tecnos, 1967), p. 586. His classification of the scale of industrial control of each of the major banks is as follows:

Bank	Enterprises in Group	Capital of Group (millions of PTS.)
Banesto	203	32371
Bilbao	147	21953
Hispano Americano	133	20515
Central	155	19299
Vizcaya	159	18902
Urquijo	145	11797

17 Tamames, *La lucha contra los monopolios,* p. 347.

18 Amando de Miguel and Juan Linz, "Los empresarios españolas y la banca," *Moneda y crédito* 84 (March 1963):3–112. See also their *Los empresarios ante el poder público.* In relation to the Spanish banking system in general, see also Jesús Prados Arrarte, *El sistema bancario español* (Madrid: Aguilar, 1958).

19 Juan de la Cierva, *Notas de mi vida* (Madrid: Instituto Editorial Reus, 1955).

20 For a sense of the "professional identity" of this group, see the *Boletín del colegio nacional de doctores y licenciados en ciencias económicas y comerciales,* 1954–57.

21 Facultad de ciencias económicas y Instituto de Economía "Sancho

de Moncada," *La contabilidad nacional en España* (Madrid: Instituto Sancho Moncada, 1958).

22 *Revista sindical de estadística* 6 (September 1961):83.

23 Francisco G. Quijano, "Sobre la distribución personal de la renta en España," *Moneda y crédito* 86 (September 1963).

24

	Bank of Spain	Hacienda (used by OECD)
Central Receipts	63179	63200
Autonomous Agencies	15718	–
U.S. Aid	3791	3800
Banking System	1077	–
Treasury: Current Account	–	2500
Bouillion	2679	7600
Central Government Issues	7917	–
Total	94361	77100

25 *Información comercial española* 10 (January 1961):148-49.

26 Alberto de Ullastres, *Política comercial española* (Madrid: Imprenta Nacional, 1963), p. 13.

27 The best source on the Movement exists at the time of writing only in mimeographed form: Juan Linz, "From Falange to Movimiento Organización: The Spanish Single Party and the Franco Regime (1936–1968)" (Mimeographed copy in possession of author, 1968). See also Payne, *Falange*, pp. 239–67.

28 See Stanley Payne, *The Army in Spanish Politics* (Stanford, Calif.: Stanford University Press, 1967).

29 For an interesting discussion of analogies between the centralized use of local government for partisan control in the Nationalist period and in the 1820s, see José Luis L. Aranguren, *Moral y sociedad: la moral social española en el siglo XIX* (Madrid: Edicusa, 1966), pp. 107–9.

30 On this point, particularly in regard to labor organization, see Edelman and Fleming, *Politics of Wage-Price Decisions*.

Chapter 4

1 París Eguilaz, *Desarrollo económico español*, p. 212, identifies these as the major economic policy measures of the 1951–57 period.

2 I will use this term to refer to a set of relatively independent journals designed for businessmen and managers, more or less like *Business Week* or *Fortune* in the United States. The number of these journals increased rapidly from 1958 to 1961, and we will

return again to their role in the proceedings. For the period under consideration, *España económica* was the sharpest of the lot. Along with *Actualidad económica, Balance,* and *La economía,* we probably have a fairly good inventory of the formal media of communications within the upper echelons of the Spanish commercial and industrial community.

3 A good example is found in J. J. Sánchez y Zabalza, "Crónica," *La economía,* 15 January 1954, pp. 2–3, a summary of the state of the economy at the beginning of 1954.

4 Editorial, *España económica,* 5 March 1955, p. 182.

5 Robert, *Perspectivas de la economía española.*

6 See Banco Urquijo, *Memoria: 1953, 1954* (Madrid: Banco Urquijo, 1954, 1955); Banco Hispano Americano, *La situación económica en 1954* (Madrid: Banco Hispano Americano, 1955); *España económica,* 26 March 1955, p. 245.

7 Banco Español de Crédito, *Memoria: 1955* (Madrid: Banesto, 1956).

8 Andrés Moreno, *Economía,* 25 September 1954, p. 6.

9 José Larraz, *La integración Europea y España* (Madrid: Espasa Capte, 1961).

10 Delegación Nacional de Provincias de FET y de los JONS, *Notas sobre política económica Española* (Madrid: Talleres Prensa Gráfica, 1954).

11 Whitaker, *Spain and Defense of the West,* p. 46; Tamames, *Estructura económica española,* p. 435.

12 *La Vanguardia* (Barcelona), 2 June 1956.

13 *España económica,* 8 October 1956, p. 833.

14 *Económica española: 1954–1955,* p. 9.

15 Ibid., p. 10.

16 Ibid., pp. 23–24.

17 Manuel Arbúrua y de la Miyar, *Cinco años al frente del Ministerio de Comerico* (Madrid: Imprenta Nacional, 1956), passim; *España económica,* 7 May 1955, pp. 379–80.

18 Tamames, *Estructura económica española; La lucha contra los monopolios.*

19 Compare any of the bank studies cited herein with Consejo Económico Sindical Nacional, *20 Años de crecimiento nacional* (Madrid: Organización Sindical, 1960), for a good idea of the contrast.

20 "Reunión económica nacional," *De economía* 9 (January–April 1956):116–17.

21 Victoriano Martín Mendicute, "Los economistas sindicales," *Bole-*

tín de colegio nacional de doctores y licenciados en ciencias económicas, 1 (January 1954):14.

22 OECD, *Cuarto informe sobre la economía española* (Madrid: Oficina de Coordinación y Programación Económica, 1962), p. 39.

23 Relations of policy to inflation in this period are well analyzed in: OECD, *Economic Surveys: Spain, 1958* (Paris: OECD, 1959), pp. 19–20 and 23–27; Tamames, *Estructura económica española,* pp. 737–38; Rogers, *Economic Surveys: Spain,* to name only three of numerous commentaries.

24 One estimate suggests that, at constant prices, taxation receipts in 1954 were about 75 percent of those of 1935. Taxation absorbed about 15 percent of national income in 1931–35, and 8.2 percent in 1952. Delegación Nacional de Provincias de FET y de los JONS, *Notas sobre política económica española,* p. 381.

25 See the study of rate of response to the recession of 1958 in the U.S. and to inflationary pressures in Europe after the Korean War, in Kirschen et al., *Economic Policy in Our Time,* 1:277–78.

26 Economic Commission for Latin America, *The Economic Development of Latin America and Its Principal Problems* (New York: United Nations, 1949).

27 The most direct application of the Prebisch thesis to Spanish conditions that I know appears in París Eguilaz's contribution to José Larraz et al., *Estudios sobre la unidad económica de Europa,* 10 vols. (Madrid: Estudios Económicos Españoles y Europeos, S. A., 1961), 1:5–85.

28 París Eguilaz, *Desarrollo económico español,* p. 79.

29 Robert, *Perspectivas de la economía española,* pp. 173, 208. See also, Cánovas del Castillo, "De como he venido á ser doctrinalmente protecionista," *Revista de economía política* 10 (September-December 1959):1025–48.

30 For an interesting essay on the personal relationships among the members of this group and for a basic treatment of their main themes, see Velarde Fuertes, *Sobre la decadencia económica de España.* One of the earliest collections of their writings is Delegación Nacional de Provincias de FET y de los JONS, *Notas sobre política económica española.* Their use of structural analysis is discussed in José Luis Sampedro, *Realidad económica y analisis estructural* (Madrid: Aguilar, 1959).

31 For a basic statement of this controversy, see Albert O. Hirschman, ed., *Latin American Issues: Essays and Comments* (New York: Twentieth Century Fund, 1961), pp. 69–94.

32 "Tres adelantados," *Boletín del colegio nacional de doctores y licenciados en ciencias económicas y comerciales* 4 (Primer trimestre 1957):1–2.

33 Cited in Welles, *Spain*, p. 317.

34 Daniel Artigues, *El Opus Dei en España: 1928–1967* (Madrid: Ruedo Iberico, 1967), pp. 158–65.

35 *España económica*, 8 December 1956, p. 856, and 28 June 1958, p. 509.

36 "El plan de estabilización de la economía española," *Moneda y crédito* 70 (September 1959):76–77.

37 A private survey, conducted in 1963 by Antonio Goxens, "¿Por qué se defrauda el fisco?" *Actualidad económica*, 1 February 1964, p. 6, apparently included an ingenuous question, asking businessmen in effect why they did not pay taxes honestly. Some of the responses were quite revealing:

"It isn't a sin not to pay taxes."

"I work and produce ten hours a day and make less than many high bureaucrats who I consider social parasites."

"My conscience objects when the State doesn't administer efficiently what it collects."

"The Government asks me for money to finance state industries that compete with me."

"The State says it needs money to provide services, but those I receive do not satisfy me."

"The State dedicates its money to instruments of war and I am a pacifist."

"I will pay like a German when we have highways like Germany."

"I try not to pay because no one else does."

"If I tell the truth and my competitor doesn't, he will ruin me."

"The State takes account of evasion when it sets the rates."

"I will pay when I can go to a Fiscal Office and find out what people I know get paid and those whose names appear most frequently in the press."

"I do not agree with the organization of the state and this is my only means of protest."

Another student of this problem found that about 24 percent of the Spanish population essentially "approves" of tax evasion, another 36 percent were indifferent toward it, and about 39 percent condemned it. Disapproval was generally strongest in lower status occupations. However, the author of this study remarks that these

Spanish attitudes may not differ too greatly from those of other Europeans. In a similar survey, 53 percent of German industrialists and professionals approved of some forms of tax evasions and 23 percent disapproved. Among similar Swiss occupational groups, 40 percent approved and 50 percent disapproved. See Burkhard Strümpel, "El español como contribuyente," *Revista de fomento social* 85 (January–March 1967):5–25.

38 The system met with mixed reactions. One survey of larger entre-preneurs reported that only 23 percent thought the global assess-ment just, but 43 percent preferred it to the system of individual assessments. Fernando Finat, "Actitudes empresariales," *Moneda y crédito* 91 (December 1964):9–15.

39 *España económica*, 18 January 1968, p. 365.

40 Banco Urquijo, *La economía española: 1957* (Madrid: Banco Urquijo, 1958), pp. 34, 37, 99.

41 Tamames, *Estructura económica española*, p. 740.

42 OECD, *Economic Surveys: Spain, 1959* and *1960* (Paris: OECD, 1960, 1961).

43 OECD, *Spain, 1959*.

44 König, "Multiple Exchange Rate Policies in Latin America," pp. 35–52.

45 Oficina de Coordinación y Programación Económica, *Contesta-ciones al cuestionario económico del gobierno* (Madrid: Oficina de Coordinación y Programación Económica, 1959).

46 *España económica*, 20 February 1960, p. 143.

47 König, "Multiple Exchange Rate Policies in Latin America," p. 147.

48 Amando de Miguel and John Linz, "El mercado común, el capital extranjero, y el empresario español," *Productividad* 27 (April–June 1963):37–62.

49 José Solís Ruiz, *Nueva conviviencia española* (Madrid: Imprenta Pueblo, 1959), pp. 122–23.

50 José Isbert Soriano, "La organización sindical y el desarrollo eco-nómico," *Cuadernos del centro de estudios sindicales* 20 (Decem-ber 1963):22–24.

51 "Consejo económico sindical nacional: Conclusiones del IX pleno," *De economía* 50 (November–December 1957):8–47, and reports in the archives of the Syndical Organization.

52 Ullastres, *Política comercial española*, p. 381.

53 *España económica*, 11 May 1957, p. 188; and 8 June 1957, p. 297.

54 Presidencia del Gobierno, Secretaria General Técnica, *Legislación económica I: Estabilización* (Madrid: Imprenta Nacional, 1965).

55 Ministerio de Hacienda, *Información estadística del Ministerio de Hacienda* (Madrid: Ministerio de Hacienda, 1960), pp. 5–6.
56 Kirschen, et al. *Economic Policy in Our Time*, 1:273–75.

Chapter 5

1 Presidencia del Gobierno, *Legislación económica I: Estabilización;* "El plan de estabilización de la economía española," pp. 76–77; Tamames, *Estructura económica española*, pp. 742–45; Whitaker, *Spain and Defense of the West*, p. 201.
2 Herbert L. Matthews, *The Yoke and the Arrows* (New York: Braziller, 1961), p. 142.
3 Solís Ruiz, *Nueva conviviencia española*, pp. 244–89; *Pueblo* (Madrid), 17 July 1959.
4 Antonio Robert, *Informe sobre la economía española y la integración europea* (Madrid: Consejo Económico Sindical Nacional, 1958).
5 José Antonio Suanzes, *Ocho discursos* (Madrid: Instituto Nacional de Industria, 1963).
6 Enrique Fuentes Quintana, ed., *El desarrollo económico de España: Juicio crítico del informe del Banco Mundial* (Madrid: Revista del Occidente, 1963), p. 32; Editorial, *De economía* 12 (May–June 1959):436.
7 Whitaker, *Spain and Defense of the West*, p. 239.
8 Welles, *Spain*, p. 319.
9 Ullastres, *Política comercial española*, p. 108.
10 "De Gaulle and Franco," *New Republic*, 14 December 1963, pp. 13–14.
11 OECD, *Cuarto informe sobre la economía española*, pp. 34–35; Fondo Monetario Internacional, *Informe sobre España*, pp. 32–33.
12 "Analisis del nuevo arancel español," *Información comercial española* 322 (June 1960):50,58.
13 OECD, *Cuarto informe sobre la economía española*, p. 35.
14 Martín Bassovs Coma, "Las disposiciones adoptadas en virtud del decreto de 23 de Noviembre 1962 sobre medias previas al Plan de Desarrollo Económico," *Documentación administrativa* 62 (May 1963):33–56.
15 Oficina de Coordinación y Programación Económica, *Informe sobre la ejucución del programa de las inversiones para el año 1959* (Madrid: Imprenta Nacional, 1964).
16 Fuentes Quintana, *Desarrollo económico de España*, pp. 56–57.
17 IBRD, *Economic Development of Spain*, p. 13; Juan Sarda Dexeus,

"Aspectos monetarios de la estabilización," in Luis Olariaga et al., *La estabilización en España* (Madrid: Facultad de Derecho, Universidad de Madrid, 1960), pp. 34–35.

18 Tamames, *La lucha contra los monopolios*, pp. 243–319.

19 Fondo Monetario Internacional, *Informe sobre España*, pp. 97–100.

20 OECD, *Spain*, 1960, pp. 9–14; Confederación Española de Cajas de Ahorros, *La economía española desde la estabilización (1960–1961)* (Madrid: Confederación Española de Cajas de Ahorros, 1962), pp. 9–15; Banco Urquijo, *La economía española: 1959* (Madrid: Banco Urquijo, 1960).

21 Jesús García Fernández, *La emigración exterior de España* (Barcelona: Ediciones Ariel, 1965), pp. 21, 25. Illegal emigration may raise the latter figures as much as 50 percent.

22 *España económica*, 3 February 1962, p. 82.

23 *Hispanic American Report* 12 (December 1959):529, and 14 (July 1961):384.

24 For a good, straightforward analysis of these unanticipated consequences, see the reflections of the Director of Studies of the Bank of Spain, Juan Sarda Dexeus, "Aspectos monetarios de la estabilización," pp. 36 ff.

25 Tamames, *Estructura económica española*, pp. 746–47.

26 *España económica*, 26 May 1962, p. 401.

27 Perpina Rodríguez, *Los salarios en la industria española y en el extranjero* (Madrid: Instituto de Estudios Políticos, 1963).

Chapter 6

1 "Al comienzo de 1960," *Actualidad económica*, 2 January 1960, p. 2.

2 Ibid., p. 102; 27 February 1960, p. 4. *España económica*, similarly, was critical of the failure of policy to move from stabilization to expansion during the first quarter of 1960. *España económica*, January–March 1960, passim.

3 *Arriba* (Madrid), 13 February 1960.

4 Sánchez Gil, *Problemas de actualidad económico-social*, pp. 3–85.

5 "Un año despúes," *Información comercial española* 337 (September 1961):3.

6 "Tres opiniones sobre la actual situación económica española," *Información comercial española* 329 (January 1961):18.

7 *España económica*, 20 February 1960, p. 211.

8 OECD, *Spain, 1960*, p. 7.

9 Robert, *Informe sobre la económia española*, p. 65.

10 De Miguel and Linz, "Los empresarios españoles y la banca," p. 111.
11 Eduardo Taragona, "Un ministro en orbita," *Actualidad económica*, 8 June 1963, p. 7.
12 Presidencia del Gobierno, *Legislación económica I: Estabilización*, pp. 201–74.
13 Instituto de Cultura Hispánica, *Estudios hispánicos de desarrollo económico*, 7 vols., mimeo. (Madrid: Instituto de Cultura Hispánica, 1956).
14 *España económica*, 13 April 1957, p. 283.
15 Ministerio de Hacienda, *Información estadística: 1961* (Madrid: Ministerio de Hacienda, 1962, pp. 33–34.
16 *España económica*, 18 March 1961, p. 231.
17 Editorial, *De economía* 13 (January–March, 1960):8.
18 Ullastres, *Política comercial española*, pp. 227–28.
19 Shonfield, *Modern Capitalism*, p. 72.
20 Walter Heller, *New Dimensions of Political Economy* (New York: W. W. Norton and Co., Inc., 1967), p. 11.
21 Shonfield, *Modern Capitalism*, p. 138.
22 Presidencia del Gobierno, Comisaría del Plan, *Hoja informativo*, 13 July 1962, pp. 5–6. (Hereafter cited as *Hoja informativo*.)
23 Whitaker, *Spain and Defense of the West*, p. 125.
24 *Hispanic American Report* 17 (April 1964):104. See also 1 (May 1963):223, of this same publication.
25 Laureano López Ródo, *Objectivos y estructuras del Plan de Desarrollo Económico* (Madrid: Imprenta Nacional, 1963).
26 IBRD, *Economic Development of Spain*, pp. 56–102.
27 "Decreto 3060 1962, 23 de Noviembre por el que se establecen directrices y medidas preliminares al Plan de Desarrollo," *Boletín Oficial del Estado* 329 (November 25, 1962).
28 Laureano López Ródo "La organización, administrativa del desarrollo económico en España," *Documentación administrativa* 51 (March 1962):60–61.
29 *Faro de Vigo* (Vigo), 11 August 1962.
30 *Hoja informativo: Resumén de 1962* (January 1963); *Hoja informativo*, 3 September 1962.
31 López Ródo, *Objectivos y estructuras del Plan de Desarrollo Económico*, p. 14. See also his *La administración pública y las transformaciones socioeconomicas* (Madrid: Real Academia de Ciencias Morales y Políticas, 1963).
32 López Ródo, *Objectivos y estructuras del Plan de Desarrollo Económico*, p. 8.

33 *Hoja informativo: Resumén de 1962.*

34 *Hoja informativo,* 11 January 1963.

35 Presidencia del Gobierno, Comisaría del Plan, *Anexos al Plan de Desarrollo Económico y Social: Servicios de Información* (Madrid: Imprenta Nacional, 1964), pp. 86–88.

36 *Hoja informativo,* 3 September 1962.

37 Soriano, "La organización sindical y el desarrollo económico," p. 29.

38 *Boletín de las Cortés Españolas* 339 (December 5, 1963); *ABC* (Madrid), 6 December 1963; *Actualidad económica,* 14 December 1963, pp. 6–8.

39 *Boletín de las Cortés Españolas* 351 (December 17, 1963); *ABC* (Madrid), 18 December 1963.

40 *ABC* (Madrid), 20 December 1963.

41 On the French experience, see Pierre Bauchet, *Economic Planning: The French Experience* (London: Heineman Books, 1964); Richard B. Du Boff, "The Decline of Economic Planning in France," *Western Political Quarterly* 21 (March 1968):98–109; Bernard Cazes, *La planification en France et le IVe Plan* (Paris: Editorial de l' Epargne, 1962); Jean Fourastie, *La planification economique en France* (Paris: Presses Universitaires, 1963); François Perroux, *Le IVe Plan Français* (Paris: Presses Universitaires, 1963). Warren Baum, *The French Economy and the State* (Princeton, N.J.: Princeton University Press, 1958), p. 28, reports on the desultory debate on the second plan in Parliament. Only twenty to fifty of the 627 members of the National Assembly attended the sessions at which the Plan was debated.

Chapter 7

1 See James Michener's impression in *Iberia: Spanish Travels and Reflections* (New York: Random House, 1968), pp. 36–37.

2 Editorial, *De economía* 13 (October–December 1960):1081–86.

3 *España económica,* 11 May 1963, pp. 377–78.

4 "Tres opiniones sobre la actual situacion española," *Información comercial española* 329 (January 1961): 22–33; Tamames, *Estructura económica española,* pp. 763–89; and *Cuatro problemas de la economía española* (Madrid: Ediciones Peninsula, 1965).

5 *España económica,* 24 March 1962, pp. 224–25. See also Fuentes Quintana's views in *Ya* (Madrid), 20 November 1962.

6 Alberto Ullastres, "El desarrollo económico y su planamiento en España," *Arbor* 50 (September–October 1961): 8–21. (Although

the issue was dated 1961 for editorial purposes, it was not actually published until March 1962.)

7 *Pueblo* (Madrid), 5 June 1963. See also "El señor Ullastres y el desarrollo disequilibriado," *España económica*, 13 May 1962.

8 (Madrid: Sanchez Ocaña y Companía, 1965).

9 Manuel Funes Robert, *Un programa para la Economía Española* (Madrid: Aguilar, 1965).

10 See, for example, *Estudios económicos* 2 (July 1961), and 3 (February–March 1962); *Actualidad económica*, 17 February and 24 February 1962. Tuñon de Lara, a far-left critic of the regime carefully documents financial and business support for integration in his *Panorama actual de la economía española*, pp. 321–22.

11 See the report of the ICADE conference of March 16, 1962, in *España económica*, 24 March 1962, pp. 3–6, and *Ya* (Madrid), 20 November 1962.

12 Raymond Aron, "Old Nations, New Europe," in Stephen R. Graubard, *A New Europe?* (Boston: Beacon Press, 1964), pp. 43–45; Cecilio Lora Soria, *Juventud española actual* (Madrid: Ediciones y Publicaciones Españolas, 1965), pp. 125–29; de Miguel and Linz, "El mercado común, el capital extranjero, y el empresario español," pp. 37–62.

13 Welles, *Spain*, p. 269.

14 *ABC* (Madrid), 8 February 1967.

15 Tamames, *Cuatro problemas de la economía española*, pp. 46–49.

16 IBRD, *Economic Development of Spain*.

17 Tamames, *Estructura económica española*, p. 748.

18 Fuentes Quintana, *Desarrollo económico de España*, pp. 9, 11.

19 *Hoja informativo*, 5 October 1962.

20 *Actualidad económica*, 13 October 1962, pp. 3–5. See also 4 April 1963.

21 *La vanguardia español* (Barcelona), 12 August 1962.

22 *España económica*, October–November 1962, passim.

23 Tamames, *Estructura económica española*, p. 748.

24 *Ya* (Madrid), 1 December 1962.

25 Juan José López Gutíerrez et al., "Aspectos sociales del estudio del Banco Mundial," *Seminarios* 16 (January–February 1963); Fuentes Quintana, *Desarrollo económico de España; Arriba* (Madrid), 17 September 1962; *Ya* (Madrid), 13 September 1962.

26 *Hoja informativo*, 17 May 1963.

27 *Actualidad económica*, 15 February 1964.

28 Miguel Siguán, "Encuesta sobre el Plan," *Revista español de*

opinión pública 4 (April–June 1966):188–214; Instituto Español de la Opinión Pública, *Encuesta nacional sobre el Plan de Desarrollo Económico y Social,* mimeographed (Madrid, 1966).

29 Juan Martín de Nicolas, "La empresa frente al Plan de Desarrollo," *Ya* (Madrid), 5 July 1964.

30 "Opiniones sobre el Plan de Desarrollo," *De economía* 18 (January–March 1965):105–11.

Chapter 8

1 See Presidencia del Gobierno, Comisaría del Plan, *Plan de desarrollo económico y social para el periódo 1964–1967* (Madrid: Imprenta del Boletín Oficial, 1964).

2 Banco Central, *Estudio económico: 1964* (Madrid: Banco Central, 1965), p. 161.

3 The syndical economic journal commissioned a series of such critiques. For two particularly interesting statements, see Glauco Della Porta, "Consideraciones sobre el Plan de Desarrollo Económico y Social: 1964–1967," *De economía* 17 (July–December 1964):413–19; and Arthur S. Burns, "Economic Development in Spain," *De economía* 18 (December 1965):807–14.

4 Manuel Funes Robert, "Plan de desarrollo y reforma fiscal," *Actualidad económica,* 8 February 1964, pp. 4–5.

5 On the wisdom, in development planning generally, of less elegant technique, see Albert Waterston, *Development Planning: Lessons of Experience* (Baltimore: Johns Hopkins University Press, 1965), p. 72; and Bertram Gross, ed., *Action Under Planning* (New York: McGraw-Hill, 1967). It is worth noting that French planning has been criticized on similar grounds.

6 See, for example, the entire issue of the journal of the Ministry of Commerce devoted to this problem: *Información comercial española* 330 (February 1961).

7 See the following bulletin of the Chamber of Industry, *Industria* 18 (October 1960):558.

8 Presidencia del Gobierno, Comisaría del Plan, *Memoria sobre la ejecución del Plan de Desarrollo Económico y Social: 1965* (Madrid: Boletín Oficial del Estado: 1966), pp. 19–20.

9 Presidencia del Gobierno, *Memoria sobre la ejecución del Plan: 1964,* p. 27.

10 Laureano López Ródo, "Polos de crecimiento," *Actualidad económica,* 16 March 1963.

11 *Hoja informativo,* 3 April 1963; *Ya* (Madrid), 1 April 1963.

12 J. González Paz, "El desarrollo regional desde el punto de vista económico," *Revista de economía política* 37 (May–August 1964): 96–160.

13 *De economía* 9 (May–August 1956):41–42.

14 *Noticias de Avilá* (Avilá), 29 April 1963.

15 José Luis Meilan, "Observaciones acerca del regimén jurídico de los polos de promoción y desarrollo," *Documentación administrativa* 77 (May 1964):32.

16 Rafael de Mendizabel Allende, "La gerencia de los polos de promoción y desarrollo," *Documentación administrativa* 89 (May 1965): 9–26.

17 Meilan, "Observaciones acerca del regimén jurídico de los polos," p. 32.

18 Presidencia del Gobierno, *Memoria sobre la ejecución del Plan: 1965*, pp. 24–26.

19 *Actualidad económica*, 2 May 1964.

20 OECD, *Economic Surveys: Spain, 1967* (Paris: OECD, 1968), p. 12.

21 Ramón Tamames, "El primer año," *Anales de economía* 29 (January–March 1965):29–45.

22 Banco Hispano Americano, *La situacion económica en 1966* (Madrid: Banco Hispano Americano, 1967), pp. 26–27.

23 Martin Hardy, "Stabilizing an Economy: Spain," *Finance and Development* 5 (March 1968):36.

24 R. C. Carr, "General Franco's New Deputy and His Problems," *World Today* 24 (June 1968):250–57.

25 José María Peman, "Redia," *ABC* (Madrid), 14 February 1967.

26 *España económica*, 21 November 1964, p. 957.

27 *Ya* (Madrid), 2 March 1966.

28 *Panorama económico*, April 1967.

29 "Ante el II Plan de desarrollo," *Pueblo* (Madrid), 21–29 November 1966.

30 Presidencia del Gobierno, Comisaría del Plan, *Anteprojecto de directrices de política de desarrollo y informes: 1968–71* (Madrid: Presidencia del Gobierno, Comisaría del Plan, 1960).

31 Presidencia del Gobierno, Comisaría del Plan, *II Plan de desarrollo económico y social* (Madrid: Boletín Oficial del Estado, 1969).

INDEX